WITHDRAWN
HARVARD LIBRARY
WITHDRAWN

Conscience and the Reality of God

Religion and Reason 36

Method and Theory
in the Study and Interpretation of Religion

GENERAL EDITOR
Jaques Waardenburg, *University of Lausanne*

BOARD OF ADVISERS
Th. P. van Baaren, *Groningen*
R. N. Bellah, *Berkeley*
U. Bianchi, *Rome*
H.J.W. Drijvers, *Groningen*
S. N. Eisenstadt, *Jerusalem*
C. Geertz, *Princeton*
K. Goldammer, *Marburg*
P. Ricœur, *Paris* and *Chicago*
M. Rodinson, *Paris*
K. Rudolph, *Marburg*
N. Smart, *Lancaster* and *Santa Barbara, Calif.*
G. Widengren, *Stockholm*

Mouton de Gruyter
Berlin · New York · Amsterdam

Conscience and the Reality of God

An Essay on the Experiential Foundations of Religious Knowledge

John C. Staten

Mouton de Gruyter
Berlin · New York · Amsterdam 1988

Mouton de Gruyter (formerly Mouton, The Hague)
is a Division of Walter de Gruyter & Co., Berlin.

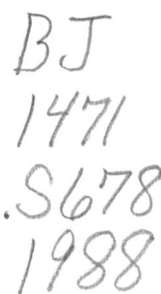

Library of Congress Cataloging – in – Publication Data

Staten, John C., 1938-
Conscience and the reality of God.
(Religion and reason ; 36)
Bibliography: p.
Includes indexes.
1. Conscience. 2. God. 2. Ebeling, Gerhard, 1912 –
1912 –   · 4. Heidegger, Martin, 1889–1976. I. Title.
II. Series.
BJ1471.S678 1988 241'.1 88-9072
ISBN 0-89925-435-7 (alk. paper)

Deutsche Bibliothek Cataloging – in – Publication Data

Staten, John C.:
Conscience and the reality of God : an essay on the experiential
foundation of religious knowledge / John C. Staten. - Berlin ;
New York ; Amsterdam : Mouton de Gruyter, 1988
  (Religion and reason ; 36)
  ISBN 3-11-010525-X
NE: GT

Printed on acid free paper.

© Copyright 1988 by Walter de Gruyter & Co., Berlin. All rights reserved, including those of translation into foreign languages. No part of this book may be reproduced in any form – by photoprint, microfilm, or any other means – nor transmitted, nor translated into a machine language without written permission from Mouton de Gruyter, a Division of Walter de Gruyter & Co., Berlin.
Printing: Ratzlow-Druck, Berlin – Binding: Dieter Mikolai, Berlin. Printed in Germany.

To Katrina
True Partner in Love and Thought

Contents

Foreword   By Paul Ricoeur ix

Preface xiii

Chapter I: The Present Theological Situation and the Need for
   a New Theological Anthropology 1
   Our Orientation and Point of Departure from Rudolf Bultmann 1
   Some Related, Representative Voices 11
   Thesis and Approach: "Conscience" as an Experiential Locus
      for the Understanding of "God"—a Contribution to a
      Theological Prolegomenon 23

Chapter II: The Centrality and Significance of
   Conscience in Ebeling's Thought 39
   Roots of Ebeling's Conception of Conscience
      in the Work of the Early Heidegger (*Being and Time*) 48
   Historical Backdrop—The "University Milieu": Marburg 50
   The "University Milieu": Zürich and Elsewhere 53

Chapter III: Heidegger's Phenomenological
   Description of Conscience in *Being and Time* 65

Chapter IV: Ebeling's Interpretation of
   the Phenomenon of Conscience 81

Chapter V: Man as Conscience and the Reality of "God" 111

Bibliography 143

Index 153
   Subjects 153
   Authors/Proper Names 160
   Biblical References 162

Foreword

I am happy to commend to John Staten's readers this work entitled *Conscience and the Reality of God*. This undertaking sets for itself a *limited* task—one that it *completely fulfills*.

The task is *limited* in at least two senses. Although it offers a positive, "constructive", contribution to the exploration of language on the subject of God, to the signification of the term "God", this effort is situated on the level of a prolegomenon to theology. Staten thus speaks of "the corroborative, hermeneutical assistance of a specific, modern philosophical perspective" (pp. 47, 97–98). In other words, he is seeking a locus from which the discourse on God could be heard at a time—our own—marked by the theoretical and practical irrelevance of language concerning God. In this respect, the modesty proclaimed by Staten is by no means a rhetorical device; it is solely a question of identifying the locus where human experience as such can be opened to language, to a *word-event*, whose specific and specifically Christian structure is not itself the object of this study. The task is limited in another sense as well: a single experience is examined, that of *Gewissen* which we translate by *conscience*. The author does not claim that conscience is the only experience in which a breach onto the Open, as Rilke would have called it, is revealed within the heart of the person. Certainly, conscience does have, as I shall underscore in a moment, weighty credentials to allow it to occupy a privileged place in these anthropological prolegomena to theology, but there is no assertion that, in our present cultural situation, the only access to a reasoned discourse on God is by way of conscience. If it be privileged, the access by way of conscience is not the sole path open to us.

A limited task, I said, but one that is *completely fulfilled*—fulfilled in a number of respects, which I would like to enumerate.

First of all, Staten had the wisdom to take as his guide two contemporary authors, a philosopher and a theologian: Heidegger and Ebeling, who are pioneers in this matter. In this respect, Staten's work can be read as an introduction to a parallel reading of Heidegger and Ebeling, in whom the central position of the phenomenon of conscience is evident, in contrast to readings which stress solely in the first, Being-towards-death and in the second, the Christological character of the *word-event*.

However, there is a more important respect in which this work is to be recommended: it is not restricted to juxtaposing a monograph devoted to conscience in Heidegger and another dealing with conscience in Ebeling. It proposes an interpretation of Ebeling's texts in light of Heidegger's texts. In this way it increases the intelligibility and the force of many terse or cryptic expressions in Ebeling, by restoring their Heideggerian background. In particular, the essay in *Wort und Glaube* devoted precisely to the phenomenon of conscience, is made somehow greater by this exegesis, which I would term an amplifying interpretation, while its place at the end of the work is shown to be entirely justified by an analysis which shows it to be the culmination of the collection of essays. By the same token, the Heideggerian reading of Ebeling opens a difficult problem of interpretaiton, namely that of the double allegiance of the Zürich theologian to Luther and to Heidegger. A recent article by Ebeling, which due to its date of publication Staten could not have known (*Das Gewissen in Luthers Verständnis*, in *Lutherstudien*, Bd. III, Tübingen: Mohr, 1985, pp. 108-125), confirms my feeling that his allegiance to Heidegger, which is well documented by Staten, renders Ebeling's position all the more enigmatic, as it is just as intimately bound up with the Lutheran thesis that conscience possesses from the very outset a theological dimension. For myself, I am tempted to consider this double allegiance which Staten helps to uncover to be the source of a creative tension at the very heart of Ebeling's analyses. Some of the measured criticisms that Staten formulates at the end of his study, after having given full credit to Ebeling, seem to me less to denounce weaknesses in the synthesis that Ebeling is held to have made between his two mentors, than to point towards the place where the two allegiances reinforce each other instead of undercutting one another.

However, it is the personal contribution of Staten's study that seems to me most fully to justify his assertion that he has fulfilled the contract signed at the start of his work: "I shall develop the primary thesis that in the experience given to man as 'conscience' we have a qualitatively unique ontological grounding for understanding the reality deemed 'God'" (p. 23; cf. also pp. 81f., 111f.). Everything revolves around the preposition *in*: "*in the experience given to man as conscience*". I should like to underscore what this preposition of *place*, already employed in my Foreward, specifically implies when it is used in reference, precisely, to conscience. It does not designate in a general way the coincidence of immanence and transcendance. It designates conscience itself as being a "*place*". If one may say, in an epistemological sense, that conscience is the "meaningful experiential *locus* for the knowledge of God" (or again: "the more fundamental hermeneutical *locus* concerning God"), this is because conscience is already, in an ontological sense, a *place*, as is signaled by the Latin preposition *coram*, "before": *coram seipso, coram Deo*, "before oneself, before God". As in all living metaphors, *coram* expresses something essential, namely that with conscience the question *who?* (who am I?) is made explicit by the question *where?* (where are you Adam?). In this way the ontological sense of place—the mathematical point where all the horizontal and vertical dimensions of experience converge—governs the epistemological sense of place as the starting point of the investigation. Conscience: "the radical place where it is decided what man truly is...where man belongs, where he is and where he has his abode".

A topology such as this undoubtedly originates in Augustine, who designates the heart (*cordia*) and the entrails (*pericordia*) as places which are at once organic and spiritual, with all the attendant dimensions, directions, orientations. John Staten's thesis, as it is completely developed, consists in placing the topology of conscience at the starting point, that is at the heart of his "prolegomenous theological anthropology". From this undertaking, two results are awaited. First, Staten foresees the resolution of the tension between a purely anthropological thesis, like that of Heidegger, for whom conscience has no theological dimension inasmuch as it is but the silent call that authentic Dasein addresses to "fallen" Dasein, delivered over to the inauthenticity of the "they"—*and* a strictly theological thesis, like that of Luther, according to which *coram Deo* arises in profane experience as the effect of the word of Salvation, as Gospel and not as the Law. According to Staten a coherent anthropology of conscience implies a reference to God, but as *preceding* any theological context, *preceding* Christian tidings in the Gospel. In this way the author believes he can place himself beyond the choice, Luther or Heidegger.

On the other hand, the author expects that his investigation will resolve the tensions within Ebeling's thought, which, according to Staten, oscillates between the clear affirmation of the coincidence of *coram seipso* and *coram Deo*, at the heart of profane experience, *and* the quasi-Lutheran recourse to the *word-event* of Scripture to awaken conscience to its transcendent dimension. Staten hopes to attain this twofold critical result, required by his "constructive" thesis, by pushing even further than his own mentors the exegesis of conscience interpreted as "joint-cognizance". Conscience is held to be *at one and the same time* the revelation of man's non-identity with himself—and hence his powerlessness to remove himself by his own means from his state of fallenness in the "they"—and the call to responsibility, by which man is summoned to unite himself in decision. It is this conjunction between the "*disclosure of non-mastery*" and the call to respond in a decisive manner, which would permit giving to Ebeling's *word-event* a pre-Christian, even a pre-theological, sense as demanded by the present state of our culture, where what is in question is the very relevance of the word "God".

The reader permitting, I should like to stress the importance of John Staten's contribution to a debate situated on the border between philosophical anthropology and theology, in a place *somewhere* between natural theology and revealed theology.

Paul Ricoeur

Preface

In the light of the distinctively secular form of our modern consciousness how is it possible to speak at all of a transcendent reality deemed "God"? In what way is the knowledge of God grounded in our everyday experience of ourselves and the world? Is the term "God" made meaningful from the beginning through the language and proclamation of the community of faith? Or is the meaning of such a term, and the reality to which it refers, already made meaningful in the linguistic experience—nay, in the very ontological structure—of man as man? Such are the basic questions which motivate this study. They are questions which stand at the center of the recent ferment in theological thought, a fermentation process, I need hardly add, which has its source not simply in the more recent upheavals of contemporary Protestant theology, but in forces embedded in the emergent life and thought of Western culture since the Renaissance.

The constructive reinterpretation presented in this book represents my own initial response to the challenge presented by these questions. I speak in this investigation as a systematic theologian concerned about the responsible future of intelligent belief in God. It is my deeply held conviction that today the problem of the meaning of God must take precedence over all other theological issues and themes; indeed, the meaningfulness of the term "God," as the meaningfulness of the category of the transcendent or extramundane itself, is the unavoidable presupposition of all discussions concerned with christology, ecclesiology, and scriptural authority.

While I am concerned in this work to speak responsibly toward the future, I recognize that no genuine progress—nor any truly fresh start—can be made without an equal attentiveness to the past, particularly the most recent past. I am convinced that we have far from exhausted the rich inheritance which has been handed on to us through the labors of a most remarkable theological (and philosophical) generation. It is perhaps fitting that I write these thoughts at a time not too distant from the final passing of this generation through the death of its last great representative, Rudolf Bultmann. Like Bultmann, I find that I have no qualms in utilizing for theological purposes the best possible philosophical resources at my disposal. I hope it will become apparent in the course of this inquiry that Heidegger's early work is anything but a once fertile field which now lies before us overworked and fallow! Furthermore, that the theologian himself must also think "philosophically", especially in the type of foundational work called for here, is something which I emphatically take for granted. The basic issue as to what it means to think "theologically" and to think "philosophically", as well as the thorny problem as to what distinguishes "philosophical" from "theological" concepts, is far from settled, particuarly in present-day Protestant theology. I hope in the course of these constructive efforts that I also manage to help clarify, even if I do not finally resolve, this vexing issue.

I along with Bultmann (and, for that matter, along with all of his neo-orthodox compatriots) feel an inestimable sense of solidarity with a living tradition which encounters us out of the more distant past. The crucial question which confronts us today may be significantly different than that which confronted this tradition—and, as the reader will discover, I believe this to be the case in one important respect—but this should in no way bewitch us into thinking that we can address our question through a severance of relations with this past. Although involving an approach and a conceptuality appropriate to our own time and situation, the constructive enterprise which follows would be sadly misconstrued if it were not ultimately understood as a faithful, though indirect, response to voices which yet beckon us from the past: the Yahwist's dramatic proposal that a human being possesses a personal knowledge of the Creator through that haunting address which concerns one's true identity, "Adam, where art thou?"; the Apostle Paul's profound, though rough-hewn conception in *Romans* which inextricably links our everyday knowledge of God to the peculiar cognizance of an opposing "law" within our "mind", "heart", "members", and "conscience"; St. Augustine's classic specification of an ineradicable awareness of the divine being in the revelatory "restlessness" of the homeless "heart"; Luther's recognition of an original knowledge given to each person in that definitive "*coram*" experience wherein one stands naked "before" self, world, and God; and Calvin's powerful and suggestive conception of "the anxiety of conscience" as that basic "*sensus divinitatis*" through which one comes to know the "presence" of the holy God as Creator and Judge.

My thesis, namely, that in "conscience" we have a meaningful experiential locus for the knowledge of God, was born rather early along in my studies out of a lengthy dialogue with this tradition. It was later sharpened and developed through a more specific dialogue with two contemporary figures, Gerhard Ebeling and Martin Heidegger. As I shall attempt to demonstrate, it is primarily through the as yet unnoticed efforts of these two thinkers that we have the resources for retrieving and reconceiving the phenomenon of conscience and for showing its revelance for the contemporary problem of God. Incidentally, along the way students of Ebeling and Heidegger as such should find much that interests them here besides the concept of conscience. In striving for a clear understanding of their respective interpretations of this phenomenon I of necessity examined, and hopefully elucidated, other major themes in their thought: the notions of "understanding" and "knowledge", "reality" and "truth", "word-event", "language" and "discourse".

As for the central concept of "conscience", a preliminary word of caution is in order in this Preface. Today there are few other terms which are as misused and abused. In technical writing as in popular parlance "conscience" has come to stand for such a wide variety of experiences that it has ceased to have any precise meaning or reference. In view of this situation I ask the reader to suspend all preconceptions of this concept as he or she proceeds into this work, especially those "moral" and "psychological" renderings which we in contemporary scholarship have appropriated all too uncritically from the intellectual tradition of Aquinas, Butler, Kant, Ritschl, Nietzsche, and Freud. What is called for today, as a long overdue project in both philosophy and theology, is a radical interpretative retrieval of the root meaning of this concept with the strictest, circumscriptive description of the experiential and onotological phenomena to which it refers. It is just such a retrieval that the reader should anticipate in the chapters which follow.

I would like to express my appreciation to those who in so many ways contributed toward the initiation and completion of this project. I am indebted to Professor Kathleen Blamey, one of Professor Ricoeur's experienced translators, for her able assistance in the English rendering of his Foreword to this work. Before this book reached its original form as a doctoral dissertation at The University of Chicago, two teachers at Princeton Theological Seminary opened new paths for which I am grateful. I am happy to express my gratitude to Professor James Barr, now of Oxford University, whose spirited work enabled me to break through the spell of the established "historical" paradigm in biblical theology and thus to discern the realm of "personal divine-human communication" as an equally significant scriptural model for the knowledge of God. My thanks are extended as well to Professor Edward Dowey, Jr. whose monograph on Calvin first directed me to the idea of conscience as a key "element of the subjective revelation of God"(1), and by implication suggested as well (over against strong counter theological currents at the time) that to pursue this "anthropological" phenomenon was not to betray the spirit of my Reformed heritage.

I wish to thank Professor Gerhard Ebeling himself who, during two busy weeks together several summers past, took the time to answer my interminable questions and to respond ever so patiently and conscientiously (as is his custom) to various aspects of my treatment of this thought.

I am most indebted, of course, to my teachers and advisers at Chicago who encouraged and assisted me throughout the many stages of this work. It was with the late Professor Joseph Haroutunian that I first launched this investigation and who along the way taught me, mainly through personal example, how the rigors of systematic thinking could at the same time occasion the silent experience of personal joy. I am especially grateful to my adviser, Professor Langdon Gilkey. It was he more than anyone else who provided, through his teaching and written work, the stimulus and direction for the specific line of inquiry reflected in these chapters. Professor Gibson Winter was also very helpful, particularly in his criticism and detailed suggestions regarding the analysis in chapters three and four. Finally I wish to thank Professor Paul Ricoeur who over several years so graciously gave of his time to read, comment on, and discuss this work. This monograph would never have seen the public light of day without his sustained interest and assistance. In more ways than can be expressed here I stand in profound personal and intellectual debt to him.

John C. Staten

1. Edward A. Dowey, Jr., *The Knowledge of God in Calvin's Theology* (New York: Columbia University Press, 1952), p. 56.

"God" is not a specifically Christian word. And by the same token the substance which this word expresses is not first discovered through Christian talk about God and then made into a subject for discussion. The problem so presents itself to us of the 20th century—whether rightly or not is a question which could still be asked—that we who live in a world which knows nothing about God have, as it were, to bring up God first. We have to introduce the word "God" first and make it understandable.
>Gerhard Ebeling,
>"The Hermeneutical Locus of the Doctrine of God"

The task of a comprehensive analysis of reality...the study of which is the constant, historically conditioned and historically motivated act of reflective questioning, would be...: to observe the radical questionableness of reality. If this questionableness which strikes to the roots of personal being and thereby proves its radicality is described as concerned with the conscience, then we could...say that the place where we experience what "God" means is the conscience.
>Gerhard Ebeling,
>*Word and Faith*

Chapter I

The present theological situation and the need for a new theological anthropology

*Our orientation and
point of departure from Rudolf Bultmann*

In varying modulation during the past several years a significant chorus of observers, theological and non-theological, has given voice to the awareness that we are living in an age which has become genuinely secular in all major spheres of our cultural life and experience(1). That this spirit of secularity, with its underlying sense of the absence of the "divine" or "transcendent", is a phenomenon that has achieved a certain normative status not only outside the church but from "the inside" as well, is a fact that has been brought home most forcefully (and painfully) by developments in American Protestant theology during the nineteen sixties and seventies(2). It is articulated quite succinctly, for example, by Paul van Buren who at one point in his controversial work, *The Secular Meaning of the Gospel*(3), distinguishes the kind of question he is asking from that which he feels is asked by certain neo-orthodox forerunners. According to van Buren, these forerunners asked "how the Christian can preach the Gospel to secular modern man so that he will be able to hear, understand, and become a Christian"(4). Their main concern was to "translate" the gospel to the modern man who was "outside" the church. But for van Buren our real concern "has to do", as he puts it, "with the 'modern man' who is *inside* the church, more or less, and who is wondering what he is doing there"(5). He concludes: "Their question is thus different from the one which introduces this study: 'How can the Christian who is himself a secular man understand his faith in a secular way'"(6). Now we may join recent critics of van Buren (which we do)(7) by noting the degree in which he fails to heed the mistake of our nineteenth century forerunners in appropriating too uncritically the presuppositions and outlook of their contemporary culture. Nevertheless, at the same time we cannot but accept wholeheartedly the general thrust of his contention that we can no longer do theology today as if the theologian himself stands somewhere in neutral territory, apart or distinct from the increasingly secular mind of his fellow man and woman. As one critic of van Buren so aptly put it: "In this somewhat restricted sense then, that theology must start with secularity and think through its message in terms intelligible to secular minds (and so to [its] own secular [mind] as well), rather than talking *at* those minds in terms of traditional or biblical language, it is true that we must now all accept the normative character of our secularity"(8). With this statement we must concur and, indeed, accept as the basic critical impulse guiding the general direction of our study.

In appropriating this fact in the formulation of our constructive task it would be short-sighted, however, to simply write off the so-called older neo-orthodox generation as being totally insensitive and unresponsive to the peculiar, radically secular nature of our modern cultural situation. The name of Rudolf Bultmann, for one, cries out once more for recognition in this regard(9). Was it not Bultmann above all others who orignally posed and attempted to deal positively with the problem of working out a theological method which fully accepted the normative character of our modern secularity(10)? Certainly the initial(11) stage for our present problematic was set, and a way was opened towards solving our methodological perplexity, in Bultmann's 1941 essay, "New Testament and Mythology", and the subsequent "demythologizing" debate which followed(12). Particularly significant was the question raised with Karl Barth and others of the necessity for clarifying the problem of "pre-understanding" in biblical hermeneutics, and, connected with this, the indispensable utilization of a philosophical anthropology in any self-critical, modern reinterpretation of theological concepts(13). Bultmann's persistence in working toward a constructive methodological position, even in the light of the most recent developments regarding the prime question of our knowledge and experience of God, can be observed in one of his later essays entitled "The Idea of God and Modern Man"(14). It would be instructive to turn our attention briefly to this essay, for here, I think, we find a perceptive sketch of the key issues involved in the more recent assessment of our cultural and theological situation. We also find, so I shall argue, evidence of the limitation of Bultmann's distinctive methodological position, but a limitation which nevertheless does succeed in pointing the way toward a fruitful solution, one with which this investigation shall be concerned.

Written in 1963 in response to the appearance of, and to the debate which centered on, John A. T. Robinson's *Honest to God*, Bultmann's essay anticipates in a remarkable way the even more radical rumblings which were to emerge, especially on the American scene, during the next several years(16). Bultmann addresses himself to what he understands as the essential thrust of Robinson's book, that "since the traditional ecclesiastical image of God is no longer credible to contemporary man, *a new image of God* is required"(17), and from the start attempts to direct his remarks toward its even more revolutionary implications with reference to the modern phenomenon of the "death of God". Significantly, Bultmann sees in Gabriel Vahanian's earlier work, *The Death of God* ("a peculiar and theologically more independent parallel to Robinson's book"), the outline of the critical theme and basic problematic which will, or should, occupy the attention of theologians in the years to follow. According to Bultmann, Robinson's concern with the obsolescence of an old image and construction of a new one only hints at, and merely begins to touch upon, the much more serious problem which really exists at the heart of our modern cultural selfunderstanding, that which is manifest in the sometimes tacitly, sometimes explicitly expressed assumption of "the death of God".

Drawing upon the analyses of Gogarten, Heidegger, Vahanian and others, Bultmann observes that the shadow of the death of God has arisen from rather distant horizons on the developing landscape of the 'Christian' West. Although reaching its high prophetic point in the nineteenth century, it takes its rise essentially in two key developments of our post-Renaissance period, the first, in certain distinctive impulses of the sixteenth century Reformation, the second (although with parallels through the history of the West since the Greeks), in generative forces of the seventeenth and eighteenth century Enlightenment. From these two originary and qualitatively important movements, we are led, according to Bultmann, toward what we understand today as the thoroughgoing "secularization of the world", the fundamental phenomenon of which the problem of the death of God is really merely a consequence. The distinction between these two forces is an important one, for Bultmann. On the one hand, we have what might be called a legitimate form of secularization, in the "de-divinization" of the world through the Reformers' concept of faith as eschatological freedom. Bultmann draws upon Gogarten's use of the term "secularity" or "secular", to describe this positive form of secularization. On the other hand, we are confronted with what might be understood as an illegitimate, or (Bultmann) "degenerate" form of secularization in the radically naturalistic (Bultmann himself calls it "explicitly atheistic", but we prefer the non-perjorative terminology) view of the world which stems, in a general sense, from the rise of the "natural attitude" (Heidegger), or autonomous standpoint of reason during the period of the Enlightenment. In describing this form of the process of secularization Bultmann utilizes Gogarten's term "secularism", or "secularistic"(18).

Can we speak then of a genuine form of secularization which would be appropriate and ultimately non-threatening to both a modern Christian understanding of the reality of God and an understanding of the reality of the world as modern, or "scientific" man? Bultmann thinks we can. Such a genuine form of secularity can be re-expressed in our time, he claims, by grasping Luther's rendering of the biblical "eschatological" conception of the authentic situation of man in the world *coram Deo*. Man is "'a free master over all things and subject to no one'" in Luther's interpretation of that dialectical understanding of the world given in the stance of obedient faith "before God"(19). Or, as Bultmann puts it: Luther's doctrine of justification by faith alone (here, of course, a recovery of the insight of Paul), "by de-divinizing the world, allowed it to appear in its pure worldliness. It disclosed and evoked the *freedom* of man from the world, freedom from all powers which can encounter man from out of the world"(20). In the consciousness of such freedom we find an authentic secularity, an authentic recognition of the death of God, if you will, by a refusal to identify and to be dependent in any way upon the world as divine. Such a genuinely secular faith, in a positive sense, "permits the world to be the world, indeed, it gives back to the world its authentic worldliness" (21). Bultmann is quick to point out, however, that this authentic de-divinization of the world, this genuine understanding of Christian secularity, or "worldliness", stands on the verge of collapse, on the brink of giving everything over to an illicit form of secularization when the second half of Luther's remark, above, is forgotten: For, just as a "'Christian is a free master over all things and subject to no one'", so, in a genuine stance of faith "before God", he or she is also "'a servant in the service of all things and subject to everyone'"(22). To put it differently, legitimate secularity gives way to illegitimate secularism "when it is forgotten that *freedom from* the world is at the same time *responsibility for* the world"(23). The maintenance of this delicate, dialectical balance is dependent of course upon the peculiar paradox of faith's "grasping the unconditional in the conditional in every now...in existential comportment, in the conscious or unconscious decisions of life."(24).

Such a balance becomes extremely precarious, to say the least, when faced with the strong erosive power emanating from the second source of our modern secular self-understanding. Bultmann warns that we must guard against seeing the rise of secularism as a mere consequence of the ascendancy of modern natural science during the last three centuries. Certainly, according to the dictum of La Place, modern natural science, with regard to its *method*, has found the hypothesis "God" unnecessary, and what we might call the methodological death of God, or the de-divinization of the world via a naturalistic reductionism, has had an enormous impact upon the spiritual outlook of modern man. But the roots of a radical secularistic view of the world lie much deeper than this and it is to a more fundamental ground than simply the "modern scientific world view" that we must go if we are to have a full understanding of this secularistic process. This more fundamental cultural Zeitgeist is best characterized by what Heidegger and others have described as the all-pervasive influence of the spirit of "subjectity" (Subjectität)(25), whereby the world is delivered over *in toto* to objectivizing thought (the methodological bracketing of the natural sciences being merely one instance of this), and is "subjected to the planning of man as subject, a planning which man himself establishes"(26). This spirit can be seen with respect to the rise of "autonomous reason" during the Enlightenment. In one sense it is possible to see a legitimate form of secularization in man's use of autonomous reason for the purposes of forming judgments and plans in the establishment and carrying out of human work and community. Subjectity enters the picture, however, when man attempts to make an autonomous use of reason, the autonomy of reason thus becoming confused with, or rather, sacrificed to, the autonomy of man. This is seen, for example, in the case of self-legislation.

Bultmann writes:
> [Autonomy is equivocal. In the genuine sense autonomy means self-legislation in the sense that the individual affirms the moral law as that in which he himself comes to win his authenticity](27). But the recogition that the rational man is a lawgiver in this sense, turns into the delusion that the individual as subject arbitrarily determines what is good and evil, as was the case already in the 'Greek Enlightenment' among the Sophists. And so today autonomy is unfortunately often spoken of as a self-legislation of the individual that understands itself to be free of obligations which transcend the individual level, and that determines value and valuelessness of itself.(28)

Subjectity works its way in the sphere of religion as well. It shows itself in the area of the history of religions, for instance, at that point when "Christianity" is judged the higher, or, if you wish, a lower religion. Such a judgment, according to Bultmann, can only be made by the autonomous evaluating subject(29). It is not necessarily the case, however, that authentic, or we might say, truly autonomous, Christianity disappears entirely in such subjectity. In a sense it still remains, but only in a partial, sublimated state. We see this, Bultmann says, in the fact that the western world, which has been a 'Christian' world since the Middle Ages, today is not so much "anti-Christian" as it is "a-Christian". To be sure, this has come about "partly in the sense that Christianity appears to [the western world] to be antiquated and the questions to which Christianity proposes to give answers have become for it irrelevant"(30). But more important, Bultmann emphasizes, it has come about because these questions still remain living issues for modern western man, but it is now this man himself who gives the answers(31). It is here that the radical secularization of Christianity emerges. Authentic and autonomous Christian faith gives way to the rise of 'Christian' *ideologies*, ideologies "which assert that they are able to reveal the meaning of the world and history;...the choice among which is left to the subjectivity of the individual"(32). This erosion is also felt in our contemporary flight to "religiosity". In the sense that our relationship to God is reduced to mere popular religious feeling, religiosity too becomes nothing more than subjectity.

But in the face of what Bultmann admits to be the antiquated and irrelevant character of so much of traditional Christian faith, in the face of what certainly must be seen as the near overwhelming force of the spirit of subjectity in our time—particularly as it has manifested itself with such apparently fruitful and promising results in the spheres of science, business, economics, and politics, to name only a few—in the face of all this, it would seem to be a Herculean task far beyond the mental and experiential capacities of modern men and women (even modern 'Christian theologian' men and women!) to appropriate, or, for that matter, to even begin to understand, that paradoxical kind of faith which in letting the world be the world in its own objectivity, "*nevertheless*" maintains a living relationship with the transcendent God in the midst of, and vitally connected to, the experiences of their everyday life. To put it in another way, that utterly essential understanding of ourselves in the world as "*coram Deo*" appears most tenuous, too brittle, and perhaps impossible in the light of that process of secularization which Bultmann has so aptly described.

It is not that Bultmann fails to see this plight of our "modern man"; nor, for that matter (van Buren to the contrary notwithstanding), can it be said that Bultmann has not faced this dilemma squarely within himself and with regard to the development of his theological method. Bultmann affirms his starting point for our time: "*Gone* is the relation of man to the transcendent as that which stands over against man and the world and is not at their disposal"(33). It can even be said that Bultmann begins with the full acceptance of the Nietzschean affirmation of the death of God. As with Heidegger he understands this vision to entail, however, not a typical philosophical discussion of atheism, but rather, a dramatic illumination of the fact that in our modern era we are all atheists to the extent that we are inextricably involved in the thoroughgoing secularization of the world, and that such a form of atheism ultimately entails nihilism(34). In underscoring this interpretation, particularly the assertion that such atheism implies nihilism, Bultmann points to the words of the precursor of Nietzsche, Jean Paul, whose prophetic vision appears in his work "Discourse of the dead Christ from atop the cosmos: there is no God":

> The whole universe is burst asunder by the hand of atheism and fragmented into innumerable quicksilver particles of I's, which twinkle, roll about, wander, flee together and from each other without unity and stability. No one is so very much alone in the universe as the one who denies God...Alas, if every I is its own father and creator, why can it not also be its own angel of destruction?(35)

We find the same counterpoint theme expressed, according to Bultmann, in the vision of Nietzsche's "madman":

> What did we do when we unchained this earth from its sun...? Where is it moving to now? Where are we moving to? Away from all suns? Do we not stumble all the time? Backwards, sidewards, forward, in every direction? Is there an above and a below any more? Are we not wandering as through an endless nothingness?(36)

Certainly it must be said that, for Bultmann (and for most all of those who participated in the rise of "crisis theology" on the Continent during the two world wars), no theologian or theology can claim the term "modern" which does not begin by facing fully the Nietzschean vision of the death of God(37). In this later essay as well as throughout his writing Bultmann either implicitly or explicitly expresses the fact that a Nietzschean atheism (or some variant form of it) is an inescapable fact of our modern secularized sensibilities. It is characterized by our shared understanding of the world and our own experience as void of the presence of the divine, especially in the sense of a Holy One who "stands over against us, and [who] is not at our disposal...". We are bereft of any meaningful or relevant sense of the "supernatural", whether it be 'located' in the "midst" of the world or "beyond". Speaking from a more philosophical-epistemological point of view, this fact of our contemporary experience may be described as the end of the era of "two-world thinking", or, as Heidegger puts it in his essay "Nietzsches Wort 'Gott ist tot'", as the end of "the supersensory world generally" (38), "God" here (for Nietzsche) being not only the "Christian God" but the name for the realm of ideals and supra-sensible value as well(39).

With Nietzsche's help Bultmann would have us meditate upon this inexorable tendency toward nihilism involved in such atheism. And curiously, for Bultmann, it is with such a form of atheism, and not with our modern Christian ideological movements, or with religiosity's flights into the beyond (the "purely otherworldly"), that the question of God is kept alive for us today. Modern secular man's movement toward nihilism is seen in our obsessive attempt to find ourselves in a frantic and unsuccessful grasping after the ultimate meaning and destiny of our world and our times. Here the question of God is not lost, but rather emerges dramatically in the tragic and often inhuman and hideous results of man's autonomous strivings in the historical-political order—a point not easily felt by those of us who did not live through the post-war period in Germany and elsewhere, but a consideration, nevertheless, not to be forgotten! In a more positive sense, the question of God is kept alive in our modern atheism at those points where it consciously or unconsciously draws back from the brink of nihilism. Thinking particularly of Julian Huxley and Albert Camus, Bultmann states that "even though [they do] not risk entertaining the ideas of the transcendent God and his revelation, [they] would still like to speak in some way of the divine as somehow immanent to the world, whether it be as the world's creative ground or as the spiritual life which lives and evolves in the world". Here, for Bultmann, the "form of the question of God does not die away; but the form of the question suggests 'that the deity is a missing link in man's unsuccessful attempts to grasp the meaning of his self and of the world'"(40).

Now it is at this juncture in his analysis that what we have spoken of earlier as Bultmann's "peculiar methodological limitation" begins to emerge. It may be summarized as follows: After having sketched out our present theological situation with regard to the radical implications presented by the thoroughgoing secularization of our modern cultural experience, and after having pointed to the fact that the most problematical aspect of this crisis, for theology, is the pervasive shared experience of the death or absence of God, we are asked to move all too suddenly and, apparently, with self-evident necessity, to the sphere of the biblical kerygma, to the affirmation of the transcendent God proclaimed in the paradoxical realm of biblical faith. It seems that both methodologically and experientially Bultmann would have us move from (1) a sober and honest recognition of our shared sense of the absence of the divine or the transcendent, with all that this implies in the way of the meaninglessness and irrelevance of so much of the traditional Christian world view, to (2) the necessary nihilistic implications of this modern self-understanding, to (3) the New Testament kerygma, with its witness to the act of the Transcendent One in the eschatological event of Jesus Christ. In the words now familiar to all of us Bultmann summarizes this third step as follows. Although

> reason remains in the sphere of subjectity...religion, particularly the Christian faith, abandons this sphere. The Christian faith speaks of a *revelation* which it understands to mean God's act as an event which is not visible to the objectivizing thought of reason, an event which as revelation does not communicate doctrines, but concerns the existence of man and teaches him, or better, authorizes him to understand himself as sustained by the transcendent power of God(41).

Aside from the question of the adequacy or inadequacy of Bultmann's own distinctive reinterpretation of biblical revelation, the real difficulty which we confront in our own day is the unquestioned assumption that after having passed through steps (1) and (2), above, we can so *easily* move, with openness and without hindrance of understanding—whether as "unbelievers", "hearing and understanding the word preached", or as "believers", "proclaiming the self-understood word"—within the sphere of step (3). We must ask: Can we assume in our own time the self-evidentness of this experiential and methodological leap? *Must* we pass through the searing heat of *nihilism* before entering the paradoxical world of the Bible? And even if we do tread this path (which I assume Bultmann and his generation did, again notwithstanding van Buren and others to the contrary), how is it that we find ourselves already so directly, so meaningfully and understandingly within the biblical or kerygmatic context as our real, positive starting point(42)? Can we any longer take *this* starting point for granted, even as Christian theologians, speaking within a tradition, thinking from within the church? I contend that we can no longer do so in our present cultural situation. Whatever the situation may have been during the twenties and thirties of this century which enables the early Barths and Bultmanns and Gogartens to move so easily to the standpoint of the "word", or "biblical faith", or "New Testament understanding", etc., surely it is the fate of *our* generation that we cannot do the same either so quickly or so uncritically. Before beginning to spell out anything like "the revelation of the Word", or "the biblical understanding" of the reality of God we must backtrack, as it were, and explore fully that fundamental question left dangling at step (1): Within the experiential context of our so-called radical secularity, how do we as human beings come at all to ask the question about "God"? With an eye to Bultmann's second step we must also ask in our backtracking whether a person must necessarily be driven to the "abyss of nihilism" before raising the question of God. Is the question of God not raised at other levels of one's secular experience? And more important, if so, would not such a question contain within itself a certain positive, tacit or prior understanding of the reality of that about which it asks, an understanding which could lend itself to explication quite apart from, even if ultimately connected to, the usual biblical or eschatological-kerygmatic starting point of revelational theology?

As I indicated earlier in this chapter, Bultmann does not leave us stranded at this juncture. Although he does choose to speak from a revelational rather than a natural theological standpoint, he does, nevertheless, affirm that the question of God is kept alive in our modern secular consciousness and that it does imply some kind of prior understanding of what "God" means. Here we recall Bultmann's insistence that the question of God has not died away in certain forms of modern "atheism". We remember his claim that out of the apparently radical secularism of such individuals as Camus and Huxley the question of God still remains alive, albeit in different form. But is this all that Bultmann has to say on the matter? Surely this does not provide an adequate answer to the questions just raised. For one thing, Bultmann admits that atheism's authentic question of God does not arise (here Camus, especially) except at that point where one stands gaping at the abyss of nihilism. Is there not an authentic question and understanding of God which may emerge simply at more ordinary, or everyday levels of our secular experience, a question and understanding which might be given simply in and through the structure of one as a human being? I would direct the reader's attention to a most crucial footnote which appears at the close of Bultmann's analysis:

> If one is persuaded that every man is basically moved by the question of God and that therefore the Christian proclamation may reckon with a pre-understanding, then one can ask whether this pre-understanding is not also concealed precisely in religiosity. Now H. G. Gadamer, in his book *Wahrheit und Methode*, Tübingen, 1960, which is of greatest significance for theologians, has contested (in the context of the hermeneutical problem, pp. 313f.) that one can speak of a pre-understanding for the understanding of biblical texts, namely, *a pre-understanding that is given with question of God that drives human existence*. I am of the opinion that *the pre-understanding is given precisely in that experience which Gadamer designates as the "authentic experience," namely, the experience in which 'man becomes conscious of his finiteness'* (339f.). This experience is certainly not always realized, *but it surely persists as an ever present possibility*(43).

By insisting upon "a pre-understanding that is given with the question of God that drives human existence", and in suggesting that such a pre-understanding may be reflected in something like that "experience in which 'man becomes conscious of his own finitude'", an experience, we should emphasize which apparently has its roots ("as an ever present possibility") in a human being's ontological structure, Bultmann does provide a most important clue as to the way in which we may move beyond his own methodological limitations toward a resolution of the kind of questions we have raised. If we take up this clue and explore its full implications, as Bultmann seemingly bids us to do, it is clear that we shall be involved in precisely that kind of "backtracking" process described above, a project which, with our own study in mind, we shall term here as a prolegomenous "theological anthropology". Returning to the sphere of our so-called "radical secularity", we must reexamine the question as to whether human beings, as we are constituted in our everyday being, are truly closed to an authentic or positive understanding of the reality "God". Our contention, of course, is that we are not, but for a constructive delineation as to exactly why and how we are not we shall have to probe farther and deeper than the brief indication given here by Bultmann (and Gadamer).

We should be quick to emphasize that the kind of anthropological study proposed here would not be undertaken with the expressed intention of constructing some kind of full-blown "natural theology"(44). A natural theology may or may not ultimately be implied in this investigation, but, at the same time we would want our study to be seen as a prolegomenon to a position which may also attempt to speak from revelation(45). By prolegomenon we mean that which is truly "*pro-legein*"(46) i.e., a methodologically and logically prior interpretation of "the things which must be said beforehand", before what is to be *meaningfully* explicated in the doctrinal expositions of systematic theology (here, God and man). We recognize that in proposing such a study we are assuming it is really possible to tread that rather precarious path between the heteronomous polarity which has characterized the theological mood at various times during the past several decades: "Either an autonomous natural theology, or an autonomous theology of revelation—we cannot have both!" But tread this path we must. The challenge can no longer be avoided: For *any* theology to lay claim to any cognitive validity in our day it must indicate how its language about God (and, for that matter, the "divine" or "two-worldly" dimension of all its language) is meaninglyfully rooted in a prior sense in the structure of our being and the possibility of our experience simply as humans. We recognize that the prolegomenous study demanded here as necessary for such a validation would administer a rather violent jolt to the general method typical of most revelational theologians, a method which, with few exceptions, has been most hesitant, if not out right hostile, to see the necessity of employing any sort of prolegomenous "anthropology" for its purposes. That Bultmann, as one of these theologians, points us in this direction with respect to God cannot now be denied. But in heeding his call we must move beyond our mentor's later work and attend to other important related voices.

Some related, representative voices

In focusing our sights elsewhere on the more recent theological horizon our attention is drawn to the work of an unrelated group of scholars which reflects a common concern for the kind of theological reconstruction described above. In order both to delineate more carefully the particular scope and direction of our own study, and, at the same time, to distinguish its differences from what would appear to be quite similar projects, we shall consider briefly several representative voices from this group. In our analysis—both by appropriation and criticism—we shall aim toward a statement of our basic constructive thesis in addition to a description of the method to be employed in its development.

One of the most challenging and prominent voices to be heard in the Roman Catholic arena, speaking in the aftermath of the Second Vatical Council, is that of Karl Rahner. In his book, *The Church After the Council*(47), Rahner cautions those who suppose with some complacency that we have entered a period of modern scholasticism, a period which demands nothing more than the calm elaboration and application of the work of a supposed golden era just behind us. This pastoral caution is coupled with a critical recognition of the truly radical nature of the theological task before us:

> It would be obvious and tempting—but ultimately a fatal mistake—to imagine that the chief task of systematic theology in the coming decades will be the annotation of the conciliar texts, and the historical justification and the systematic organization of the themes explicitly dealt with by the Council...The Council had no wish to invite theology to become the ways and means of the introversion of the Church upon herself. The Council wished to confront the Church of today...[with] far more radical questions than simply those which relate to a more subtle ecclesiology, or to any of the other themes explicitly treated by the Council(48).

The "newest" and most pressing "radical question" of our time, as Rahner sees it—although, as he rightly emphasizes, it is a question which is "at the same time the oldest and most radically fundamental"(49)—is the problem of the relationship of the reality of God to the everyday experience of contemporary man/woman. The radicality of this problem is to be found in the peculiar nature of our everyday experience which, perhaps more than any other time in our Western historical consciousness, is marked through and through by a fundamental sense of the absence or death of God. This problem, Rahner stresses, calls for a decisively new kind of theology, or at least a decisively new way of 'doing' theology. Such a theology, he states, must be one

> which inquires about God and yet may not deny the classical distinction between a metaphysical recognition of God and the theology of revelation about God, must invade it and bring it to new unity—this theology must take most seriously the quandary of contemporary man and his

experience (no matter how badly misinterpreted) of the 'death of God'. It must identify with this experience...*[This] theology must ask...precisely where and how contemporary man can experience the existence of God to such an extent that he can genuinely and voluntarily make it a real factor in his life*; and theology must so do this that it does not give the hopeless impression that one ought to say nothing about something about which nothing can be said, and thereby situate the 'unsaid God' somewhere within the range of option between a bitter and absurd existence and the blind courage of action(50).

Rahner emphasizes that we must take great care from the very start in the way in which we characterize this modern form of godlessness. The contemporary sense of the death of God is not to be confused with an explicit, intentioned disavowal of the divine, such as we might find, for instance, at a more reflective level in certain forms of modern logical positivism(51). For Rahner, the spirit of atheism which dominates our modern consciousness is much less assertive than this, much less confident or dogmatic than the usual forms of thoroughgoing naturalism against which theologians in the past have been so used to jousting. For modern men and women, God is "dead" quite unrhetorically and uncaringly in the sense that *the divine just simply "does not 'happen' in the world" anymore*(52). Hence, in order to speak of God in our time we must become capable of speaking of a reality that does, somehow, "happen". Or, as Rahner has put it elsewhere, the possibility of our speaking meaningfully of God as the Transcendent One, rests basically in the possibility of our speaking of man/woman as *"a being open to transcendence"*. In the case of Bultmann we were brought to ask: In this period of the experience of the death of God, how is it that one comes at all to talk about "God"? Now, with Rahner, along very similar lines, we are urged to ask ourselves first and foremost: How can we speak of ourselves as "beings open to transcendence" from the standpoint (even as "theologians") of our seemingly godless experience?

Significantly, Rahner points directly to the development of a "Christian anthropology" as a means of working toward an answer to this question. Such a study, he states, must attempt to show "the man of today who and what he really is, how his existence entails more than the *animal rationale* of an abstract metaphysics"(53). Above all, at the concrete, human level such an anthropological inquiry must attempt to "comprehend the original unity of nature and grace, and not confine that which we call Christian grace to a realm beyond concrete existence"(54). Such words could well describe the general purpose and scope of our own study, yet, we want to press on to ask what would be the most appropriate and fruitful point of departure for such a study. Bultmann pointed in a general way to that self-understanding which arises out of the genuine experience of our finitude. Rahner, painting in somewhat more precise strokes, points briefly to such experiences as interpersonal communication, love, and death(55). We must attempt to be even more specific, and in our specificity we must aim toward a more precise understanding of what is meant by the possibility of man/woman as "a being open to transcendence".

The work of several representative American theologians seems to be aimed at the kind of methodological concerns expressed by Rahner. In the context of earlier discussions concerning the "new quest for the historical Jesus" and the theological program of "biblical hermeneutics" in the mid-sixties a book appeared with the provocative title, *Understanding God; The Key Issue in Present-Day Protestant Thought*(55). In it, the author, Frederick Herzog, recognizes the necessity to redirect the basic focus of this dual program toward the consideration of the more fundamental hermeneutical locus concerning "God", a task which he describes, significantly, as rediscovering "the method of elementary theological understanding" in the human "historico-ontological" realm(57). In a passage which could well reflect the basic scope and direction of our own study ("prolegomenous, theological anthropology" seen here as a "foundational, theological hermeneutic")(58), Herzog states:

the theological question about God *is* a hermeneutical question: How can we understand God as the referent of language about God? The stress on *hermeneutic* in this context suggests that God is not a scientific problem in terms of the objectifying thought still widely prevalent in natural science...Understanding relates to 'something much more simple and fundamental' than objectifying knowledge. Wilhelm Dilthey defined hermeneutic as interpretation: 'Interpretation would be impossible if expressions of life were completely strange. It would be unnecessary if nothing strange were in them. It lies, therefore, between these two extremes. It is always required where something strange is to be grasped through the art of understanding'. *In this vein the theological question about God as a hermeneutical question asks whether the word 'God' relates to some aspect of human experience: Is language about God completely strange to man? The hermeneutical question relative to God wants to understand in what sense it is true that God is, as theology claims.* It wants to understand this primarily on the level of non-objectifying thought(59).

And, at another point, in addressing the question of the relationship of language to understanding, he writes:

even if language could create understanding, *it always addresses itself to man's experience. The question is whether God is completely strange to man's experience. Is there any awareness in man's experience of the reality to which 'God' refers?* In this respect the emphasis on hermeneutic tries to establish that Christianity is a truth claim and not merely a language game. Theological hermeneutic seeks to check the reality claims of the Christian faith(60).

In these introductory insights, and, especially, in his sustained critique of

14 *The present theological situation*

most hermeneutical studies for having failed to see that, as he puts it, "the *first* step in discussing the hermeneutic of theological language must be the examination of the *ontological roots* of the word 'God'"(61), Herzog's work does break significantly new ground. Regrettably though, after a closer examination of Herzog's own further attempt to identify and develop these more fundamental "ontological roots", the verdict is inescapable that, in the full light of the problem as set forth above by Bultmann and Rahner, the author, in spite of his penetrating criticisms of others, has not really probed deep enough himself. Happily, we would want to recognize and approrpiate those points where Herzog's concern steers very close to that which may guide our own study, as, for instance, in addition to the above insights, when he emphasizes the fact that the prime problem which confronts the theologian is not "a new quest of the historical Jesus", but a "new quest of God", and more significantly, it is not (*contra* Ernst Fuchs, especially) primarily a question of the recovery of a "christological understanding of language", but a question of the recovery of the "theological factor" *already* implied in any christo-, or ecclesio-, or special historico-language(62). We are helped in defining the scope of our own project by Herzog's statement that although his book "does not intend to develop a comprehensive theological hermeneutic", it will deal in depth with "the *primal components* of theological understanding as they function methodologically"(63). What ultimately proves unhelpful is not such an expressed intention, but the fact that the "components" Herzog considers "primal" are simply, in the final analysis, *not primal enough.*

Herzog's main difficulty stems, I believe, from a misunderstanding of the true radicality of the question that should be asked in the "new quest of God". On the one hand, he appears to recognize the full, radical nature of the problem, as, for instance, at one important point when he quotes with approval Langdon Gilkey's observation: "'Our primary problem is...to discover how the God who has almost disappeared may appear to us again in power and in truth...We must have some certainty that there is a referent to our word 'God'...no revelation, no Christ of faith, no ecclesiology is ultimately possible or intelligible if the category of deity remains totally empty'"(64). On the other hand, he fails to grasp the thoroughgoing implication of this dilemma (i.e., the emptiness of the "category of deity" in itself precludes any *starting* point such as revelation or biblical faith) when he states, for instance, at the close of his introductory section: "Our aim here is not to move from a general understanding of God to the more specific Christian understanding. Rather...[our] own response to the present theological situation is argued through in terms of our understanding of *the inner rationale of the Christian faith*"(!) (65). It is worth quoting Gilkey's observation in full here, for not only does it lay bare the limitations of Herzog's attempt to come to grips with the real issue involved in a new quest of God, but it also serves to illuminate more clearly the precise nature of the path we shall want to follow. The quote by Herzog, above, appears in the article entitled "Dissolution and Reconstruction in Theology", published in *The Christian Century*, February 3, 1965(66). Gilkey writes:

> We must go back to the very beginning, must defend the reality of God and the possibility of language about him in a world in which no prior assumptions, metaphysical or religious can be taken for granted, and in which ordinary experience seems swept clean of cosmic coherence and ultimate meaning alike. Our primary problem is to find where we can begin in this effort—to discover how the God who has almost disappeared may appear to us again in power and in truth.
>
> These questions we must answer first. For only if we can legitimately discourse about the dimension and category of deity, about God and his works, can we speak of other theological issues and problems of which those divine works are the presupposition...Our theological question about God precedes the hermeneutical, the christological and the ecclesiological questions. *We must have some certainty that there is a referent to our word 'God' and must be self-consciously aware of where that certainty comes from if we are to talk intelligibly of his divine works among us in Christ, in Scripture and in the church.*

He continues:

> It may well be, of course, that the certainty about God comes to us through our knowledge of Christ, or our perusal of Scripture—this is not here at issue, and I am not pleading for a new natural theology. What I do say is that however God may be known, the knowledge of his reality is logically prior to all else; no revelation, no Christ of faith, no ecclesiology is ultimately possible or intelligible *if the category of deity remains totally empty.*

If we can no longer begin speaking about God from the standpoint of Scripture, or revelation, etc., where are we to start? Gilkey answers:

> *Our theological analysis must begin with man.* If we felt sure that the divine word in Scripture was the truth, then the Bible might be our starting point. Or if we felt some assurance that existence as a whole was coherent, a metaphysical beginning might be possible. But in our situation these two certainties are lacking. What remains for us, as remained for Augustine and Schleiermacher in not unsimilar straits, is man as we see him acting out his life around us, and as we feel the shape and depth of that human existence in ourselves.

Perhaps we could say, in keeping with the analogy in Gilkey's last point, that Herzog would have more to contribute to the problem at hand had he drawn the circumference of his "hermeneutics" along the lines akin to that of a Schleiermacher— or a Dilthey too, for that matter! Instead of starting with the understanding of God given in the "inner rationale of the Christian", i.e., as presented in the Gospel of John(67), he should have started with the question of the sense of the reality of God as it is grounded in the structures and possibilities of human understanding in general. Here then the real "primal" questions would be, in logical succession: (1) How does basic "human understanding" take place at all in the realm of our common, concrete experience? (2) How is it that such understanding may include the meaning, or at least the possibility of the meaning, of what is spoken of in other contexts (e.g., "Christian" faith) as "God"? Such a "hermeneutical" starting point as this would be appropriate for describing the nature of the study which we are proposing, although we shall prefer to initiate and develop our "hermēneia" by way of a specific mode (or component) of our everyday being and experience.

If Gilkey's first stricture against a starting point in Scripture applies in the case of Herzog's work, certainly his second, against a "metaphysical beginning", might well be applicable in the case of Schubert Ogden, another representative to be noted in this 'reconstructionist' group. Of course, Ogden himself would probably be the first to admit that prior to the appearance of his essay "The Reality of God" (1965) his own "metaphysical" position had not really come to grips with the radical nature of our present problem of God(68). And in all fairness it should be said that Ogden's failure to recognize this fact stems, perhaps, not so much from a peculiar methodological blindness inherent in his earlier position as it does from the rather surprisingly sudden change that has come about in our contemporary theological *milieu* in general. Be this as it may, it is instructive in the formulation of our own particular approach to see how Ogden's metaphysical solution proves inadequate as a starting point and is forced to give way to a new exploration of certain anthropological foundations which, at least in terms of spirit, comes very close to those which we are seeking. We should add that Ogden's program has a particular relevance for our own study in that he too has chosen to work in one respect within the sphere of the so-called Bultmannian problematic. For this reason we must treat his program in some detail.

Ogden's earlier failure to come to grips with the more radical implications of the problem of God can be seen basically in his tendency to construe the epistemological dilemma along the lines simply of the question of an adequate versus an inadequate *conceptualization* of God(69). In his earlier work Ogden was primarily concerned to answer the query, which seemed "basic" at that time: How can the idea of God be best analyzed and conceptualized so that it is both true to the faith in which it is grounded, and meaningful to the modern man/woman to whom it must be communicated? The dual aspect of his question reflects a constructive reconsideration of the positive concerns of nineteenth century Protestant liberalism(70) with respect to (1) the recognition of the necessary role of philosophy in clarifying theological concepts, and (2) the awareness of the ultimate apologetic end toward which this philosophical clarification is aimed. And Bultmann's theological program is seen by Ogden as a fruitful resource for fulfilling these concerns, although, as he points out in his study *Christ Without Myth*, it stands in need of correction at one very crucial point(71). If there is a point of vulnerability in Bultmann's program, Ogden argues, it is not in its demand for radical "de-mythologization", but rather in its failure to apply this methodological insight consistently to the concept of God. As Ogden puts it after a rather exhaustive analysis of this issue:

> [Bultmann] is unlike some of the existentialists because he consistently holds with Heidegger that there can be such a thing as an 'objective' science of *man's* inner life.... Nevertheless, it cannot be said that Bultmann displays a similar consistency in acknowledging that God also may be spoken about in 'objective' but not 'mythological' terms(72).

Actually, according to Ogden, Bultmann's position is really ambiguous on this latter point. On the one hand, in theory, Bultmann "is unable to affirm...that God is an 'object' of thought as well as the inescapable 'subject' of existential encounter, and therefore may be as appropriately considered as man by philosophical analysis"(73). On the other hand, in practice, "Bultmann implies precisely this by constantly speaking about God in terms of 'analogies' drawn from Heidegger's existential philosophy"(74). Ogden agrees with other critics on the "right" and the "left" in concluding that as long as Bultmann fails to overcome this crucial ambiguity his constructive work with respect to God will always be justifiably vulnerable to the charge of "subjectivism", the criticism of having sacrificed faith's "objective reference" to a mere "anthropological" interpretation. In Ogden's opinion, this can be avoided only by the full development of the theory of existential "analogy" applied to God. But in order to achieve this Bultmann's basic position must be opened up as it were and rendered capable of including the full recognition and development of what his position has hitherto ambiguously implied and rejected, namely, the idea that with reference to God we have not simply one but two modes of understanding, i.e., not only an *existentiell* understanding (a "knowledge of" God in and through our personal encounters with God as acting "subject"), but also an *existential* understanding (a "knowledge about" God which, on the basis of our *existentiell* understanding, may be clarified "objectively" by philosophical analysis)(75). As Ogden sees it, Bultmann's program is "handicapped" in developing this point primarily because of its lack of a more adequate philosophical resource. But such a resource is quite near at hand, Ogden tells us, in the general ontology of process philosophy—especially as developed in the work of Charles Hartshorne—where "divine existence...is appropriately analysed and conceptualized"(76).

We cannot now go into the implications of Ogden's proposal regarding the fruitfulness of augmenting Heidegger's phenomenology with Hartshorne's "dipolar theism". Indeed, we do not need to, for as we have seen in our earlier discussion, there is yet a *prior* question which demands answering before we can even begin to consider such a proposal as this. Just as we were led to ask in the case of assertions about God made on the basis of Scripture, so now we must also ask in the case of assertions that are to be made on the basis of "metaphysics", *What to start with is their experiential grounding?* If, as Ogden suggests, metaphysical(77) concepts of God *are* connected in an originary sense to existential realities, certainly the *first* task is to show just *how* this is so. Surely in face of the radicality of the problem of God today the metaphysician no less than the "biblical revelationalist" must, as a first order of business, attempt to answer how it is that an understanding of "God" is possible at all at the level of our everyday experience.

Actually, in the early analysis of Bultmann's thought to which we have been referring, Ogden does seem to recognize this problem between conceptuality and everyday experience. In his concluding chapter he observes, for instance: "Until process philosophy is informed by the insights of existential analysis, its lack of an explicit anthropology, which handicaps it for theological employment, can hardly be remedied in keeping with its own implicit principles"(78). Unfortunately, after having put his finger on this most important corrective insight, Ogden by and large fails to implement it in the constructive studies which follow his first book.

The one important exception to this criticism is, as we have mentioned, his later essay "The Reality of God". In Section Two of this study(79) Ogden presents what might well be taken as an exploration of the kind of anthropological grounding pre-supposed by a Hartshornian metaphysical theism, or, for that matter, by *any* reflective theism. Curiously, as we would expect from the point made in his earlier work, Ogden does not attempt to develop his position from the standpoint of Heidegger's phenomenological interpretation of human existence. Rather, he chooses to work instead within the context of British language philosophy, specifically, by way of a particular position advanced by the philosopher Stephen Toulmin. Focusing upon the final chapter of Toulmin's book, *An Examination of the Place of Reason in Ethics*(80), where he directly takes up the question of "religious" language, Ogden elaborates three points in Toulmin's argument which he feels to be most suggestive to his own purposes. The first and second points have to do with the now familiar critique against the positivistic narrowness which characterizes certain forms of analytic philosophy(81). Here, Ogden applauds Toulmin's criticism of those philosophers who exhibit a "too narrow view of the uses of reasoning", due to their dogmatic adherence to the assumption that "a mathematical or logical proof or a scientific verification can be the only kind of 'good reason' for any statement"(82). "Contrary to this assumption", Ogden writes, "Toulmin holds that we must always understand both our language and the reasoning of which it is the expression in relation to the larger reality of life to which they belong"(83). The all-important presupposition supporting this view is that the "different uses of language, like the different kinds of argument, arise in function of the various situations and activities of human existence in the world"(84). For example, the fundamental experiential situation from which "scientific" language and reasoning take their rise is that "everyday situation where one is suddenly surprised by a phenomenon that his previous experience had not led him to anticipate"(85). "Scientific explanation" and its own peculiar logic emerges in one's successful attempt to overcome this surprise by understanding his experience in such a way as to predict—without further surprise—future events and developments. It is in a parallel sense, according to Ogden, that Toulmin understands the experiential genesis of "moral" language and reasoning. In the case of the latter the "underlying life activity" (Ogden) is the common pursuit of our varied interests and desires in a social context with our fellow man/woman. "Moral reasoning", and its accompanying "logic", come into being through our efforts to cope with and decide effectively in the face of the conflicts and tensions which arise in the pursuit of these varied interests. Without elaborating these examples further, Ogden moves on to consider in much greater detail the third and most important point in Toulmin's argument(86), namely, the way in which he understands both "science" and "morality" to point beyond themselves to a decidedly unique context of experience from which "religious" or "theological" language emerges. This process of pointing beyond is seen in the phenomenon which Toulmin describes as the "limiting question". In his very brief development of this insight Ogden comes close to the kind of constructive program we shall want to undertake. I say "close" because, as I shall indicate, it does suffer from a crucial deficiency which restricts its otherwise fruitful developments.

According to Ogden, Toulmin rightly sees that although both scientific and moral reasoning each have their roots in specific experiential concerns which, for their own separate purposes, include certain kinds of reasoning while they exclude others, they nevertheless are not completely self-contained. This is attested by the fact of the emergence of certain questions at the level of our everyday activities as moral agents and scientific knowers which, although appearing ostensibly as "moral" and "scientific" questions, cannot really be answered by the systems of reasoning appropriate to these spheres. Such a limiting question can be seen in the moral sphere, for example, when, even after he has been referred (and re-referred) to the logical rule that a certain action must always be done, or has been shown that only such an act makes for the greatest possible harmony of human interests, one still persists in asking: "But why ought I to do such and such anyway"? Although such a question may indeed arise out of the sphere of moral experience, it is nevertheless a question to which no moral reason can as such give an answer. Toulmin argues that the only kind of answers appropriate to such limiting questions are those which come from that reasoning appropriate to "religious" language. As Ogden is quick to add, what Toulmin is really saying is that although the experiential spheres from which such questions arise are ostensibly "moral" or "scientific", in reality they are really "religious"(87). Apparently, for Toulmin, we somehow tread over an invisible threshold into a truly "religious" sphere of experience and reflection at those subtle points in our everyday living when we are faced with the fact of "accepting ourselves and the world, of pursuing scientific knowledge and embracing moral duty, *in spite of* conditions that make for the profoundest uncertainty about what the future finally holds"(88). Now for our purposes we would like to know a great deal more not only about the typical language which emerges either out of or as an answer to this peculiarly "religious" mode of experiencing, but also about the nature of this experiencing itself, beginning first of all with the peculiar *conditions* under which such experiencing is precipitated. Precisely what are these conditions and what kind of pre-reflective understanding emerges within them? In what way does this pre-reflective understanding lend itself to conceptualization, and particularly a conceptualization of the reality "God"?

Unfortunately, Ogden tells us that Toulmin does not come close to answering any of these questions. In fact, he states, "Toulmin is not very specific as to just what is to be included among these conditions"(89). We should add— and here the limits of Ogden's work for our study emerge—Ogden himself is not very specific either! After surmising that because of Toulmin's fondness for Pascal, Tolstoy, and Dostoevsky, he must have in mind such "boundary situations" ("finitude" and "death") which certain existentialist philosophers have defined as the distinctive elements of our "human condition", Ogden says simply, and all too briefly: "At any rate, men, as Toulmin sees them, are sufficiently threatened by their actual life situation that they are moved by a deep 'desire for reassurance, for a general confidence about the future'. And so there arise the limiting questions in which this desire finds explicit expresssion"(90). On this basis Ogden does go on to argue suggestively that such limiting questions reveal that all human activities are existentially possible only because they already presuppose a certain "underlying confidence in the abiding worth of our life"(91). He argues further that "the primary use or function of 'God' is to refer to the objective ground...of [this] ineradicable confidence in the final worth of our existence"(92). He states:

> It lies in the nature of this basic confidence to affirm that the real whole of which we experience ourselves to be parts is such as to be worthy of, and thus itself to evoke, that very confidence. The word 'God,' then, provides the designation for whatever it is about this experienced whole that calls forth and justifies our original and inescapable trust, thereby meaning existentially, as William James once said, 'You can dismiss certain kinds of fear'. From this it follows that to be free of such fear by existing in this trust is one and the same thing with affirming the reality of God(93).

On the basis of this contention Ogden attempts to justify once and for all his fundamental premise, by way of allusion to John Baillie, that although one may reject "God" "in the top of the mind", as an existing being one must necessarily affirm him "in the bottom of the heart"(94). Also, by thus identifying "God" not as a separate referent apart from our commonly experienced reality, but the very meaning of "reality" itself, Ogden attempts to successively counter the charge made by certain philosophers that, so the argument goes, the word "God" is ultimately vacuous because it has no reference to any verifiably objective reality. The point I wish to make here, however, is that as much as we may share and appropriate Ogden's central concerns and methodological insights, his constructive energies, as they stand, will inevitably be limited, both for our purposes and the purposes of the present situation, as long as they fail to develop a fuller *anthropology* supportive of the kind of ontological affirmations claimed above. We could learn much from Ogden had he not moved so quickly (Section III of his essay) to Hartshorne's theistic metaphysics to show, as he puts it, "how the ground of our confidence is most appropriately understood or conceived..."(95). Ogden should have remained longer with Toulmin, or better, should have penetrated more deeply than Toulmin to a full explication of the anthropological ontology(96) toward which the latter's analysis explicitly points. Parenthetically, we might add that only by arguing from a more adequate philosophical *anthropology* can Ogden's "dialogue" with British analytic philosophy really gain any force. It seems to me that Ogden's (and our) differences with someone like Antony Flew are ultimately not over the issues of language and logic (as important as these may be), but over the rock-bottom issue of a more accurate and meaningful ontological interpretation of "human being", or of the "reality" that is disclosed in "human experiencing". It is my feeling that this crucial deficiency in Ogden's constructive program might best be overcome with the help of an anthropological phenomenology such as Heidegger's. And is this not what he suggested in the first place?

For our own purposes we shall want to heed fully Ogden's basic argument that there can be no understanding of the reality of God, no cognitively meaningful talk of "God", unless some kind of understanding of that vocable is already given in, with, and through our everyday experience as human beings. Further, we shall want to heed Ogden's contention that in interpreting and clarifying this basic understanding we can no longer start from the particularistic standpoint of faith(97), even though, as "historically conditioned" creatures we cannot ultimately escape speaking from a particular confessional perspective. As he states in his article, "The Possibility and Task of Philosophical Theology": "Not even faith can assert something as true which is in principle lacking in cognitive meaning"(98). It is primarily philosophy's role to clarify the kind of cognitive meaning implied in faith's object, i.e., theology must rely upon this extra-theological discipline, in its description function, for the "hermeneutical" clarification of its subject-matter—here, "reality, as inclusive of both "human experiencing" and the category of deity.

Hence, initially, we can appropriate Ogden's observation that with respect to God it is possible to have not simply one, but two types of "understanding": not simply an existentiell understanding, but also an existential understanding, a formal "knowledge about" (God), on the basis of that understanding which emerges in and through our prior existentiell encounter(s) with ourselves and the world.

In the progress of our own work we must not lose sight of the extremely problematical nature of this very last point, the fundamental grounding of philosophical concepts in one's prior, *existentiell* self-understanding. Because of its importance for our constructive efforts we should carefully consider the following.

Bultmann maintains that knowledge of the "existence" of God can be given *only in* the concrete *existentiell* encounter of (Christian) faith; the philosopher—and even Bultmann himself as "philosophical-theologian"—cannot have access to the "existence" of God in the same way that he has access to human "existence"(99). He holds that it is possible to develop, starting from an analysis of a person's basic *existentiell* encounter with one-self and the world, certain ontological concepts which may legitimately be used to clarify the meaning of the concept "God"(110). But this means that the philosopher (and philosophical theologian) is only speaking about the "idea" of God and in no sense about that reality itself(101). Because of the crucial issue involved here we should quote Ogden's reply to Bultmann in full:

> Such a view...I can only regard as inadequate...[Bultmann] himself has often cautioned against *a false separation of a knowledge of concepts from a knowledge of the existential realities to which they refer.* Why, then, should we suppose that the philosopher can at best know the *concept* of God, not God himself? But perhaps Bultmann's point is not simply to deny that the philosopher can know God's existence, but to insist that he can know it only negatively, as it is known in man's *question* for God. In that case, however, we would have to inquire as to *the conditions of man's being able to ask that question. Can he ask for God without some positive knowledge of God's reality? And if he cannot, is there any reason why such knowledge of God as man already possesses should not be philosophically explicable?*(102)

As we have suggested, the answer to these last two vital questions, and to the fundamental issue lying between these two theologians, can be resolved ultimately not by any quick, a priori appeal to the "logically necessary scope" of philosophical knowledge(103), but only by appeal to the "existential realities" themselves, that is, to the nature of that pre-reflective understanding which emerges on the fundamental level of our *existentiell* encounter with ourselves and the world. Gordon D. Kaufman puts this point quite well when he states, in his article "The Meaning of 'God': Trancendence Without Mythology": "We must begin our investigation by asking about the purpose or intention of

'God-language'...that is, *which experience or problems in this world seem to require some people to talk about extramundane reality?*"(104) Again:

The problem to which we shall initially address ourselves is not the abstract and general problem of proving to any rational mind the meaningfulness and even truth of the concept of 'God': it is, rather, the concrete problem of locating the context and situation in which the word 'God' is used and found appropriate and meaningful. Clearly, only if this latter task is performed first can the former be undertaken with any hope of significant outcome. Indeed, it may turn out that this word or its context has a peculiar character which makes impossible such general logical justification(105).

Apparently, for Ogden, even Bultmann implies that that special understanding given in the *existentiell* encounter of faith, is dependent for its own ultimate understanding upon that primary understanding which we possess via our basic *existentiell* encounter(s) with the world. So far though we look in vain in Ogden's work for an analysis of the *kind(s)* of *existentiell* encounter(s) that would be applicable at this point. He seems to have made a start toward this end in his examination of Toulmin's position regarding the experiential conditions wherein the "limiting question" arises. But we must dig deeper and carry forth our analysis in greater breadth at the anthropological level. In keeping with Ogden's own criteria(106) let us ask: *On what kind of specific experiential basis can we affirm with Paul that we are "without excuse" because "what can be known about God" has already been manifested to us* (Rom. 1.19f.)? Whether the kind of experiential disclosure of the divine implied here is "positive" and not simply "negative", whether it yields more than an "idea" of God, a mere quest or desire for an ultimate reality known only in the form of a "question", is something we can only answer after we have looked at the "experiential disclosure" itself. This leads us to a statement of our constructive thesis and a description of the method and nature of our study.

Thesis and approach: "conscience" as an experiential locus for the understanding of "God"—a contribution to a theological prolegomenon

As a contribution to the development of a prolegomenous theological anthropology which will meet the demands delineated above, we shall focus our sights upon a single, key dimension of our everyday experience and being: the phenomenon of *conscience*. In recent years there have been several noteworthy attempts by theologians to reinterpret this phenomenon(106). Among these the work of Gerhard Ebeling stands out distinctively as showing promise for our particular constructive problem. On the basis of an analysis of the idea of conscience in Ebeling's work (so I shall argue), and the key philosophical resource upon which it draws, specifically, Martin Heidegger's important reinterpretation in *Being and Time*, I shall develop the primary thesis that *in the experience given to man/woman as "conscience" we have a qualitatively unique ontological grounding for understanding the reality deemed "God"*.

In working towards this thesis I will assess along the way the ultimate adequacy of Ebeling's own attempt to ground the understanding of "God" in conscience. As we shall discover, although Ebeling's thought does prove to be extremely helpful for the purposes of developing a theological prolegomenon, certain presuppositions and tendencies in his theological perspective impose unnecessary and unwarranted limitations upon his fruitful insights. In venturing beyond these limitations and developing these latter insights into the nature of conscience more fully, I shall attempt to further explicate my primary thesis.

In singling out the experience of conscience for the kind of prolegomenous study described above I am not, of course, unaware of the fact that in our time this phenomenon has ostensibly been rendered useless for theological purposes. I have in mind conscience's so-called historical "domestication", "decline", and "fall"(108): in the first case, e.g., in the "*synderesis*" doctrine of the medieval Scholastics (especially in the work of Aquinas and the ensuing tradition of moral theology and philosophy)(109), secondly, in the thought of Kant and German Idealism (together with the accompanying theological development in the later, far-flung Ritschlian school)(110), and, finally, in the various social and psychological reductionistic conceptions of the nineteenth and early twentieth centuries (exemplified above all by the thought of Nietzsche and Freud)(111). In the face of this importune demise of conscience the theologian is faced (as Professor Lehmann so aptly reminds us) with the sharp alternative: "either 'do the conscience over' or 'do the conscience in!'"(113) The contention of this investigation is that in the reinterpretation undertaken by Ebeling, with Heidegger, we have the most promising resource for "doing the conscience over" in our day.

With the stress placed upon this last point, we would not want to foster the misleading impression that Ebeling's reinterpretation stands alone in recent Christian thought as a responsible attempt to overcome the challenge of the conscience's historical demise. One must cite the work by Nathan Söderblom(112), John Baillie(114), Karl Heim(115), and Paul Tillich(116), and the interpretations of conscience in the beginnings of dialectic theology found in the work of Bultmann(117), Gogarten(118), and, yes, even Karl Barth(119). These earlier interpretations are certainly at one with Ebeling's to the extent that they responsibly take cognizance of, and attempt to overcome, the relativistic and positivistic tendencies of those previous interpretations noted above. Ebeling's effort differs, however, from these earlier neo-orthodox writers in two important respects. First, he gives the phenomenon of conscience a decidedly central place in his basic conception of the divine-human relationship and in his doctrine of the knowledge of God. Secondly, and most crucially, Ebeling's analysis develops out of, in clear dependence upon (as I shall argue), a major philosophical resource which reflects a significant, new stage of development in the modern interpretation of conscience.

Because of the importance of this second point, and because Ebeling himself does not make this point sufficiently clear, I shall devote considerable space in my analysis to this key philosophical resource which lies behind Ebeling's constructive effort. The attempt to critically explicate and explore the full implications of Heidegger's phenomenological-existential description of conscience and to establish its influence upon and import for Ebeling's theological labors constitutes what might be termed the secondary thesis of this work.

Despite the crucial role which conscience plays at the heart of Ebeling's theology, it is odd, I think, that it has been given little, if any, recognition by his respective interpreters and critics. It goes without saying that in the development of our study we shall advance several steps toward correcting this situation. It could be charged that in attempting to extrapolate this particular "anthropological" theme in Ebeling's thought and to recast its constructive implications within the context of our own problematic concerning the prolegomenous issue of the experiential grounding for "God" language, we are attempting to achieve what in essence his own "theology" does not really in principle allow for. In response, let me make clear in a preliminary fashion that this study is concerned not with the examination and clarification of "a system of thought" as such (actually, in our case it would really be two systems!), but rather with assaying the potentialities of one key aspect in the thought of a contemporary theologian (and philosopher), as it applies to a specific problem at hand. Our investigation is, then, "problem oriented", rather than "thinker or system oriented". Surely in such a study the application of the insights from a particular source to the constructive solution of a problem which may not have been within the 'original' purview of this source is a legitimate procedure, provided, of course, that we do not misread or misuse these insights as they stand either in themselves or, as the case may be, in their logical extension.

Notes

Notes to page 1:
1. I cannot begin to list the many excellent studies that have appeared on this subject during the last several decades. The reader can consult the bibliographies in the following works for pertinent references on "secularization", "secularism", etc.: Thomas J. J. Altizer and William Hamilton, *Radical Theology and the Death of God* (Indianapolis: The

Notes to page 2:
Bobbs-Merrill Company, Inc., 1966), pp. 193-202; and C. W. Christian and Glenn R. Wittig, eds., *Radical Theology: Phase Two; Essays on the Current Debate* (Philadelphia: J. B. Lippincott Co., 1967), pp. 215-218; and Hans Küng, *Does God Exist?* trans. Edward Quinn (New York: Vintage Books: 1981), pp. 703-796.

The following key works stand behind the formulation of the problem presented in this study: Charles C. West, ed., *Consultation for University Teachers Report on "The Mean of the Secular"* (Bossey: Ecumenical Institute [editor's edition, personally circulated], 1959; Martin Stallmann, *Was ist Säkularisierung?* (Tübingen: J. C. B. Mohr [Paul Siebeck], 1960); Franklin L. Baumer, *Religion and the Rise of Scepticism* (New York: Harcourt, Brace and Co., 1960); Gabriel Vahanian, *The Death of God; The Culture of Our Post-Christian Era* (New York: George Braziller, 1961); Ronald Gregor Smith, *The Whole Man; Studies in Christian Anthropology* (Philadelphia: The Westminster Press, 1969); Gordon D. Kaufman, *God the Problem* (Cambridge, Mass.: Harvard University Press, 1972); Eberhard Jüngel, *God as the Mystery of the World*, trans. Darrell L. Guder (Grand Rapids, Mich.: William B. Eerdmans, 1983); and most particularly, Langdon Gilkey, *Naming the Whirlwind; The Renewal of God-Language* (Indianapolis: The Bobbs-Merrill Company, Inc., 1969).

2. Cf.,e.g., Altizer and Hamilton; Christian and Wittig, eds.
3. (New York: Macmillan, 1963).
4. *Ibid.*, p.11. I am aware of the noninclusive character of such references to the generically human ("modern man", "man as man", etc.) in modern historical, theological, and philosophical parlance. The editing requirements in so much of the literature quoted here and elsewhere in this study have presented insurmountable obstacles in terms of grammar, syntax, and basic readability. Rather than butchering such texts unmercifully I have allowed them to remain intact while modifying as much as possible the language of my own discussion through such terms as "modern man/woman", "modern man and woman" and "human being". I apologize to the justifiably sensitive readers that my ultimate resolve to reform these and other noninclusive expressions is as yet only partially realized.
5. *Ibid.*, (emphasis is mine).
6. *Ibid.*
7. See, e.g., Schubert M. Ogden's critique in his *The Reality of God and Other Essays* (New York: Harper and Row, 1966), pp. 14f., 85-90. See also the criticism by Gilkey, *Naming the Whirlwind*, pp. 107-228.
8. From Langdon Gilkey's unpublished essay entitled "The God is Dead Theology and the Possibility of God Language" (originally delivered at

Notes to page 2:
the faculty retreat of The Divinity School of The University of Chicago in the fall of 1964, and subsequently circulated in mimeographed form by the author), p. 27. See also his statement in *Naming the Whirlwind*, pp. 9.

There are those who would try to minimize the significance of the *problem* of secularism by claiming that it is presently the mere *outlook* or *perspective* of a social-intellectual class which stands on the periphery of cultural life when statistically portrayed. A reply to such criticism is not really warranted. To attempt to nullify a problem by stressing that those who recognize it speak out of a particular perspective in a rapidly changing social context is not to present a refutation at all. Hence the lack of force I see in the criticism of Michael Novak, Harvey Cox, and others. E.g., see Michael Novak's argument in "The Religious Consciousness of the Professional-Managerial Class," *The Christian Century*, 93 (1976): 217-224. Harvey Cox's provocative though weakly developed exhortation (!) is found in his recent book, *Religion in the Secular City; Toward A Postmodern Theology* (New York: Simon and Schuster, 1984).

9. Certainly van Buren and others have failed to grasp the real intentions of such an older progenitor as Bultmann when he is depicted simply as one who wrote "as a professional Christian or qualified theologian who understood the Gospel perfectly clearly and was only looking for a technique of communication or popular idiom to reach the man of today 'out there', outside the church". Van Buren, p. 2. Although van Buren's reference is only indirect here, it is nevertheless illustrative of the rather irresponsible kind of historical myopia that has become so much the fashion in contemporary theological literature. Cf. Schubert Ogden's much more perceptive understanding of Bultmann's (and, for that matter, the early Barth's) real methodological posture and intentions in his essay "The Significance of Rudolf Bultmann for Contemporary Theology", in *The Theology of Rudolf Bultmann*, ed. Charles W. Kegley (New York: Harper and Row, 1966), pp. 112ff. Cf., also Ogden's discussion in his Introduction to *Existence and Faith; Shorter Writings of Rudolf Bultmann*, ed. and trans. Schubert M. Ogden (Cleveland: Meridian Books, 1963), p. 18.

10. One could think perhaps of Paul Tillich and Friedrich Gogarten in this connection as well. Of course one could also think of the theological agenda enumerated in the prison letters of Dietrich Bonhoeffer under the dual heading of the "world come of age" and the "nonreligious interpretation of biblical concepts".

11. By "initial" stage I mean, of course, the most recent phase of a theological development which has its historical roots in the 1700's with the rise

Notes to page 2:
of the liberalized theologies of the *Aufklärung*. Bultmann's work opens the "initial stage" of our present problematic—as a continuation of the earlier liberal problematic—in the sense that it came to the surface *after* Barth's return to the "strange new world of the Bible" against modern culture (a position which Bulmann in part also shared).

12. *Kerygma and Myth*, 3 vols., ed. H. W. Bartsch, trans. Reginald H. Fuller (London: S.P.C.K., 1953-1962), 1:1-44. As Ogden has pointed out, although the term "demythologizing" did not appear until Bultmann's programmatic essay of 1941, the essential constructive features of this program were sketched out over a decade and a half earlier in his book *Jesus*. See the English translation by L. P. Smith and E. H. Lantero entitled *Jesus and the Word* (2nd ed.; New York: Charles Scribner's Sons, 1958), pp. 1-15, 51-56, *passim* (cited by Ogden, "The Significance of Rudolf Bultmann", p. 110).

13. The crucial work here is of course Bultmann's essay "The Problem of Hermeneutics", *Essays, Philosophical and Theological*, trans. James C. G. Greig (New York: The Macmillan Company, 1955), pp. 234-261; but cf., also his other important statements in such works as *Jesus Christ and Mythology* (New York: Charles Scribner's Sons, 1958), pp. 53f.; *Glauben und Verstehen*, 3 vols. (Tübingen: J. C. B. Mohr (Paul Siebeck), 1933-1962), 1:303f. ("Aber es bleibt auch dabei, dass es von Gott reden möchte, auch und gerade dann, wenn es sich sträubt, von Gott zu reden. Gott ist ausserhalb des Christentums nicht in dem Sinne unerkennbar..., dass der Mensch nicht den Gottesgedanken fassen könnte. *Auch der natürliche Mensch kann von Gott reden, weil er in seiner Existenz um Gott weiss.*" [emphasis is mine.] In this latter connection it is well to recall Bultmann's fondness for summarizing his methodological intentions by quoting Augustine's famous remark, "*Tu nos fecisti ad te, et cor nostrum inquietum est, donec requiescat in te*" ("Thou hast made us for thyself and our heart is restless, until it rests in thee"), e.g., Bultmann, *Kerygma and Myth*, 1:192f. For Barth's dialogue cf. his essay "Rudolf Bultmann—An Attempt to Understand Him", in Bultmann, *Kerygma and Myth*, 2:83-132.

14. Trans. by Robert W. Funk, *Journal for Theology and the Church*, 2 (1965):83-95. (Hereafter we shall refer to this journal by the abbreviation *JThC*.)

15. (Philadelphia: The Westminster Press, 1963).

16. On the Continent cf. the work of Herbert Braun, e.g., his essay "The Meaning of New Testament Christology", *JThC*, 5(1968): 122-123.

17. Rudolf Bultmann, "The Idea of God and Modern Man", *JThC*, 1 (1965): 83.

18. *Ibid.* pp. 85f. Cf. the distinction in Friedrich Gogarten, *Verhängnis und*

Notes to pages 2–5:
> *Hoffnung der Neuzeit* (Stuttgart: Friedrich Vorwerk Verlag, 1953), pp. 129ff.; see, also, the same kind of distinction in Chapter IV of Vahanian, especially pp. 65- 69 ("This is a reflection of the Biblical insistence to steer clear both of dualism and of monism—respectively, the separation and confusion of sacred and secular. For the Bible there is only one valid distinction: the holy and the not yet holy. Once these characteristics have been understood, it is easy to distinguish secularity from secularism. While the former is that realm in which religion can show its relevance, the latter is an inverted or concealed religious attitude. Secularism is a form of religiosity, for which the present and the immanent are invested with the attributes of the eternal and the transcendent...Protestantism and, indeed, Biblical thought are not compatible with secularism. This would contradict the basic understanding of man's nature as a creature, created in the image of God. And it would contradict the original Biblical view according to which one's faith in God and involvement in the world, or secularity, belong together. These two are united and can be separated only at the expense of one kind of fanaticism or another". [p. 67]; cf., also, Ronald Gregor Smith's discussion in West, ed., pp. 23ff., and the excellent analysis by Baumer, Chapter III, *et passim*.

19. As quoted by Bultmann, "The Idea of God", p. 86.
20. *Ibid.*
21. *Ibid.*
22. As quoted by Bultmann, *ibid.*, p. 86.
23. *Ibid.*
24. *Ibid.*, p. 92.
25. *Ibid.*, pp. 85ff. (On the use of the neologism subjectity see the translator's explanation, *ibid.*, p. 85, n.9). For Heidegger's provocative elaboration of this view see his essay "Nietzsches Word 'Gott is tot'", in *Holzwege* (Frankfurt am Main: Vittorio Klostermann, 1950), pp. 236ff., especially. In addition, see the interpretation by Martin Heidegger in *Nietzsche*, 2 vols. (Pfulligen: Günther Neske Verlag, 1961), 2:450-454.
26. Bultmann, "The Idea of God", p. 86. Cf. Ronald Gregor Smith's reference to Gabriel Marcel's remark in the latter's *Being and Having*: "'I am tempted to think that the idea of autonomy is bound up with a kind of narrowing or particularisation of the subject'". (Quoted in West, ed., pp. 24-25).
27. Here Bultmann refers to Kant's statement in his *Critique of Practical Reason* (Pt. I, Bk. II, Chapter II, Sec. V), *ibid.*, p. 87, n. 15: "'In this manner the moral law leads through the conception of the *summum bonum*, as the object and final end of pure practical reason, to religion, that is, to the recognition of all duties as divine commands, not as sanc-

Notes to pages 5–6:

tions, that is to say, arbitrary ordinances of a foreign will and contingent in themselves, but as essential laws of every free will in itself, which, however, must be regarded as commands of the supreme being...'".

28. *Ibid.*, p. 87. Here Bultmann refers to Gerhard Ebeling's statement in *Word and Faith* to clarify this point, *ibid.*, n. 16: "'But now, to the reality that concerns modern man there belongs...the discovery of the autonomy of the reason and accordingly the inescapable duty to make use of the autonomous reason—not, be it noted, to make autonomous use of the reason; for it is not man himself but reason which, rightly understood, is autonomous, whereas to confuse the autonomy of the reason with the autonomy of man results precisely in a new heteronomy of the reason...'".
29. *Ibid.*, pp. 87-88.
30. *Ibid.*, p. 88.
31. *Ibid.*
32. *Ibid.*
33. *Ibid.*, p. 89 (emphasis is mine)
34. For Heidegger's illuminating interpretation of Nietzsche's conception of the death of God and nihilism see the discussion in *Holzwege*, pp. 193-247.
35. Quoted by Bultmann, "The Idea of God", *JThC*, 1 (1965): 84 (emphasis is mine).
36. Quoted by Bultmann, *ibid.*, pp. 84-85.
37. This requirement is recognized in even the most recent theological debate. See the Introduction to Eberhard Jüngel's *God the Mystery of the World*, pp. 3-104. Jüngel understands clearly the phenomenon of "subjectity" which lies at the heart of Nietzsche's vision and its significance for our inability to speak meaningfully of God today: "It would seem to be agreed that we are living in an age of the verbal placelessness of God. This placelessness finds its counterpart in the increasing inability to think God and the speechlessness of theology, which is only poorly concealed in its opposite. Theology is thus in a bad state. This is the way in which a consideration of God as the mystery of the world must probably begin today, if one does not want to forego from the outset being in tune with the times.... One simply cannot ignore the fact that the dubiousness of talk about God has intensified in the course of what has been called the Second Enlightenment...". (pp. 3-4) "This basic theological aporia of the modern age is expressed anthropologically in our experience that man can be human without God. Man no longer has the criterion for his own necessity and reality in God; rather, he understands himself on the basis of himself, whether accidentally or necessarily.... Ejected from the center of the universe,

Notes to pages 7–10:
man had to secure himself by himself. After he had lost the objectivity of his centralized existential position through the discoveries of science, he had to secure his subjectivity and rebuild the entire universe anew on that basis, if he did not want to end up in endless uncertainty. In this sense he became the point of reference for everything that exists" (p. 16).
38. Quoted by Bultmann, *ibid.*, p. 84.
39. Cf. Heidegger, *Holzwege*, pp. 199-200. "Aus diesem Satz wird klar, dass Nietzsches Wort vom Tod Gottes den christlichen Gott meint. Aber es ist nicht weniger gewiss und im voraus zu bedenken, dass die Namen Gott und christlicher Gott im Denken Nietzsches zur Bezeichnung der übersinnlichen Welt überhaupt gebraucht werden. Gott ist der Name für den Bereich der Ideen und der Ideale. Dieser Bereich des übersinnlichen gilt seit Platon, genauer gesagt, seit der spätgriechischen und der christlichen Auslegung der Platonischen Philosophie, als die wahre und eigentlich wirkliche Welt. Im Unterschied zu ihr ist die sinnliche Welt nur die diesseitige, die veränderliche und deshalb die bloss scheinbare, unwirkliche Welt. Die diesseitige Welt ist das Jammertal im Unterschied zum Berg der ewigen Seligkeit im Jenseits. Nennen wir, wie das noch bei Kant geschieht, die sinnliche Welt die im weiteren Sinne physische, dann ist die übersinnliche Welt die metaphysische Welt". For the implications of the death of God with respect to the ultimate valuelessness of our era, cf. pp. 205ff. ("Nietzsche stellt in einer Aufzeichnung aus dem Jahr 1887 die Frage (W.z.M.A.2): 'Was bedeutet Nihilismus?' Er antwortet: '*Dass die obersten Werte sich entwerten*'". [p. 205]).
40. Bultmann, "The Idea of God", p. 88; (Bultmann quotes Vahanian here: see the latter's *The Death of God*, p. 78).
41. *Ibid.*, p. 89.
42. After all is said and done Eberhard Jüngel's admirable work, *God the Mystery of the World*, falls prey to the same limitation here as Bultmann. Invoking the seeming godlessness of the world under the paradigm of the cross of Christ as the answer to the problem of understanding the meaning of God in the modern era, Jüngel moves too quickly to the kerygmatic perspective of biblical faith. See the movement he makes, following his reading of Bonhoeffer, pp. 61-63.
43. Bultmann, "The Idea of God", pp. 89-90 (emphasis is mine).
44. Clearly, any suspicions that our project is aiming disguisedly toward the resuscitation of an empirical "proof" for the existence of God should be dispelled at this point.
45. It is here that I would resist the kind of typology ("religious", "theistic", and "secular") Gordon Kaufman might initially impose upon such a prolegomenous study as ours. See his *God the Problem*, pp. 8, n. 1, 213-

32 The present theological situation

Notes to pages 10–16:
225.
46. Van A. Harvey, *A Handbook of Theological Terms* (New York: The Macmillan Co., 1964), pp. 192f.
47. (New York: Herder and Herder, 1966). (Cf. also Karl Rahner's essay, "Theology and Anthropology", in T. Patrick Burke, ed., *The Word in History* [New York: Herder and Herder 1966].)
48. *Ibid.*, p. 93.
49. *Ibid.*
50. *Ibid.*, p. 94 (emphasis is mine).
51. This criticism might well be applied to Schubert Ogden sizing up our present theological situation. Cf. certain points, as e.g., *The Reality of God*, pp. 17ff. See our discussion of Ogden below.
52. Rahner, p. 94 (emphasis is mine).
53. *Ibid.*, p. 95. (See Rahner's more recent anthropological investigations, e.g., the important essay, "Experience of Self and Experience of God", in *Theological Investigations, Vol. XIII; Theology, Anthropology, Christology*, trans. David Bourke (New York: Crossroad, 1975), pp. 122-132.
54. *Ibid.*
55. *Ibid.*
56. (New York: Charles Scribner's Sons, 1966).
57. *Ibid.*, cf. Chapters III and IV.
58. This comparison will be elaborated in our constructive treatment of Gerhard Ebeling's thought.
59. Herzog, pp. 13-14 (emphasis is mine).
60. *Ibid.*, p. 14 (emphasis is mine).
61. *Ibid.*, p. 96 (emphasis is mine).
62. *Ibid.*, pp. 92-93.
63. *Ibid.*, p. 15 (emphasis is mine).
64. *Ibid.*, p. 12.
65. *Ibid.*, p. 15 (emphasis is mine).
66. *Ibid.*, pp. 136-137 (emphasis is mine). See Gilkey's subsequent elaboration of this point in *Naming the Whirlwind*, pp. 179ff.
67. After all has been said and done, Herzog's real starting point remains within the confines of a "scriptural pneumatology"; e.g., cf. Herzog, Chapter III, pp. 83-88.
68. Subsequent discussions with Professor Ogden have revealed he disagrees with the "radical" reading of our present theological situation sketched out in the pages above.
69. See Schubert M. Odgen, *Christ Without Myth* (New York: Harper and Row, 1961), p. 138. In this regard, we recall Bultmann's criticism of Robinson, as well as Rahner's comment above.
70. *Ibid.*, pp. 14ff.

Notes to pages 16–18:
71. Ogden's second point of correction, Bultmann's Christological particularism, does not fall within the purview of our study here.
72. *Ibid.*, p. 149 (emphasis is mine).
73. *Ibid.*, p. 150.
74. *Ibid.*
75. *Ibid.*, p. 151. For my reader's benefit let me quickly recall the meaning of these two terms, as they have come to us through the writings of and on Heidegger and Bultmann. It is customary to leave the terms "*existentiell*" (or "*existenziell*") and "*existential*" (or "*existenzial*") in their original German forms. The first, *existentiell*, always denotes specific concrete acts of existing and the type of immediate, prereflective understanding which accompanies such acts. The second, *existential*, always denotes "a universal pattern or structure that is embodied in some particular or concrete act", and which can be described formally through philosophical reflection. (See Van Harvey, *A Handbook of Theological Terms*, p. 94). We should also note that in certain contexts *existentiell* and *existential* are used interchangeably for the respective Heideggerian terms "ontic" (German: "*ontisch*") and "ontological" (German: "*ontologisch*").
76. *Ibid.*, p. 56.
77. In Ogden's position the reference here is, of course, to Hartshorne's so-called "neo-classical metaphysics".
78. *Ibid.*, p. 152.
79. It certainly must be said that except for this one important section in his essay Ogden does not depart radically from the methodological approach which typified his earlier work. For instance, he sizes up the present crisis concerning the "death of God" by saying: "...the problem now confronting us is posed, not by the real death of God, but the demise of a '*cast of thought*,' of *some particular conceptuality* through which the witness of Christian faith has traditionally been expressed". He responds characteristically by stating: "The point I would emphasize is that the major obstacle to real progress in dealing with the problem of God is *the supernaturalistic theism of the metaphysical tradition*. Thus my own way of responding...is to seek a *conception* of God's reality in which the inadequacies of this traditional theism can be overcome". Ogden, *The Reality of God*, p. 19 (emphasis is mine).
80. (Cambridge: Cambridge University Press, 1950), pp. 202- 221.
81. Cf. Ogden's sizing up of the picture here in the light of Father Rahner's criticism above, p. 11.
82. Quoted by Ogden, *The Reality of God*, p. 27.
83. *Ibid.*, p. 28.
84. *Ibid.*

Notes to pages 19–22:
85. *Ibid.*
86. That is, from Ogden's point of view. In fact, Toulmin's consideration of this problem comprises only a few pages of his work.
87. Although the point cannot be pursued here, I should note that even though Ogden (with Toulmin) wants to avoid the apparent fallacy of converting the statement, "'Religious' experience and language entail 'limiting questions'" into the statement "All experience and language which entail 'limiting questions' is 'religious'," he is not entirely clear as to what precisely constitutes and distinguishes "religious" language and experience *per se*.
88. Ogden, *The Reality of God*, p. 31 (emphasis is mine).
89. *Ibid.*
90. *Ibid.*
91. *Ibid.*, p. 36.
92. *Ibid.*, p. 37.
93. *Ibid.*, pp. 37-38.
94. *Ibid.*, p. 23; cf. John Baillie, *Our Knowledge of God* (New York: Charles Scribner's Sons, 1959), p. 52.
95. Ogden, *The Reality of God*, p. 39.
96. This is admittedly a difficult term. In order to avoid as much confusion as possible let me note that I intend it to connote something like the sense in which Heidegger uses the phrase "*Fundamentalontologie*" ("fundamental ontology") in relation to an "*existenzialen Analytik des Daseins*" ("existential analytic of Dasein") in *Being and Time*, trans. John Macquarrie and Edward Robinson from the 7th German ed. (New York: Harper and Row, 1962). (Hereafter Heidegger's *Being and Time* shall be cited as *BT*).
97. See, Schubert M. Ogden, "The Possibility and Task of Philosophical Theology", *Union Seminary Quarterly Review*, 20 (1965):275; cf. the discussion by Bultmann and Hartshore in the two articles preceding Ogden's. (Hereafter we shall refer to this journal as *USQR*.)
98. *Ibid.*
99. See, Rudolf Bultmann, "On the Question of a Philosophical Theology", trans. Orus C. Barker, Jr., *USQR*, (1965): 262f.
100. *Ibid.* See, also, Bultmann's discussion in Kegley, ed., *The Theology of Rudolf Bultmann*, p. 273.
101. Bultmann, "On the Question of Philosophical Theology", pp. 262f.
102. Ogden, "The Possibility and Task of Philosophical Theology", p. 273 (emphasis is mine). Cf., also, Ogden's statement (p. 275): "...only a view of the possibility and task of philosophical theology which is less restricted than Bultmann's can do justice either to certain of his own basic intentions or of the needs of our present theological situation. The

Notes to pages 22-23:
notion that human existence is in any instance the primary or exclusive reality of knowledge—even of *philosophical* knowledge—I regard as mistaken. Against it, I would set the dictum of Thomas Aquinas, *Omnia cognoscentia cognoscunt implicite Deum in quolibet cognito* (*De veritate*, 22, 22 ad 1) or (what is not different) Hartshorne's statement above, that the reality of God is 'inherent in all basic secular conceptions and only intellectual inhibitions can keep it from being formulated'. In both cases, we are reminded that philosophical theology is possible because the original encounter in which all our knowledge has its basis is an encounter not merely with ourselves or our fellow creatures, but also with our infinite ground and end." I cannot but agree with Ogden's fundamental point here, but I would have to take serious issue with his assumption (via Hartshorne) that "only intellectual inhibitions" keep us from a formulation of our tacit, pre-reflective understanding of God. To use Ogden's own terms, our knowledge (i.e., understanding-relationship) of others, including the "divine Other", surely is more than a question, or problem of the "mind". It is also—and perhaps more fundamentally—a question of the "heart" or "will". Ogden's and Hartshorne's Thomism must somehow come to grips with Bultmann's 'Augustinianism'! So far, it seems to me, they have managed to skirt the issue. In our study we shall attempt to confront it squarely.
103. See Ogden's full argument, *ibid.*, p. 275f.
104. *New Theology No. 4*, ed. Martin E. Marty and Dean G. Peerman (New York: The Macmillan Company, 1967), p. 74. The article originally appeared in *Harvard Theological Review*, 59 (1966): 105-132. It was republished in Kaufman's important collection of essays, *God the Problem*, pp. 41-71. Of importance for our discussion, see especially the essays in this volume entitled "The Problem of God", pp. 3-16, "Two Models of Transcendence", pp. 72-81, "God as Symbol", pp. 82-115, "Secular, Religious, and Theistic World-Views", pp. 203-225, "The Foundations of Belief", pp. 226-256, and "The Secular Utility of 'God-Talk'", pp. 257-270.

It should be mentioned in passing that while there is much in Kaufman's work with which I entirely agree, his basic position regarding the problem is fundamentally different than mine. While he recognizes the problem of meaning today for all language about "God", he deliberately chooses not to turn to what I have called our everyday experience as human beings for the recovery of meaning. Such attempts to ground the meaning of language (about God) are misguided, according to Kaufman; talk about God (in what he calls "*theistic* world-views") ought to be grounded "directly on itself in its own terms", (*God the*

Notes to pages 23–24:

Problem, p. 8, n. 1). Kaufman's criticism of the position I have taken in this study might fall under that which he levels at Schleiermacher, Tillich and Gilkey. See the essay, "Secular, Religious, and Theistic World-Views", cited above. While at times helpful, Kaufman's typology of "religious", "theistic", and "secular" experience is too confining, and initially too prejudicial, for my purposes. From my perspective Kaufman's more recent work *The Theological Imagination; Constructing the Concept of God* (Philadelphia: The Westminster Press, 1981), does not break any new significant ground regarding the problem of God today.

105. Kaufman, *God the Problem*, p. 46. The similarity of Kaufman's constructive effort to that which we have observed in the case of Bultmann and Ogden (via Toulmin) can be seen in his thesis: "It is in the context of these questions and problems about man's finitude and the significance of his existence in the light of this finitude that the meaning and use of the word 'God' should be understood. That is, our speech about this Other arises because certain features of experience force us up against the limit(s) of all possible knowledge and experience. If there were no experiences within the world which brought us in this way up against the limit of our world...then there would be no justification whatsoever for the use of 'God-language'" (p. 49). Although Kaufman does deal with this "experience of finitude" in greater detail in Section IV of his article, its "highly complex character" demands, as he admits, far more refined and extensive treatment.

106. See e.g., Ogden's familiar contention in "The Possibility and Task of Philosophical Theology", p. 276: "In principle, then, it must always be possible to explicate our encounter with [God] conceptually in the form of a philosophical theology. One is...driven to this conclusion if he reflects carefully on the Christian understanding of man. For faith, man is nothing if not a self, or person, who is created as the express image of God himself. This is to say that every man has a 'capacity for God', which establishes his radical freedom and responsibility. If he falls away from God into the misunderstanding of sin, then he is, as Paul tells us, 'without excuse', since 'what can be known about God' has already been manifested to him (Rom. 1.19f). But from this, too, it follows that a philosophical knowledge of God must always be possible. If every man's encounter with God is sufficient to ground this kind of responsibility, it also provides more than a sufficient basis for a philosophical theology". See, also *Christ Without Myth*, pp. 141f.

107. See references following below.

108. See Paul Lehmann's account in Chapter XIII of his *Ethics in a Christian Context* (New York: Harper and Row, 1963), pp. 326-343. Lehmann's remark regarding the need for a critical, comprehensive study of the his-

Notes to page 24:
tory of conscience in Western theological and philosophical thought is worth noting: "A full- length study of what has happened to conscience in the Western cultural tradition is overdue. A carefully documented and sufficiently comprehensive account of what might be called 'the shape of conscience', i.e., of an interpretive framework other than that offered by moral theology in which the ethical nature and behavioral effectiveness of the conscience might once again be clearly and persuasively understood, is not at hand", pp. 327f., n. 2.

I am indebted to Lehmann's incisive sketch of the "principal episodes of the decline and fall of conscience" in assessing the significance of Heidegger's and Ebeling's attempt to achieve a radical reinterpretation of the phenomenon.

Also helpful has been H. G. Stoker's comprehensive monograph, *Das Gewissen, Erscheinungformen und Theorien, Vol 2* of the series *Schriften zur Philosophie und Soziologie*, ed. Max Scheler (Bonn: Friedrich Cohen, 1925), which, though dated, comes closest to the kind of investigation Lehmann calls for. Incidentally, as I shall note later, Stoker's analysis of the critical status of conscience in Western thought played an important part in Heidegger's constructive effort in *Being and Time*, published soon afterwards.

109. See Lehmann's discussion, *Ethics in a Christian Context*, pp. 330-332, and Stoker's survey, *Das Gewissen*, pp. 25-30. A more detailed examination of the development of the concept of conscience, with special treatment of Aquinas' decisive contribution, is Eric D'Arcy, *Conscience and Its Right to Freedom* (New York: Sheed and Ward, 1961). The most important texts reflecting Aquinas' position are *Summa Theologica* I, Q. 79, art. 12 and 13, and *De Veritate*, QQ. 16 and 17.

110. See Lehmann, *Ethics in a Christian Context*, pp. 333- 337, and Stoker, *Das Gewissen*, pp. 32ff., 69ff., 111ff. and 192-199. Cf. also the oblique, but nonetheless relevant study by Edward Engelberg, *The Unknown Distance, From Consciousness to Conscience, Goethe to Camus* (Cambridge, Mass.: Harvard University Press, 1972), pp. 15-39. The two classical loci for Kant's description of conscience are *The Metaphysical Principles of Virtue* [Part II of *The Metaphysics of Morals*], especially Section 13, and the earlier, pre-Critical *Lectures on Ethics*. Also important is the apparent, though disputed, move which Kant makes toward identifying the 'voice of God' with the 'voice of conscience' in his last notes collected in the *Opus Postumum*.

111. See Lehmann, *Ethics in a Christian Context*, pp. 337-343, and Stoker, *Das Gewissen*, pp. 38ff. and 246ff. Chapter IX contains an illuminating placement of Nietzsche in relation to the wider psychological and social philosophical background of the modern period. The classical loci of

Notes to page 24:
> Nietzsche's interpretation are found in *Beyond Good and Evil, On the Genealogy of Morals* (especially the Second Essay), and various notes from the posthumously published projected work, *The Will to Power*. The major studies in Freud's case (moving chronologically): *Totem and Taboo, Group Psychology and the Analysis of the Ego* (Chapters 7ff.), *The Ego and the Id, The Problem of Anxiety, Civilization and Its Discontents*, and *New Introductory Lectures on Psychoanalysis*.

112. Lehmann, *Ethics in a Christian Context*, p. 327.
113. For example, Söderblom's view of the conscience as a "portal of revelation" in *The Nature of Revelation*, trans. Frederic E. Pamp (Philadelphia: Fortress Press, 1966), pp. 107-112.
114. For example, the role of conscience in Baillie's early book, *The Roots of Religion in the Human Soul* (London: Hodder and Stoughton, 1926), pp. 205ff., and in the well-known study *Our Knowledge of God*, pp. 131, 153, 159f., 191, and especially 242-258. Cf. its conspicuous absence in his later Gifford Lectures, *The Sense of the Presence of God* (New York: Charles Scribner's Sons, 1962).
115. For example, the place of the conscience in Heim's conception of "suprapolar space" as developed in *Christian Faith and Natural Science*, trans. N. Horton Smith (New York: Harper Brothers, 1953), pp. 225ff.
116. Here, of course, Tillich's essay, "The Transmoral Conscience", in *The Protestant Era*, trans. James Luther Adams (Chicago: The University of Chicago Press; Phoenix Books, 1962), pp. 136-149.
117. Bultmann's development of the idea of conscience in his elaboration of Gogarten's position, in the essay, "The Historicity of Man and Faith", *Existence and Faith*, ed. and trans. Schubert M. Ogden (New York: Meridian Books, 1960), pp. 103ff. See also his interpretation in *Theology of the New Testament*, 2 vols., trans. Kendrick Grobel New York: Charles Scribner's Sons, 1951), 1:211-220, and in the essays, "The Concept of the Word of God in the New Testament" and "The Problem of 'Natural Theology'" in *Faith and Understanding, Vol. I*, trans. Louise P. Smith, ed. Robert W. Funk (New York: Harper and Row, 1969), pp. 301-303, 317-321.
118. See, for example, the implicit presence of conscience as "call" in Gogarten's *The Reality of Faith; the Problem of Subjectivism in Theology*, trans. Carl Michalson and others (Philadelphia: The Westminster Press, 1959), pp. 39f., 134ff.
119. For example, especially the central role of conscience alongside the Bible in Barth's early essay, "The Righteousness of God", *The Word of God and the Word of Man*, trans. Douglas Horton (New York: Harper and Row, 1957), pp. 9-27.

Chapter II

The centrality and significance of conscience in Ebeling's thought

Our first task in this study is to set forth the centrality and significance of the concept of conscience in Ebeling's thought. Although a great deal of attention has been given to such themes in Ebeling's work as the "historical Jesus", the "linguisticality of existence", language as "word-event", and "hermeneutic" as a methodological basis for a "theology of the Word", to my knowledge no one has sought to explore the meaning and implications of his crucial doctrine of "man as conscience"(1). This oversight has not only prevented this most important concept from bearing significant fruit in our present theological situation, but it has also led to a regrettable attenuation, if not an outright misinterpretation, of those programmatic themes for which his work has become known. Ebeling concludes an important essay which has become widely known in this country(2) with the key, definitive statement, "With an eye to the real sphere of the word-event I suggest for consideration the formula: the hermeneutic principle is *man as conscience*"(3), yet none of his American "discussion partners" who contributed to the volume in which Ebeling's piece appeared as a "focal essay" felt the need to explore the ramifications of this formula. Had they done so I suspect that Ebeling's methodological program might well have been cleared of what seemed to be the unanimous indictment, namely, that it had fallen prey to "the danger of becoming an empty abstraction"(4), because of its "blindness" to the concrete "human character" of the historical situation.

It seems to me that Philip Hefner's biting criticism of Ebeling's theological method, in his book, *Faith and the Vitalities of History*, suffers from the same lack of responsible critical attentiveness. Completely bypassing Ebeling's understanding of the hermeneutic function of man as conscience, Hefner faults Ebeling's theological program for its failure to be "rooted in life itself", due to its tendency toward "too narrow a commitment to an abstract philosophical category" (Ebeling's description of human reality as "word-event")(5). Robert Funk presents a far more judicious view of Ebeling's method in his work *Language, Hermeneutic, and the Word of God*(6), yet, with due respect to the confessedly limited scope of his study, it is still puzzling how Funk can present an interpretation of Ebeling's "biblical hermeneutics" (Funk's special concern) without some attention given to Ebeling's conception of the significance and function of conscience. Among many examples, consider, for instance, the key point that Ebeling formulates specifically with regard to the question of biblical interpretation in his "Discussion Theses for a Course of Introductory Lectures on the Study of Theology":

8. The text of holy scripture can open up to very different ways of approach. No angle is *a limine* forbidden, although considering the nature of the text questions from certain angles forbid themselves. And not every possible approach is really appropriate to the character of the text as a linguisitic event. The question which is ultimately appropriate to the biblical text is, how it affects the *conscience*. The hermeneutic principle of proper exegesis of holy scripture is therefore *man as conscience*(7).

To my knowledge Amos Wilder is the only critic who has taken note of the importance of the idea of conscience in Ebeling's thought. Wilder's reference, however, is at best indirect; its thrust is negative. Lumping Ebeling's anthropology together with "the view of man that New Testament theology has worked with of late", Wilder chides: "It tends to be moralistic, as though the whole problem of salvation were that of the forgiveness of sins.... Theology is focused too exclusively on man rather than upon all beings and the great theater of all beings and the glory and activity of God in which they all share in varying degrees. We are too obsessed with man and with his moral inwardness"(8). But surely, if Ebeling can be seen as the target of this cantankerous scolding (and we must assume he is since Wilder's essay appears as an "American response" to the Ebeling-Fuchs symposium on "The New Hermeneutic"), he would be the very first to challenge this kind of reading of the soteriological character of his work ("moralistic"), and especially of such an interpretation of his concept of "man as conscience" ("moral inwardness" and "the forgiveness of sins"). If anything, it is precisely this kind of moralistic rendering of the human situation that Ebeling hoped to transcend by means of his existential interpretation of man and, particularly, man as "conscience".

Let us put aside for a moment the question of misinterpretation and ask why it is that Ebeling's doctrine of conscience has, for the most part, gone so unnoticed by his various interpreters. Surely it has not been because the doctrine is of a peripheral nature, playing merely an ancillary role to other more important themes in his systematic work. To the contrary, even a cursory reading of Ebeling's work indicates that the doctrine of conscience lies at the heart of his thought, and, furthermore, is an absolutely crucial (if not the most crucial) notion for interpreting correctly the other various themes in his constructive work (theology as "hermeneutic", reality and revelation as "word-event", etc.). A catena of passages from his earliest to his latest work should forcefully confirm this claim beyond any doubt.

In the volume *The Nature of Faith*, the first systematic presentation of Ebeling's thought, an important juncture is reached in Chapter 13 with a question whose answer appears essential for a proper understanding of all that has gone before: "What is the sphere of the world, and the sphere of time, that the world and time can be the true sphere of faith"? Ebeling's answer:

> The sphere of the world and of time, the sphere where the world is encountered as the world, where it is experienced as the world, the sphere

where time presses upon us and is received as time, abused or gained, this sphere where such important things happen that the world and time are decided in them, is the *conscience*. Because the world is the sphere of faith, conscience has in fact to do with faith. For only when faith makes the conscience free, and takes possession of it can the conscience allow the world and time to be themselves(9).

In Chapter 15 we reach an even more dramatic climax in his interpretation with the decisive questions which Ebeling places on the lips of Everyman:

Is there nothing left, is man finished and balanced and purified, when there is no more time left? Has death the last word, in the sense that the man who is falling silent in death is asked nothing more, and has nothing more to say? Or is there a word which disputes the last word with death, and which matters for the dying or the dead man, and calls to him as the man he was, even if his last hour has struck? Or we could put it thus: what is the real future of the future? Is it death, or is it God(10)?

"The radical interpretation of this confusion of voices", Ebeling states, "and failure of all speech, in the relation between man and the future is to be found at the point which is like a mathematical point, where everything meets, namely, the *conscience*. The future is not an empty stretch of time, but *that which is still to come and is already stirring in the conscience*"(11). In one of his later essays, entitled "Existence between God and God", (1965), we find the following:

Theology is...not the theology of the essence of God in his majesty, but *the theology of revelation as the veiling of God in the fragile nature of man*. This is the reason christology, too, must be kept free from the neutralizing effect of metaphysical interpretation, in favor of *the true hermeneutical situation of* theology, which consists in the troubled conscience....(12)

According to Ebeling, it is as "conscience", above all, that man

experiences himself as being in between that which incomprehensibly withdraws from him, and that which incomprehensibly grants itself to him. *[This] plight of being in between is the locus for speaking about God.* The word 'God', in its elementary sense, is an interjection, a cat-call, it is the cry of existence for God between God and God...this is an interpretation of the word 'God' that originates only in that faith which takes seriously the last outcry of Jesus(13).

Taken together, these references to conscience as the "true hermeneutical situation of theology" and the "locus for speaking about God" serve as unmistakable indicators of the critical role which the doctrine plays in the important volume *Word and Faith* (1960). Certainly it is by no mean design that this series of essays, which as Ebeling explains in his preface to the English edition reflects a definite, purposive ordering of a systematic vision rather than a mere chronological collation of published articles, culminates in the work entitled "Theological Reflexions on Conscience"(14). In this volume, Ebeling's doctrine of conscience might well be seen as a prismal plane through which all the multi-faceted elements of his thought achieve their final distinctive focus and illuminative power. Note, for example, his historical-systematic essay on the theology of the Reformers, "Reflexions on the Doctrine of the Law" (1958), in which we find:

> Paul indicates in Rom. 2.14ff. that even outside the sphere of the Mosaic Law we can and must speak of the reality of the law.
>
> The theology of the Reformers derived from this its justification for the extension of the Pauline concept of law, which it took to mean, transposed into universal terms, the law written in every man's heart.... For the elucidation of this view of the law written in the heart Luther made use of the traditional view of the *lex naturalis*, which...is supposed to belong to man inalienably from birth.... We have become aware today of the flaws in this method of arguing from natural law. *But that does not by any means do away with the Reformers' doctrine of the law written in the heart. It merely requires a different grounding and elucidation. And a basis for that is provided precisely by Luther's doctrine of conscience*....(15)

As for the nature of this fundamental interpretive ground:

> Luther knows very well that the conscience is no infallible source of information about the ideal contents of the law.... The decisive question put to the conscience is concerned not with its knowing but with its hearing. For conscience is the question 'Where'? knocking at man's door, and by conscience that question is decided to the effect: in prison or in freedom.... Hence even the so-called 'man without the law' is not outside the real event of the law...the law written in the heart [must] be interpreted [not] as a detailed legal codex, but only as the state of being utterly open to question. The law written in the heart is so to speak the question mark that is branded upon man: Where are thou?(16)

To this thesis Ebeling adds: "It would then be the task of a detailed doctrine of the law to show how *this question mark that is branded upon man sets in motion the whole reality that concerns man and brings it to expression, thereby summons to the interpretation of reality*...(17).

This last thread is picked up and carried further in an article published the following year, "Reflexions on Speaking Responsibly of God" (1959)(18). Here the meaning of "God" emerges alongside "reality"—in the phenomenon of conscience:

> The task of a comprehensive analysis of reality, which cannot be completed once for all, but the study of which is the constant, historically conditioned and historically motivated act of reflective questioning, would...be: to observe the radical questionableness of reality.... Radical questionableness—or...the problem of true transcendence—seems to us to

arise at a totally different point from where the question of the *primum movens* or such like, but with the problems relating to personal being, like the question of meaning, the question of guilt, the question of communication, etc.... *If this questionableness which strikes to the roots of personal being and thereby proves its radicality is described as concerned with the conscience, then we could...say that the place where we experience what 'God' means is the conscience*(19).

This important statement should be viewed alongside the statement to which we have already referred, that which concludes the essay "Word of God and Hermeneutics" (1959): "With an eye to the real sphere of the word-event I suggest for consideration the formula: the hermeneutic principle is man as conscience"(20). Both themes merge in Ebeling's constructive argument in the essay "Worldly Talk of God" (1959)(21):

Our talk of God as such,...must be called to account. Before whom? ... Man has in fact to answer for himself before God and before the world at the same time... To answer for (*verantworten*) God before the world means: to let God and the world come together by means of 'word' (*das Wort*). Only so will man be affected by our talk of God. And the only responsible talk of God is that which aims at the place where God and the world meet as it were in a mathematical point. That place is the conscience.... For as conscience man stands between God and the world(22).

And in case we have missed the fundamental import of this central thesis, Ebeling elaborates in the conclusion of the same article:

It is true that our talk of God aims solely *at the inmost being, the conscience*. But precisely what happens in the inmost being, his conscience, is grasped only when it is clearly realized that here it is not a case of man in the abstract, separated from the world, and of his then necessarily likewise abstract relation to God; rather, the conscience is, as we said already, *the place where God and the world meet*(23).

In the final analysis the question of the meaning of "God" and the truth of "who" and "where" man is, is decided in the conflict of faith and unbelief concerning the true nature of "reality". In the important article bearing this provocative title, "Faith and Unbelief in Conflict about Reality" (1960)(24), Ebeling's argument concludes with these remarkable series of passages:

Faith has its proper place where it is a case of understanding reality. And indeed, understanding reality as a whole. This wholeness is not a sum of individual parts, but the experience that at one particular point everything stands of falls together. That sounds very strange. But perhaps it can be guessed what I am after when I say: *this one point at which everything stands or falls together is the conscience of man*(25).

And we should pay close attention to the qualifying remarks which follow. Ebeling continues: "Not the conscience in the common, moralized sense as a moral law written in the heart. *But the conscience in the radical sense as the place where it is decided what man truly is*"(26). This means that if man

is there under the pressure and anxiety of despair, then that does not merely effect the whole of his own being, but he also finds the whole world dragged into his despair. If on the other hand his conscience is cheerful and confident, *then the whole of reality also takes on a different shape for him. Whatever binds him in conscience, decides how reality as a whole concerns him.* If his conscience is set free, then he is absolutely free and no power on earth can alter that. It is therefore better not to call conscience a place *in* man but—however surprising it may sound—the place *of* man. *For in the conscience it is decided where man belongs, where he is and where he has his abode*(27).

Observing the centrality of conscience in the foregoing, it should come as no surprise that Ebeling sees fit to conclude the final essays of this volume (between which is inserted his crucial article "Theological Reflexions on Conscience" [1960]), "The Necessity of the Doctrine of the Two Kingdoms" (1960)(28) and "Discussion Theses for a Course of Introductory Lectures on the Study of Theology" (1960)(29) respectively, with the following assertions:

The *regnum Christi* remains a kingdom of the Word whose proper proclamation encounters the perdition of the *regnum mundi* at the point where that perdition has its source and develops its real virulence: in the heart, in the *conscientia* of man. The *conscientia* is the mathematical point at which the *regnum Christi* becomes one with a *regnum mundi* stripped of its power and freed from itself in order to be mere world(30).

11. The systematic aspect of systematic theology is not to be confused with the closed architectural structure of a theological doctrinal edifice, which may be useful on occasion, but is not to be overestimated and not without danger. Rather it is a question of grasping the coherence of the subject in two respects: on the one hand the coherence between faith and reality in the whole range of experience and in all the manifold ways of perceiving truth, on the other hand, the coherence between the individual statements of faith as mere modifications of one single statement (not, however, as independent factors to be summed up together). *Both forms of the question as to the coherence of theology coincide in this: that systematic theology is concerned with the question of what is absolutely necessary, and must therefore be studied with a constant eye to man in his sensitivity to the question of what is absolutely necessary, i.e., with an eye to man as conscience*(31).

Certainly, in the light of the above, there should be no question as to the absolutely crucial role the idea of conscience plays in Ebeling's thought. In fact, when faced as such with Ebeling's own words, the question becomes only more acute as to how and why his interpreters and critics have remained so unanimously silent on the subject. No doubt, as Ebeling himself suggests, one reason is due to a certain "justified aversion to [past] idealistic interpretations of conscience"(32). This aversion is familiar in our Anglo-American setting where, among other things, the anti-Idealistic current runs particularly strong. Where conscience is spoken of at all in this context (and here we make no mention of its flagrant misinterpretation in popular usage), it is associated with a number of empirical definitions utilized in the social and psychological sciences, or with the domesticated ethical-casuistic formulations of Roman Catholic and Anglican moral theology. Clearly, Ebeling's understanding of conscience shuns these usual interpretative formulations as much as it attempts to part company with the caricature of modern idealism(33).

In the essay, "Theological Reflexions on Conscience", Ebeling cites four basic misconceptions of conscience which, he argues, must be rejected once and for all: (1) the understanding of conscience as a faculty or organ in man, (2) the sometimes exclusive rendering of conscience as an authority over against man, (3) the conception of conscience as a codex of general truths and commands, and (4) the idea of the voice of conscience as the voice of God. Regarding the first misconception, Ebeling writes: "To call conscience an organ (even a vitally necessary organ) in man misses the basic fact that conscience is a matter of the coming to expression of man himself"(34). He adds: "Strictly man does not 'have' a conscience, but he is conscience". According to Ebeling, in this distinction may be seen in the etymology of the Greek "*syneidēsis*" the root-term for the Latin "*conscientia*" and our "conscience". Interpreted literally, *syneidēsis* points to the fact that the root of the phenomenon of conscience lies in *the basic ontological determination of man as the being whose relation to himself is that of joint cognizance*"(35). "Hence", Ebeling reasons, "in explaining the concept of conscience the distinction of subject and object is not applicable, since here the point at issue is the selfhood of man as identity of subject and object"(36).

It is for this reason that Ebeling also rejects the accepted misconception of conscience as an internalized "authority" over against man. Ebeling states that "without detriment to the question whether something standing over against man does not present itself in conscience, the *first* thing where the phenomenon of conscience is concerned is to grasp that the structure of human nature itself is confrontation...that man is the being who is answerable." "Instead of speaking of an authority (*Instanz*)", he continues, "it would therefore be more appropriate to speak of the 'dissociation' (*Distanz*) which is given with conscience in human nature itself." And he adds: "Man [as 'conscience'] experiences himself as one who is not identical with himself, but whose essence it is to be questioned about his identity with himself. Only in being thus questioned is his identity given"(37). We shall elaborate the implications of this key statement at a later point in our analysis.

It should be obvious from the above why the content of the so-called "call of conscience" must not be viewed as a "codex of general truths and commands", or, as Ebeling puts it, "a law written in the heart, which is conceived as a sum of inborn ideas that by nature form part of the content of human consciousness"(38). "Conscience", Ebeling cautions, "makes no speeches". The phenomenon of conscience, is man as he "is", calling himself, asking about himself, demanding that he be responsible for his self(39). This calling of man himself, to himself, in his essence, points ultimately to the essential "temporal being" of man. In that "joint cognizance" given in conscience, according to Ebeling, man hears himself "as one who is continually questioned as to what attitude he takes to himself in his own past and future", that is to say, "whether he identifies himself with himself, confesses to his past and decides for his future, and thus (though this of course is a secondary mode of the identification in question) whether he identifies himself with his deeds and his potentialities"(40).

Just as such an understanding rules out the designation of conscience as an inborn codex of general truths and laws, so it equally negates any interpretation which equates conscience's call with the "voice of God". This does not mean (and here we should take careful note) that, for Ebeling, there is no connection between the phenomenon "God" and the phenomenon of man as conscience. Indeed, Ebeling posits: "Conscience is the condition on which it becomes possible to understand what is meant by the word 'God'". Furthermore, he states:

In the interpretation of conscience it must become clear what we mean when we say 'God'...the fact of man's identity being open to question opens also the question of God. And indeed not least also in the sense that man can find himself asking how in spite of his constant non-identity with himself he yet remains upheld in that identity, in remaining questioned about it and summoned to it(41).

It is on the basis of this last important observation that Ebeling ventures to assert, in the same essay on conscience, the startling proposition: "God—as phenomenon, and that is precisely a way of saying as *Deus* ABSCONDITUS—is a phenomenon of conscience"(42).

Clearly, with this statement Ebeling begins to tread on rather embarrassing, or even forbidden, ground for one speaking in the tradition of "post-Liberal" theology! Does he not raise again that presumably settled question of an experiential grounding for our knowledge of God? Does this not imply that the revelatory process is indeed linked integrally to what has been called man's/woman's "natural" self-understanding? Ebeling admits it does. In fact, this apparent implication is the second prime reason he gives for the "widespread antipathy towards the use of the concept of conscience in theology today..."(43). Regardless of this antipathy, he argues, we (i.e., those who claim the title of neo-Reformation theologians) of all people should be the last to deny that "the concept of conscience is of decisive importance for theology"(44); and we should be the first to follow the implications of this insight to wherever and whatever it leads us. To drive this point home Ebeling reminds his fellow neo-Reformers that for Luther '*theologice*' was *synonymous* with '*in conscientia*':

> (on Gal. 5.1) *Est libertas a lege, peccatis, morte, a potentia diaboli, ira dei, extremo iudicio. Ubi? in conscientia, Ut sic iustus sim, quod Christus sit liberator et reddat liberos, non carnaliter non politice, diabolice, sed theologice i.e. tantum in conscientia* (WA 40/2, p. 3.5-8)(45).

To be sure, the function and nature of conscience in Luther's thought is of the utmost importance for Ebeling's own interpretation, and we shall have cause to explore certain implications of this influence at another point in our analysis. Here though it should be emphasized that in spite of the distinctive understanding of conscience in the theology of the Reformation, and of Luther in particular, Ebeling is really operating in his systematic and constructive thought with "an exactly defined concept of conscience" conceived primarily through what is perhaps best termed the corraborative, hermeneutic assistance(46) of a specific, modern philosophical perspective. Furthermore, I venture the judgment that it is primarily because of this philosophical perspective (or perhaps, because theologians outside the Continent have either been suspicious towards, or, which is perhaps more truly the case, have simply not imbibed long or deeply enough in this perspective), that the lack of comment on the doctrine in Ebeling's thought has been what it is. The nature of this important philosophical influence is correctly (although disapprovingly) observed by Philip Hefner when he states, regarding Ebeling's thought in general:

> Ebeling's systematic theological achievement to date is constituted by his application...of existentialist philosophy to an interpretation of biblical and historical materials of the Christian faith. Riding the crest of a European wave of theological thought that has thoroughly absorbed existentialist thinking, Ebeling's work may be considered to be the ultimate refinement of its type(47).

Hefner correctly identifies the prime philosophical figure behind the "European wave" when he refers specifically to the distinctive "Heideggerian provenance of his [Ebeling's] thought"(48). It is important to note also the point made by Ernst Fuchs in *New Frontiers in Theology II*, that the lack of communication between the continental and American theologians who participated in the Consultation on Hermeneutic at Drew University was due primarily to an almost unanimous antipathy toward, and at times an even "absurd" (as Fuchs puts it) misunderstanding of, the particular Heideggerian orientation of their (Fuchs' and Ebeling's) thought(49). John Cobb also confirms the lack of a common meeting ground on precisely this same issue in his final summation essay to that volume(50). It seems to me—and this is the main point I wish to make—the most unfortunate aspect of this situation is that when the contentious dialogue in the hermeneutic discussion turned to the question of philosophical resources, the focus was centered exclusively upon the work of the later Heidegger. The result of this has been the creation of a regrettable lacuna regarding the significant implications of the *early* Heidegger for Fuchs' and Ebeling's programs, especially with respect to the important role it plays in the constructive formulation of that central theme in the thought of the latter, the idea of the nature of man/woman as conscience. Until this particular hiatus is filled, I contend, all that Ebeling has to say to those outside the Continental context concerning conscience will be brought to naught. It is of the utmost importance, therefore, that one proceed in his investigation of the theological function of conscience in Ebeling's work by way of a careful analysis of Heidegger's original reinterpretation of the phenomenon. My thesis, I should emphasize, is not only that the phenomenological description of conscience in the latter's early study, *Being and Time*, serves as the prime foundation for the concept as it is conceived and functions in Ebeling's thought, but also, and certainly much more significantly for estimating the value of its role in the latter's thought, that in Heidegger's phenomenological description we have the groundwork for decisively overcoming, or moving positively beyond, the traditional post-Kantian and post-Freudian formulations which have so far dominated our anthropological landscape.

Roots of Ebeling's conception of conscience
in the work of the early Heidegger (Being and Time)

We must ask ourselves explicitly the extent to which we are justified in singling out the philosophy of the early Heidegger as the fundamental extra-theological source behind Ebeling's interpretation of conscience. One might object, for instance, that Ebeling has presented no programmatic statement of the role which the early Heidegger plays in his systematic thought. In fact, one might well question our thesis at its inception by simply pointing to Ebeling's expressed methodological acceptance of Luther's admonition found in *Word and Faith*. Here, quoting Luther, Ebeling directly takes up the question of the role of philosophy in "the formation of theological concepts": "*'Omnia vocabula fiunt nova, quando e suo foro in alienum transferunter.... Si tamen vultis uti vocabulis istis, prius quaeso illa bene purgate....'*"(51). This caution and its recommendation to give philosophical concepts "a good bath", should not lead us astray however. In emphasizing that theology, as every scientific, reflective discipline, has its own distinctive "linguistic usage", Ebeling by no means wishes to deny that philosophical concepts both do and ought to play an important role in theological formulations. Indeed, in this same section Ebeling explicitly states that although "it is beyond question that every science...forms its own particular concepts", and that theology "has naturally to watch over the forming of specifically theological concepts", still "it can only in exceptional cases...be a question of using special theological terms"(52). He adds, "It is chiefly a case of giving precise definition as theological concepts to words which are also used elsewhere, in everyday life as in other sciences"(53). Ebeling elaborates with the following critical thesis: "...to deal with concepts in a responsible manner is to know oneself bound to two cardinal points: attentiveness to the history of language and openness towards the reality that confronts us"(54).

Although theology finds its point of divergence from philosophy in the fact that it is rooted inextricably in a specific language tradition (philosophy, Ebeling observes at another point, is not so rooted)(55), there is a definite, unavoidable convergence of the two reflective disciplines in the fact that they both have a common stake in, and hence come to share between themselves a joint-interpretation of, "the reality that confronts us". The fundamental, mutual encounter between philosophy and theology at the point of their interpretation of reality is a requisite aspect of the hermeneutical task of theology, whether it be in the area of biblical interpretation, historical theology, or dogmatics. In saying this Ebeling anticipates the question: "Is this not a case of being enticed on to the false paths of empirical theology and natural theology"? Ebeling's response, although indirect in his early work, definitely implies that there is indeed an authentic "natural" theology when this unavoidable relationship betweeen philosophy and theology is properly understood, that is to say, at the point of their reciprocal joint-interpretation of "reality".

Ebeling's position, expressed indirectly here in his earlier work, would seem to be unmistakably clear in his later "conversation with Bultmann", *Theology and Proclamation*(56) when the question is raised (not by Bultmann, of course, but by their common antagonists) as to whether dogmatic theology becomes "mere anthropology" when it utilizes a philosophical analysis with regard to the "subject-matter" of "the reality of man". Ebeling's response appears to be unequivocal: "It is high time that theologians freed themselves from the polemical use of the word anthropology, as meaning that treatment of a subject which is (supposedly!) limited to the 'mere human' side of things, and which as such stands in antithesis to theology"(57).

But what about the actual and specific contribution of Heidegger's philosophical 'anthropology' to Ebeling's thought, and particularly to his interpretation of the idea of conscience? So far we have only spoken of this influence in a general way, building upon Hefner's typical observation that Ebeling's work is to be seen as the "ultimate refinement" of a type of theology which finds itself moving "at the crest of a European wave of theological thought that has thoroughly absorbed existentialist thinking...."(58). We should not forget that there are those who, even while admitting a general "Heideggerian", or "existentialist" cast to Ebeling's work, nevertheless, contend that it is really "Luther" who exerts the prime influence upon the method and content of his thought. Such interpreters would insist, for example, that Ebeling's idea of conscience is no more (nor less) than a characteristic outgrowth of the Reformers' doctrine of "law and gospel". Our own argument is that although Luther's theology does indeed play a vital role in the selection and development of Ebeling's central theological concepts, there are more direct formative factors operating in the latter's work, even, we might add, in his Luther interpretations(59)! The following observations are offered to support our contention that the most important of these forces is the work of the so-called early Heidegger.

Historical backdrop
The "university milieu": Marburg

I am sure were we to ask Ebeling to account for the influence of Heidegger's early "anthropological hermeneutic" (our term) upon his thought, he would no doubt point, as his teacher Bultmann did before him (although with reference to the influence of "existential thinking" in general)(60), to the "university *milieu*", the "internal discussion with the intellectual situation" of his formative academic development. It is important to recall, first of all, that a large part of Ebeling's major academic preparation (specifically, from the Summer Semester of 1930 through the Winter Semester of 1932), was spent in Marburg under Bultmann. The powerful and fruitful impact of Heidegger's *Being and Time* during this period(61) upon Bultmann and his students, the so-called "old-Marburgers"(62), is elaborated elsewhere and need not be reiterated here in detail(63). Of pertinence for our own particular concern, however, is the remarkably important role the concept of conscience plays in both Bultmann's and Heidegger's work during this period of their closest acquaintanceship. As we shall see, the phenomenon of conscience is the key, hinge concept in the latter's anthropological hermeneutic, *Being and Time*, and, although it has not been generally recognized by Bultmann's interpreters, the idea of conscience also assumed an equally central position in his early writings. Needless to say, in these early formulations of Bultmann, Heidegger's "existential" description of the concept finds an agreeable 'extra-philosophical' application. It is noteworthy to observe that these essays, wherein the conscience appears as a central motif(64), were composed and published precisely during the period of Ebeling's academic sojourn at the German university. In the first essay, "The Concept of the Word of God in the New Testament", we find thoughts which comprised the subject-matter of Bultmann's seminars at that time: "Throughout the New Testament it is assumed that every hearer can understand what forgiveness is and can understand that forgiveness is life. This holds true since it is assumed that every man, when he asks about his salvation, must be asking about *God*"(65). The "Word of God", Bultmann says, "has the power to show man his sins and at the same time to forgive his sins". "But", he adds, "the Word can do this only as true summons, by asking the hearer whether he is willing so to understand himself, whether he is willing to see his real situation before God, and therefore whether he is willing to understand the Word, which confronts him here and now, as God's Word"(66). But where does this "hearing" take place? Wherein does man hold the possibility for understanding his actual, and true, "situation before God"? Paul provides us with the clue, Bultmann answers, and the clue is "conscience":

> The missionary preaching of Paul, the substance of which we learn from Rom. 1.18f., assumes that the heathen have the possibility of understanding the wrath of God which is kindled against them. They have a knowledge that God decrees righteousness (1.32) and 'what the law requires' is 'written on their hearts'; they have a conscience (2.14f.). And since they have a conscience, they can understand the word of forgiveness(67).

This interpretation is carried much further in Bultmann's second essay, "The Problems of 'Natural Theology'". We should not be surprised to hear some rather remarkable methodological and terminological echoes from this important study in Ebeling's later work! Bultmann writes:

> The task which 'natural theology' might undertake would be to discover how far the unbelieving existence and its self-understanding is ruled and affected by the *questionableness* which only becomes clear as such in the understanding of existence in faith. *Conscience*, for example, would be interpreted as such a phenomenon; and that interpretation corresponds to the fact that the Christian kerygma is addressed to the conscience (IICor. 4.2). That is why it is possible for the kerygma to be a call to decision and for faith to be a decision(68).

As for the influence of Heidegger's "existential clarification" of this concept, it can be observed clearly in this early formulation by Bultmann:

> The 'supreme being' can be claimed [by the intellect] as the guarantor of the moral law, as the origin of the knowledge of good and evil, as the voice of conscience. Here what is really meant is only the *idea* of the moral law, the idea of the good. *The conscience is not the voice of God, but a call issuing from a particular existence to itself*(69).

It is on the basis of this peculiarly "existential" rendering of the reality which is truly involved in this phenomenon, that Bultmann ventures the following constructive position:

> In the knowledge of good and evil, in the 'ought' under which man places himself, is there not hidden the knowledge of the demand of God at each specific moment? Is not the interpretation of this knowledge as an obligation which a man in freedom pronounces upon himself really the rejection of the bondage of which man is dimly conscious when he

rejects it? And if in fact the conscience does develop in the historical intercourse of man, is not the phenomenon of conscience the sign that man does know that God's demand becomes audible at the moment of encounter with a *Thou*?(70)

Of course we must not forget that the Heidegger-Bultmann relationship during this period was by no means a one-way affair. The internal "theological" discussions in the "university milieu" of which Bultmann speaks, also made their impact upon Heidegger. Among the key "theological" sources cited by Heidegger is his interpretation of conscience, we should note first the thought of Kierkegaard. It is significant that of all of Kierkegaard's "theoretical" writings, Heidegger considers to be most "penetrating" the one wherein the Dane presents his interpretation of the phenomenon of "conscience". Observe Heidegger's evaluation of Kierkegaard in this most important note in *Being and Time*:

In the nineteenth century, Søren Kierkegaard explicitly seized upon the problem of existence as an *existentiell* problem, and thought it through in a penetrating fashion. But the existential problematic was so alien to him that, as regards his ontology, he remained completely dominated by Hegel and ancient philosophy as Hegel saw it. Thus, there is more to be learned philosophically from his 'edifying' writings than from his theoretical ones—*with the exception of his treatise on the concept of anxiety* [English translation *The Concept of Dread*](71).

Heidegger's phenomenological description draws upon other extra-philosophical sources, two of the most important of these being Martin Kähler's monograph *Das Gewissen, erster geschichtlicher Teil*(1878), and his article on "Gewissen" in Hauck's *Realenzyklopädie für Protestantische Theologie und Kirche*. For Heidegger, Kähler's researches illuminated once again the original "ontological" implications of the Greek term *syneidēsis*. (As we shall see, this etymological analysis of *syneidēsis* is crucial both for Heidegger and Ebeling.) According to Heidegger, Kähler's careful historical analyses confirm the thesis that *syn-eidēsis* (or the Latin *con-scientia*) should be translated, in accordance with its reference to man as essentially that being who exists, or "is" in terms of "joint-cognizance (or consciousness)" of himself, as "self-knowledge"(72). In addition to illuminating this fundamental existential rootage of the concept, Kähler also performed the additional service of disentangling the genuine phenomenon from the various "objectivized", "popular" and "scientific" misconceptions(73) which have persisted from the ancient Greeks to the present(74).

In spite of his high regard for Kähler, we should bear in mind that Heidegger still maintained fundamental reservations regarding the ultimate ontological-hermeneutical limitations of the theologian's researches. This is true in fact of every source utilized in Heidegger's existential analysis of the phenomenon. For example, concerning one of the most useful of these sources(75), H. G.

Stoker's *Das Gewissen*(76), "a wide-ranging investigation [which brings] to light a rich multiplicity of conscience-phenomena", and in addition reflects a further development of Kähler's original insights, Heidegger states: "Stoker underestimates from the outset the hermeneutical conditions for a 'description' of 'conscience as something which subsists objectively and actually'...." Hence, in final evaluation: "...Stoker's monograph signifies notable progress as compared with previous Interpretations of conscience, *though more by its comprehensive treatment of the conscience-phenomena and their ramifications than by exhibiting the ontological roots of the phenomenon itself*"(77). Clearly, it would follow that the most appropriate hermeneutic description of "the ontological roots" of this phenomenon is to be found in Heidegger's own study! But let us not be offended by what appears as a most immodest claim. Although Heidegger's analysis is not the "last word" on the matter, it may well be justified in its claim to have presented a more "correct", or "genuine" "ontological description" of this phenomenon than most analyses which have preceded it. Bultmann, for one, was convinced of this fact(78), and my supposition is that one of his most important students was equally impressed(79).

The "university milieu": Zürich and elsewhere

In sketching out the "university milieu" in which Ebeling was immersed we should take additional note of the important influence of Heidegger's study upon the students of Fritz Blanke at the University of Zürich, for it was under Blanke that Ebeling himself completed his doctoral studies in 1938(80). Apparently a great deal of interest was generated at this time among Blanke's (as well as Brunner's) pupils concerning Luther studies in general, and the phenomenon of conscience in particular. It is of significance to note the influence of Heidegger's recent phenomenological description of conscience in the work, for example, of Willy Bremi, a contemporary of Ebeling's at Zürich. Bremi's study, entitled *Was ist das Gewissen?; seine Beschreibung, seine metaphysische und religiose Deutung, seine Geschichte*(81), was a doctoral dissertation carried out under the direction of Blanke (as well as Professors Brunner and Gut), and published at Zürich in 1934. That Heidegger's phenomenological description was considered at Zürich, at that time, as a most important advance beyond, or rather out of, the cul-de-sac created in the psychological-philosophical discussion of the modern period, can be seen by the positive role it plays in both Bremi's "up-dated" constructive, "theological description" of the phenomenon(82), and in his extended summary account of the conscience's circuitous, historical odyssey(83). Although maintaining at all times a decisively "theological" position on the matter (in contrast to Heidegger's "neutral" anthropological description), Bremi betrays no hesitancy in affirming that Heidegger's reinterpretation represents an important recovery of the real "ontological" understanding of the phenomenon which was articulated at various moments in the course of Western intellectual history, and most authentically, as he sees it, in the work of Luther and Kierkegaard. Significantly, Bremi finds it appropriate to complete his study with a section on Heidegger, a section which opens with the following thesis:

> Finally, a renewal of the Lutheran-Kierkegaardian idea is heard in a most up-to-date manner, the idea that the conscience is disclosed in its essence (in the latest metaphysical formulation) through *Angst*. Under the religious and theological setting of this idea Martin Heidegger has taken new steps along this way(84).

Can we doubt that Ebeling was influenced by these intellectual winds blowing at Zürich during this period? Even Brunner, under whom Ebeling also studied at Zürich, and whose academic chair the younger theologian was later to fill, shows evidence of having quite freely—and fully—appropriated the German philosopher's recent, "important", reinterpretation of conscience. In 1938, Brunner stated quite explicitly (and perhaps surprisingly for some of us) that Heidegger (the Heidegger of *Being and Time*) is "the most important philosophical anthropologist of the present day"(85). In spite of his overriding "theological" point of departure, and, like Bremi, his reservations toward any philosophical anthropology which claimed to be "neutral" with respect to "God as Creator", Brunner felt no hesitancy in utilizing the insights, and even the language, of Heidegger's "Dasein-analysis". The influence of the latter can be seen clearly in Brunner's two works, *Man in Revolt* and *The Divine Imperative*, especially when the subject concerns the phenomenon of "conscience", that "sense of contradiction at the very heart of existence, at the point of responsibility"(86). In the latter work, for instance, Brunner writes:

> Conscience is not the "Voice of God", as it used to be described in the theology of the Enlightenment, and as it has since then been usually regarded by popular natural theology. Nor is it the consciousness of the Moral Law, of the "Thou Shalt," nor the judgement of the intellect concerning the agreement or non-agreement rationalizations of the original phenomenon of conscience, which conceal from us its true character(87).

For Brunner, as we shall find clearly spelled out by Heidegger, conscience is *"simply the man himself as he feels himself in the centre of his existence"*(88). To be sure, he continues, conscience "makes its presence felt on certain occasions of actual wrongdoing or of failure; but as soon as it makes its voice heard it announces more than this particular instance of wrongdoing or failure. It proclaims this fault as an outbreak of [man's] contradiction as a whole...."(89) And he concludes:

> In the experience of conscience we learn that 'we have lost ourselves', we learn our loneliness, we find that we have been 'cast out' and 'excluded', and we discover that this is not due to the workings of Fate but is the result of our 'guilt' [i.e.] our decision for action (*Entschlossen-*

heit: Heidegger) is seen to be actually reserve (*Verschlossenheit*), and we see...that the possibility we thought existed does not exist at all(90).

Like Bremi, Brunner sees in Heidegger's "existential" description of this phenomenon an authentic reinterpretation of its primordial "ontological" character. In this sense, according to Brunner, Heidegger stands as a prime, modern representative—in the philosophical camp—of a line of tradition which stretches from Hellenism and the Bible (especially Paul) to Augustine and Luther, and finally, in its most articulate form, to Kierkegaard(91). The real advantage of Heidegger's interpretation for theology is that it convincingly argues this classic tradition on precisely those grounds, philosophical and psychological, where the most severe modern challenges have been leveled. In short, Heidegger's phenomenological description in *Being and Time* should be understood as decisively overcoming and, if its evidence and method be taken seriously, as finally refuting those "rationalizations" which—to the loss of philosophy, psychology, and theology alike—have misconstrued this human phenomenon from the Rennaisance onward(92).

We must point out, however, that in spite of this positive assessment of Heidegger's work, and the obvious imprint of the latter's actual formulations upon his own systematic descriptions, Brunner, nevertheless, wished to maintain, in characteristically perplexing fashion (no doubt with an eye to the criticism of Karl Barth), a proper and necessary "theological distance" from the philosopher—as from all "philosophers". Hence, Brunner would never think of going as far as Bultmann in appraising Heidegger's work as "the 'right' philosophy", i.e., as "one which has worked out an appropriate terminology for the understanding of existence, an understanding involved in human existence itself"(93). In this regard it must be emphasized that, in spite of his later Swiss experience, and in spite of certain "public"(94) indications, I believe Ebeling stands closer to "Marburg" than to "Zürich". In his own interpretation of conscience, both in his systematic work and in his historical approach to the phenomenon in Luther, Ebeling cites two principal sources which, as he sees it, stand closest to his own position. The first, is the early Heidegger, a rather brief, direct reference in his short essay on conscience(95); the second is the work by the two Luther scholars Günther Jacob and Emanuel Hirsch(96). It is more than a curious fact, for example, that while Jacob's study, *Der Gewissensbegriff in der Theologie Luthers*(97), was criticized by Brunner and Bremi for being "unfortunately too much influenced by the terminology of Heidegger" (Brunner) and, because of this, for having ultimately "forced Luther into a procrustrean bed" (Bremi), it was cited and recommended without qualification, in terms of both its method and its results, by Bultmann, Gogarten,—and Ebeling. We should recall, in this example, that Jacob's study appeared in the midst of the debate surrounding Karl Holl's epoch-making studies on the early Luther during the mid-twenties. Jacob's monograph was an attempt to support Holl's interpretation of Luther's theology as "Gewissensreligion", (a religion of the conscience), a reading of Luther which was hotly contested by Theodosius Harnack, Erich Seeberg, Hans Michael Müller, and others. Although Jacob commends Gogarten's earlier attempt to "correct" Holl's thesis vis-à-vis several of its detractors, the results of this effort always remain questionable, according to Jacob: "because Gogarten has not confirmed his interpretation of Luther's theology through an exact analysis of the basic anthropological ideas standing here in question"(98). But such an "exact analysis" of the basic anthropological idea, conscience, is present for our use, according to Jacob. It is to be found in Heidegger's study *Being and Time*(99). So important is Heidegger's phenomenological analysis for Jacob, that he can state, regarding the method of his own approach to the idea of conscience in Luther:

> We have, therefore, deliberately waived a classification of materials in separate discussion with Heidegger's analysis of Dasein, to which the critical line of sight of our inquiry is indebted, in setting forth the proper interpretation of Luther's conception of existence(100).

Because Heidegger's interpretation of conscience is so intertwined with the whole complex of his "Analyse des Daseins", Jacob foregoes any separate presentation of the philosopher's work and simply assumes that his readers are by this time familiar with this indispensable source. I suggest that, in both his historical and systematic investigations, this is precisely the way in which Ebling (much like his co-wroker, Ernst Fuchs) treats Heidegger's early phenomenological study(101). Indeed, writing in the Continental "university milieu" in the late 1950's and early 1960's, one could assume—and with greater justice than Jacob, Gogarten, and Bultmann in the late 1920's—that one's readership was familiar enough with this epoch-making work to dispense with a direct explication of its basic approach and central themes. Hence, when Ebling repeatedly calls in his historical work for an "existentialist interpretation", or "existential rendering", of theological concepts (e.g., Luther's concept of the "law"(102), "heart"(103), and "conscience"(104)), it is primarily in Heidegger's early phenomenological anthropology that we should seek basic hermeneutical, and even material, insights and directions. The same, I hold, is true of Ebling's systematic work, especially with regard to the interpretation of the key anthropological concept "man as conscience". Thus, Ebling's brief direct reference to Heidegger in his essay, "Theological Reflexions on the Conscience"(105), should not mislead us in its brevity: the philosopher's early phenomenological analysis must be seen as standing behind what Ebling has to say concerning "the genuine nature" of this phenomenon. Nor should this methodological state of affairs be lamented by "theologians", as such, for ultimately, I would argue, it is because of Heidegger's definitive "ontological-existential clarification" of this phenomenon that Ebling's "theological" interpretation becomes defensible and, indeed, is enabled to move critically and responsibly beyond all of its modern-day "extra-theological" detractors.

With this brief historical and biographical backdrop behind us, let us turn now to a careful analysis of Heidegger's interpretation of conscience. I recognize that no matter how much "historical data" I might muster to clarify and support the thesis concerning the integral relationship of the work of the early Heidegger to that of Ebeling, only a "demonstration by comparison" of the work of both will be ultimately convincing.

Notes

Notes to page 39:
1. A seeming exception to this overview is the book by Eric Mount, Jr., *Conscience and Responsibility* (Richmond, Va.: John Knox Press, 1969). This book is a product of a dissertation of the same title completed under the direction of Professor Waldo Beach in 1966 at Duke University. It is noteworthy that Mount does address himself to the concept of conscience in Ebeling, as well as in H. R. Niebuhr, the latter (together with James Gustafson) providing the main insights for Mount's constructive efforts. In view of the seeming affinity between this work and ours I venture the following brief evaluation with respect to its bearing on this phase of our inquiry. Mount's work is to be commended for focusing upon the concept of conscience as a fundamental motif in Ebeling's thought. Unfortunately, in spite of such a promising start, Mount's study of Ebeling bears little "corrective" fruit, and for the following reasons. First of all, Mount approaches Ebeling's formulation of the idea of conscience from the usual ethical, or moral perspective, ignoring entirely the latter's explicit objections to such a reading of his interpretation of this phenomenon. As we shall show, for Ebeling, conscience must be understood and interpreted from the start as fundamentally an ontological phenomenon, standing prior (both ontologically and methodologically) to any "ethical", "moral", "rational", or "theological" distinction. That this would, or rather, must involve the theologian in philosophical anthropology (Ebeling: "*Fundamentalontologie*") as a basic methodological starting point, Mount fails to recognize. The most lamentable weakness in Mount's analysis, however, is the inexplicable failure to grasp the crucial role which the *early* Heidegger (*Being and Time*) plays in Ebeling's concept of conscience. In fact, Mount commits a serious error in his attempt to explicate Ebeling's statements on conscience in light of the impact of Heidegger's *later* work (cf., for example, pp. 41, 58-60), and, unfortunately, this error only further compounds the confusion and misunderstanding to which we refer in the initial pages of this chapter. As I shall contend, before bring-

Notes to pages 39–41:
ing in the influence of the so-called later Heidegger to one's interpretation of Ebeling, one must first of all be quite clear as to the nature of the impact of the latter's *early* thought on the Zürich theologian. To miss this cardinal connection (cf. Mount's summary analysis of Heidegger's early interpretation on p. 14!) is to lead one into the greatest kind of misunderstanding and confusion not only concerning Ebeling's concept of conscience, but even with respect to the real meaning and import of his special "hermeneutical" concepts. Furthermore, the implications of such a lack of connection in Mount's analysis suggests quite clearly that Heidegger's later "hermeneutical" phase can be interpreted (let alone understood) on its own, separate and apart from the earlier phenomenological studies in *Being and Time*. We know of Heidegger's protestations to such a reading of his later work (cf., for example, Heidegger's remarks in his letter to William J. Richardson, published as a Preface to the latter's *Heidegger; Through Phenomenology to Thought*, 2nd ed. [The Hague: Martinus Nijhoff, 1967] pp. xiv-xxiii), but apparently Mount is also unaware of Ebeling's objections as well! (With respect to the latter, see especially Ebeling's discussion in his essay, "Verantworten des Glaubens in Begegnung mit dem Denken M. Heideggers", *Zeitschrift für Theologie und Kirche*, Beiheft 2 [1961]:119-124.) (Hereafter we shall refer to this journal as *ZThK*.)

2. "Word of God and Hermeneutic", James M. Robinson and John B. Cobb, Jr., eds., *New Frontiers in Theology, II; The New Hermeneutic* (New York: Harper and Row, 1964), pp. 78-110. This essay was first written for an editorial conference of the journal *ZThK* in April, 1959, and was printed in volumne 56 (1959) of that publication, pp. 224-251. This same essay also appears in Gerhard Ebeling, *Word and Faith*, trans. James W. Leitch (Philadelphia: Fortress Press, 1963), pp. 305-332. Hereafter Ebeling's *Word and Faith* shall be cited as *WF*.)
3. Robinson and Cobb, ed., *New Frontiers in Theology, II*, p. 110.
4. *Ibid.*, p. 190; cf. Amos Wilder's criticism, p. 208.
5. Philip Hefner, *Faith and the Vitalities of History* (New York: Harper and Row, 1966), p. 166.
6. (New York: Harper and Row, 1966).
7. Ebeling, *WF*, p. 428 (emphasis is mine). (Cf. Funk in Robinson and Cobb, eds. *New Frontiers in Theology, II*, pp. 180ff.)
8. Robinson and Cobb, eds, *New Frontiers in Theology, II*, p. 216.
9. Gerhard Ebeling, *The Nature of Faith*, trans. Ronald G. Smith (Philadelphia: The Fortress Press, 1961), pp. 160-161 (emphasis is mine). (Hereafter cited as Ebeling, *NF*.)
10. *Ibid.*, pp. 180-181.
11. *Ibid.*, p. 180 (emphasis is mine).

Notes to pages 41–46:
12. Gerhard Ebeling, "Existence between God and God: A Contribution to the Question of the Existence of God", trans. James P. Carse, *JThC*, 5 (1968):150 (emphasis is mine).
13. *Ibid.*, p. 154 (emphasis is mine).
14. Ebeling, *WF*, pp. 407-23.
15. *Ibid.*, pp. 276-77 (emphasis is mine).
16. *Ibid.*, p. 277.
17. *Ibid.*, pp. 277-79 (emphasis is mine).
18. *Ibid.*, pp. 333-353.
19. *Ibid.*, p. 349 (emphasis is mine).
20. *Ibid.*, p. 332.
21. *Ibid.*, pp. 354-62.
22. *Ibid.*, p. 356 (emphasis is mine).
23. *Ibid.*, p. 360 (emphasis is mine)
24. *Ibid.*, pp. 374-85.
25. *Ibid.*, p. 384 (emphasis is mine).
26. *Ibid.* (emphasis is mine).
27. *Ibid.* (emphasis is mine).
28. *Ibid.*, pp. 386-406.
29. *Ibid.*, pp. 424-33.
30. *Ibid.*, p. 406.
31. *Ibid.*, pp. 432-33 (emphasis is mine).
32. *Ibid.*, p. 407.
33. See *ibid.*, p. 332, n. 1, where Ebeling cites "the need to form an exactly defined *concept* of conscience". Also, see Ebeling's statement, *ibid.*, p. 349, that our present situation requires "an interpretation of conscience which takes a critical view of its customary use, in order to guard against the misunderstanding that the conscience delivers definite material teachings and instructions, whereas in fact it is man himself under the aspect of his involvement in radical questionableness".
34. *Ibid.*, p. 417.
35. *Ibid.* (emphasis is mine). Suffice it to say, for the present, Ebeling's argument here and elsewhere rests upon more than mere etymological analysis. Certainly one can justifiably reason that the latter becomes convincing only when seen in the light of a fuller ontological description of this root phenomenon. In fact, this is precisely what we shall attempt to show in the following investigation of the philosophical underpinnings of Ebeling's thought. See chapter III, below.
36. *Ibid.*
37. *Ibid.*, p. 417.
38. *Ibid.*, p. 420.
39. *Ibid.*

Notes to pages 46–49:
40. *Ibid.*, p. 418.
41. *Ibid.*, pp. 418-19.
42. *Ibid.*, p. 412.
43. *Ibid.*, p. 407.
44. *Ibid.*
45. *Ibid.*, p. 332, n. 1. Cf. the English rendering of this passage from Jaroslav Pelikan's translation in Martin Luther, *Luther's Works*, Vol. 27 (*Lectures on Galatians* 1535, Chapters 5-6; *Lectures on Galatians* 1519, Chapters 1-6), eds. Jaroslav Pelikan and Walter A. Hanson (St. Louis: Concordia Publishing House, 1964), p. 4: "This is the freedom with which Christ has set us free, not from some human slavery or tyrannical authority but from the eternal wrath of God. Where? In the conscience. This is where our freedom comes to a halt; it goes no further. For Christ has set us free, not for a political freedom or a freedom of the flesh but for a theological or spiritual freedom, that is, to make our conscience free and joyful, unafraid of the wrath to come" (Matt. 3.7). Here one might assume that the lack of recognition given to Ebeling's idea of conscience stems also from a certain basic unfamiliarity with the Reformers' (and especially Luther's) interpretation of conscience. But this can hardly be the case, particularly when one reckons among Ebeling's critics such students of Luther as John Dillenberger, Philip Hefner and others.
46. I would stress that my way of stating this relationship has been chosen with extreme care. I believe it describes more accurately the Heideggerian connection of Ebeling's interpretation than do such terms as "dependence upon" or "determined by". I recognize Ebeling's sensitivity to, and persistent rejection of the latter terminology (a sensitivity and resistance, incidentally, that we do not find in Bultmann), and I feel encouraged, through discussion with Professor Ebeling, that my way of putting it achieves a more accurate (if still, from his point of view, not entirely acceptable) understanding of the nature of this relationship.
47. Hefner, *Faith and the Vitalities of History*, p. 156.
48. *Ibid.*
49. Robinson and Cobb, eds., *New Frontiers in Theology II*, p. 240.
50. *Ibid.*, pp. 219-20. See also, Amos Wilder's remarks, *ibid.*, pp. 199-200, and especially 207-08; John Dillenberger, *ibid.*, pp. 150-52.
51. Ebeling, *WF*, p. 249. "All words acquire a new meaning when they are transferred from one context to another.... If you want to use these words, then give them a good bath..." (my translation).
52. *Ibid.*
53. *Ibid.*
54. *Ibid.*, p. 248.

Notes to pages 49–50:
55. *Ibid.*, p. 251. For example, Ebeling states: "The task of forming theological concepts is consequently perceived to be an uncommonly difficult matter. More difficult in a way than, say, the task of forming philosophical concepts. The latter is, of course, also bound to concern itself with the history of language and cannot behave towards it in a completely arbitrary fashion. But it is not bound to a definite linguistic tradition, as is the case in theology."
56. Gerhard Ebeling, *Theology and Proclamation; Dialogue with Rudolf Bultmann*, trans. John Riches (Philadelphia: Fortress Press, 1966). (Hereafter Ebeling's *Theology and Proclamation* shall be cited as *TP*).
57. *Ibid.*, p. 141.
58. See above
59. It is striking fact that nowhere in Ebeling's two major works on Luther does he treat systematically the Reformer's conception of conscience. See the brief references in the volume, *Luther; An Introduction to His Thought*, trans. R. A. Wilson (Philadelphia: Fortress Press, 1970). (Hereafter cited as *Luther*.) See the even more remarkable absence of any treatment of the concept in his earlier published doctoral dissertation, *Evangelische Evangelienauslegung; Eine Untersuchung zu Luthers Hermeneutik* (München: Christian Kaiser, 1942), a work which many cite as decisive for showing the Luther provenance of Ebeling's thought!
60. As related in 1926 in a letter to Erich Förster, pastor and professor in Frankfurt. Cf. Walter Schmithals, *An Introduction to the Theology of Rudolf Bultmann*, trans. John Bowden (Minneapolis, Minnesota: Augsburg Publishing House, 1967), p. 10.
61. According to Schmithals, "Heidegger, five years younger than Bultmann, became ordinarius professor of philosophy in Marburg in 1923, where his epoch-making work *Being and Time* appeared in 1927. In 1928 he went to Freiburg. Bultmann and Heidegger soon came in contact with each other, had regular meetings, and also put their common work into practice in joint seminars. When Bultmann published the first volume of his collected articles in 1933, under the title *Faith and Understanding*, he deliberately dedicated the volume to Martin Heidegger; all the articles collected here from the years 1924-30 show the significance of Heidegger's thought for Bultmann's theological work. We may remark in passing that this collaboration also proved fruitful for Heidegger, who was at that time intensively occupied with Paul and Luther...". *Ibid.*, pp. 14-15. Cf., also, the observation, *ibid.*, p. 66: "One may certainly ask to what extent in their years together not only Bultmann learnt from Heidegger, *but also Heidegger, who at that time was intensively occupied, among other things, with Luther, learnt from Bultmann...*". (Emphasis is mine).

Notes to pages 50–52:
62. Cf. James M. Robinson and John B. Cobb, eds., *New Frontiers in Theology I, The Later Heidegger and Theology* (New York: Harper and Row, 1963), p. 77; Robinson and Cobb, eds., *New Frontiers in Theology II*, pp. 5, 6ff., 62-76.
63. See the illuminative recollection of Hans Georg Gadamer in his book, *Philosophical Apprenticeships*, trans. Robert Sullivan (Cambridge, Mass.: The MIT Press, 1985), pp. 7-19 (Marburg), 45-54 (Heidegger), 55-60 (Bultmann). See also the extended discussion by James M. Robinson in Robinson and Cobb, eds., *New Frontiers in Theology I*, pp. 3-76, and Robinson and Coibb, eds., *New Frontiers in Theology II*, pp. 43-77. Cf., also, Robert Funk's discussion in *Language, Hermeneutic and Word of God* (New York: Harper and Row, 1966), pp. 20-71. For an indication of the impact of Heidegger's *Being and Time* upon Bultmann's students at Marburg during the late 1920's and early 1930's, cf. for example the observations by Robinson in Robinson and Cobb, eds., *New Frontiers in Theology I*, pp. 65-66, n. 144 and n. 145, and by Funk, *Language, Hermeneutic and Word of God*, p. 49, n. 16.
64. "The Concept of the Word of God in the New Testament" (1931), and "The Problem of Natural Theology", (1931) in Rudolf Bultmann, *Faith and Understanding, I* trans. Louise Pettibone Smith, ed. Robert W. Funk (New York: Harper and Row, 1969), pp. 286-312 and 313-331.
65. *Ibid.*, p. 302.
66. *Ibid.*
67. *Ibid.*, p. 303. Cf., *ibid.*, pp. 300f., and 301, n. 45.
68. *Ibid.*, p. 317 (emphasis is mine).
69. *Ibid.*, p. 320 (emphasis is mine).
70. *Ibid.*, pp. 320-321.
71. Heidegger, *BT*, p. 494, n. vi (Division Two, Section 45) (emphasis is mine).
72. It is significant to note that in the conceptual and etymological analyses of *Being and Time* Heidegger nowhere explores the possible relation of the German term "Gewissen" to the Greek notion of "joint-consciousness" in *syneidēsis*. Apparently the same connection cannot be made between the German and the Greek and Latin terms as can be made between *syneidēsis* and "*conscientia*" and the term "conscience" in French where the idea of conscience as a distinctive mode of "knowing" or "self-awareness" comes out most clearly. Interestingly, Heidegger explores the term "Gewissen" only as it relates to two phenomena connected with the so-called "good conscience", a "making certain" and a "becoming certain" ("Sichvergewissen" and "Gewisswerden"). As we shall see, these do not represent true conscience phenomena for Heideg-

Notes to pages 52–55:
ger (see our discussion below, Chapter III, and Heidegger's own analysis in *BT*, p. 338).
73. Cf. Ebeling's discussion of these "objectivized" misconceptions in chapter I, above..
74. Heidegger, *BT*, p. 495, n. vi (Division Two, Chapter Two).
75. As other sources Heidegger cites the interpretations in Kant, Hegel, Schopenhauer, and Nietzsche; see *ibid.*
76. *Ibid.* Stoker's monograph (full title) *Das Gewissen, Erscheinungformen und Theorien*, appears as Vol. 2 in the series edited by Max Scheler, entitled *Schriften zur Philosophie und Soziologie* (Bonn: Friedrich Cohen, 1925).
77. *Ibid.*, pp. 495-96, n. vi (Division Two, Chapter Two) (emphasis is mine).
78. Cf. especially, Rudolf Bultmann, *Faith and Understanding, I*, pp. 330f. Cf., also, Bultmann's remarks in his essay, "The Historicity of Man and Faith", in *Existence and Faith; Shorter Writings of Rudolf Bultmann*, ed. and trans. Schubert M. Ogden (Cleveland: Meridian Books, 1963), pp. 92ff., and in his book, *Jesus Christ and Mythology* (New York: Charles Scribner's Sons, 1958), pp. 77f.
79. In anticipation of Ebeling's possible dissatisfaction with this way of putting it, I would add: "—equally impressed, if not in words (as in the case with Bultmann), at least in practice!"
80. Cf., Robinson and Cobb, eds., *New Frontiers in Theology, II*, p. 63, n. 187.
81. (Zürich: Art Institut Orell Füssli, 1934).
82. *Ibid.*, parts I-II, pp. 11-76.
83. *Ibid.*, part III, pp. 77-158.
84. (My translation.) *Ibid.*, pp. 153-154: "Endlich hat...der lutherisch-kierkegaardsche Gedanke eine Wiederbelebung modernster Art erfahren, die Idee, dass Gewissen seinem Wesen nach ein Erschliessen letzter metaphysischer Zusammenhänge sei—eine Offenbarung durch das Mittel der Angst. Unter Beiseitelassung der religiösen und theologischen Fassung dieser Idee hat Martin Heidegger diesen Weg aufs neue beschritten".
85. Emil Brunner, *Man in Revolt; A Christian Anthropology*, trans. Olive Wyon (New York: Charles Scribner's Sons, 1939), p. 195.
86. *Ibid.*, p. 202.
87. Emil Brunner, *The Divine Imperative*, trans. Olive Wyon (Philadelphia: The Westminster Press, 1947), p. 156.
88. *Ibid.* (emphasis is mine).
89. *Ibid.*, pp. 156-57.
90. *Ibid.*, p. 157. Cf. also, Brunner, *Man in Revolt*, pp. 46-47, 114-15, 164, 189, 195.

Notes to pages 55–56:
91. See Brunner, *Man in Revolt*, pp. 47, 195-204, and especially 512.
92. See Brunner *The Divine Imperative*, pp. 155-57, 599, and especially 701-03; also Brunner, *Man in Revolt*, pp. 47, 195.
93. Bultmann, *Kerygma and Myth*, I:193. Cf. Brunner, *The Divine Imperative*, pp. 607f.; also, Brunner, *Man in Revolt, pp. 217, n. 2, 462, n. 2, and 542-44.*
94. In conversations with Professor Ebeling at Regis College, Toronto, I found it significant that he felt freer to elaborate his ties to the so-called Marburg tradition when speaking in an Anglo-American context than when speaking on the Continent.
95. Ebeling, *WF*, p. 420, n. 1.
96. *Ibid.*, p. 277, n. 3.
97. Beiträge für historischen Theologie, No.4 (Tübingen: J.C.B. Mohr [Paul Siebeck], 1929).
98. *Ibid.*, p. 1 (translation is mine).
99. See, *ibid.*, p. 7, nn. 1, 2.
100. *Ibid.*, p. 7 (translation is mine).
101. I should stress here that I am not emphasizing the uncritical acceptance of Jacob's study as a model of Luther interpretation by Ebeling (a point to which he has drawn my attention), but rather the more general and almost overlooked manner in which the Heideggerian transformation of philosophical and theological language and thought became a *fait accompli* in that generation of theological students.
102. Ebeling, *WF*, pp. 277-81; see also, Gerhard Ebeling, *Luther*, pp. 133-36, 147.
103. Ebeling, *WF*, p. 276; see also, *Luther*, pp. 136-38.
104. Ebeling, *WF*, pp. 276-78; see also, *Luther*, pp. 119-20, 130, 147-49, 170-76, 219-20, and 261-62. Cf., e.g., "...the will is always committed, always determined by something. Consequently, the concept of 'free will' can also represent a contradiction in terms, in so far as it refers to a will which is not yet decided, but still has to come to a decision, so that it is not yet the will. Luther realizes that it is a completely abstract mode of thought to speak of an 'absolute' will, that is, the will completely isolated and undertermined. The will is always already decided, involved and committed, and is not the natural will in the situation of absolute freedom of choice, the will considered in purely unhistorical terms". (*Luther*, p. 220.)
105. Ebeling, *WF*, p. 420.

Chapter III

Heidegger's phenomenological description of conscience in *Being and Time*

The second chapter of division 2 of Heidegger's *Being and Time*, entitled "Dasein's Attestation of an Authentic Potentiality-for-Being, and Resoluteness," represents a crucial hinge in the development of his phenomenological interpretation of human existence (*Dasein*)(1). Prior to this section Heidegger presents a description of Dasein's "everyday being-in-the-world", giving particular emphasis to its ontological character as "disowned" or "inauthentic" existence. This description reaches its climax in the comprehensive concept of "Care" (*Sorge*) where the ontological structure of Dasein's everyday existence is set forth in all its complexity. Through a thematic breakdown and analysis of the 'care-formula'(2) Heidegger attempts to show how the disclosure of Dasein's "Authentic potentiality-for-Being-oneself" is made possible by and grounded in its basic ontological character as Care. This analysis places a capstone on the first part of Heidegger's inquiry and sets the stage for the phenomenological interpretation of "time" as the fundamental ontological "ground" of the wholeness of Dasein's Being. But before passing on to this final interpretation, Heidegger must first deal with a basic question left unanswered in his analysis of the concept of Care, namely, the actual ontic attestation of the possibility for Dasein's understanding its authentic potentiality for Care-Being.

The possibility of such an attestation seems at first sight to be difficult, if not impossible, in view of the dilemma presented in the Preparatory Analysis. Heidegger summarizes this dilemma as follows:

The question of the "*who*" of Dasein has been answered with the expression 'Self.' Dasein's Selfhood has been defined formally as a way of existing, and therefore not as an entity present-at-hand. But for the most part *I myself* am not the "who" of Dasein; the they-self is its "who".... With Dasein's lostness in the "they," that factical potentiality-for-Being which is closest to it...has already been decided upon. The "they" has always kept Dasein from taking hold of these possibilities of Being. The "they" even hides the manner in which it has tacitly relieved Dasein of the burden of explicitly *choosing* these possibilities. It remains indefinite who has 'really' done the choosing. So Dasein makes no choices, get carried along by the nobody, and thus ensnares itself in inauthenticity.(3)

In order for Dasein to 'bring itself back' from its lostness (or fallenness) in the "they", and to recover its capacity to "choose", it must first of all "find" itself. Now, we have seen that Dasein's "authentic Self" has been brought into view phenomenologically in terms of Care-being: "In terms of its *possibility*,

Dasein is already a potentiality-for-Being-its-Self...."(4). But, Heidegger asks, exactly "where" and "in what way" can this ontological possibility be shown to Dasein, shown, that is, so that it may be grasped as a real ontic, or *existentiell* possibility for its everyday mode of being? To answer this question Heidegger introduces his phenomenological interpretation of the "*voice of conscience*" (*Stimme des Gewissens*).

According to Heidegger, the phenomenon of the voice of conscience is not something that can be attested by an "inductive empirical proof". As in the case of the first part of his study, Heidegger makes it clear that his interpretation is not a "scientific" one: "The ontological analysis of conscience on which we are thus embarking, is prior to any description and classification of Experiences of conscience, and likewise lies outside of any biological 'explanation' of this phenomenon (which would mean its dissolution)"(5). But that this phenomenon cannot be established as any "fact", or that its "reality" cannot be legitimized by objective investigation does not in any way lessen its worth for an existential interpretation, according to Heidegger. Like other phenomena presented in Dasein's common-sense experience, the 'voice of conscience' can also be approached and brought into view through phenomenological analysis.

In contradistinction to what Heidegger refers to as the "Vulgar" or ordinary interpretation of conscience(6), which pictures the phenomenon more or less as a substantial "faculty" which Dasein "has", his analysis begins by focusing upon the phenomenon as a primordial "*existentiale*", that is, a basic ontological structure of Dasein as existing. As a mode of disclosure, he writes, "Conscience gives us 'something' to understand...."(7). This 'something', as stated at an earlier point in his analysis, is Dasein's own authentic self as Care. It will be noted that, as a general mode of self-disclosure, conscience appears similar to those other ontological states-of-mind connected with Dasein's "factical thereness"(8), e.g., "fear" (*Furcht*)(9), "dread" (*Grauen*)(10), "alarm" (*Erschrecken*)(11), "terror" (*Entsetzen*)(12), etc. It differs significantly, however, from these modes of disclosure in two important respects: (1) founded in the more fundamental state of "uncanny anxiety" (*unheimliche Angst*)(13), the 'voice of conscience' presents to Dasein's understanding a more complete picture of its true ontological potentiality (i.e., its *wholeness* of Being, as Care), and (2) through its ownmost *existentiell* "choice" which its authentic potentiality-for-Being would require. Heidegger takes up this latter point first.

Viewed phenomenologically, Heidegger tells us, the 'voice of conscience' has the fundamental character of a "call", it is essentially a *linguistic* phenomenon. If we ask *who* it is that is called, we must answer, Dasein itself, although not Dasein absorbed in the "they-self" of its average, everyday understanding. Now this call that is made to Dasein is quite different from a mere vocal "utterance". Although silent, conscience announces itself as an "appeal", or, more technically, a "summons" (*Aufruf*). And *to what* is one "summoned" by the silent but abrupt)(14) voice of conscience, Heidegger asks? "To one's own Self"(15).

By "one's own Self" Heidegger, of course, has in mind Dasein's original, ownmost potentiality-for-Being which it has lost in the world of its everyday concern. It is worth noting that in this *summoning* process, what is called up for question by the voice of conscience is not some specific, concrete aspect of Dasein's everyday manner of being. Heidegger writes: "*What* does the conscience call to him to whom it appeals? Taken strictly, nothing. The call asserts nothing, gives no information about world-events, has nothing to tell.... Nothing gets called to [*zu-gerufen*] this Self, but it has been summoned [*aufgerufen*] to itself—that is, to its ownmost potentiality-for-Being"(16). Nor is the Self brought to question as if in some kind of courtroom-style soliloquy within itself. As Heidegger puts it: "The tendency of the call is not such as to put up for 'trial' the Self to which the appeal is made; but it calls Dasein forth (and 'forward') into its ownmost possibilities, as a summons to its ownmost potentiality-for-Being-its-Self"(17). The voice of conscience, in short, *is a call to Care.*

Now that the voice of conscience has been described as a call or summons to one's own authentic Self, Heidegger asks, phenomenologically conceived, "Who is it that calls in the conscience?" "Who, or what is the source of the voice?" The answer: "In conscience Dasein calls itself"(18). Properly interpreted, the caller is not to be understood as 'someone else' who is with Dasein in its world. And neither is it to be taken as some arbitrary, external 'power', i.e., God the Supreme Lawgiver, who, at his own bidding, breaks in upon man via a "faculty" of conscience, calling to question and bringing to judgment. Nor, following a typical "psychological" description, can the phenomenon be "explained away" as man's "superego", as with Freud. All these explanations, according to Heidegger, "*pass over the phenomenal findings too hastily*". *They are founded upon an unexamined ontological interpretation of man.*

Now, in the description of Dasein itself as the caller, certain difficulties immediately arise, for Heidegger. He has shown how, in its everyday mode of being, Dasein has 'lost' or 'surrendered' its ownmost Self to the 'crowd', the world of the "they". How, therefore, can Dasein, as "fallen" Dasein, call itself to Care-Being? Having surrendered its true identity to the "they", how can Dasein's authentic potentiality-for-Being be brought once again to understanding?

Heidegger would remind us that in asking these questions we have forgotten that Dasein, as Care, is more than a "mere object". Its ownmost Self is more than a mere 'something' that can be owned or given up as its other possessions. To understand Dasein in this way is to completely overlook its fundamental ontological structure as "possibility", as "potentiality-for-Being". If, then, Dasein is ontologically always a possibility, or potentiality, and never a mere thing, its ownmost Self is still 'there' as a live possibility for being even when Dasein has lost itself to the everyday world of the crowd or the "public".

Having answered the question as to how it is possible for Dasein's authentic potentiality-for-Being to be brought to understanding, the further question remains as to the way in which this occurs: *From whence* and *in what manner* does Dasein as conscience call? Heidegger answers this question by pointing to the affective mode of disclosure: "Uncanniness" (*Unheimlichkeit*). "Uncanniness", he writes "is the basic kind of Being-in-the-world, even though in an everyday way it has been covered up. Out of the depths of this kind of Being, Dasein itself, as conscience, calls"(19).

It is out of the state of uncanniness, therefore, as the innermost dimension of one's experience of "anxiety", (*Angst*), that Dasein calls to itself as conscience. Heidegger has already described how the mood of anxiety, above all other states of mind, discloses to Dasein its full ontological situation as a thrown possibility of Being-in-the-world(20). In the mood of anxiety Dasein is brought face to face with the world, and its previous understanding of itself and its place in the world is radically thrown into question(21). In this state of 'radical questionableness' Heidegger has indicated how Dasein approaches the threshold of an authentic discovery of itself in terms of its Being as Care. But it should be pointed out that in the mood of anxiety Dasein reaches only the threshold of an authentic transcendence, that is to say, in its anxiety, Dasein only catches a glimpse, as it were, of its true potentiality-for-Being. And this "glimpse", although 'seen' clearly, is nevertheless only deficiently present as the 'other side' of its fully disclosed, thrown and scattered being-in-the-world.

The concept of uncanniness is to be seen as an analytical elaboration and refinement of that centermost aspect of the mood of anxiety which Heidegger refers to as the state of radical questionableness(22). This state of being thrown open to question is interpreted in two ways by means of its most basic nature as uncanniness. First, Heidegger describes how in the feeling of uncanniness Dasein is questioned as to its "peculiar indefiniteness"(23). This indefiniteness is Dasein's "nothing and nowhere"(24), i.e., man's non-finitude, his non-possibility for Being 'there' (thrownness) in the world. This "nothing and nowhere" comes to expression and receives fuller content in the second aspect of uncanniness, the feeling of "not-being-at home". Here Heidegger draws upon the literal meaning of the German word for uncanny, "*unheimlich*", to point to the way in which Dasein is brought, in its state of anxiety, to question its hitherto accepted familiarity with and at-homeness in its average, work-a-day world. This state of questionableness brings into view Dasein's usual mode of being (i.e., Dasein in its "fallenness") as a "fleeing from" and a "fleeing towards"(25). This is to say that, in the state of anxiety, Dasein's average being-in-the-world is laid bare (or disclosed) as a fleeing *from* the uncanny awareness of its not-being-at-home in the world, and as a fleeing *towards* the illusionary security of the at-homeness offered by the they-world to which it is most used.

It is out of this kind of a state then that Dasein itself, as the voice of conscience, calls. Here, Dasein summons itself at the very threshold of authentic self-discovery. The call of conscience emerges from that silent and uncanny in-between-state of self-disclosure wherein Dasein is presented with the possibility of understanding itself in its authentic potentiality-for-Being—the only true alternative to the radical picture of its fallen condition to which it has been brought face to face.

To speak of the summons of the conscience as the very "threshold" of authentic self-discovery here may appear to be somewhat misleading. Actually, it is a useful descriptive term at this point in our analysis in that it suggests an important aspect of the phenomenon of conscience hitherto left unmentioned, viz., the all-important temporal dimension of the call as it arises out of Dasein's projection of itself in the mood of anxiety. It has already been indicated how the mood of anxiety brings into view Dasein's ontological situation as a thrown possibility of being-in-the-world. In the state of uncanniness Dasein's temporal horizon is thrown open to radical questionableness. In this openness (significantly, Heidegger refers often to this state of questionableness as an openness) Dasein is left free for the possibility of "projecting" (understanding and willing)(26) itself towards the future in terms of its true potentiality-for-Being. But, so far, Dasein's present ontological situation has been disclosed to itself only in terms of its past, i.e., only in terms of its sheer "thrownness" in the world. At the other end of its finitude lies the final, end prospect of "Death", the "possible impossibility" of Dasein's existence. According to Heidegger, it is only as Dasein comes ultimately to grasp itself in its anxiety as "Being-destined-for-death" that it becomes truly free for the authentic projection of itself in terms of its inmost potentiality. But this leads to yet another point.

In grasping itself between the uncanny extremity of its "thrownness", on the one hand, and its "Being-towards-death" on the other, Dasein comes face to face with the "Nothingness" of its own Being. We have already seen how Dasein, in the feeling of uncanniness, is disclosed in terms of its "nothing and nowhere". In one sense, this refers ontologically to Dasein's past, i.e., its non-possibility for being thrown 'there' in the world. At the other end of the spectrum is the disclosure of Death, i.e., the future limit of Dasein's finitude as the "possibility of no-longer-being-able-to-be-there"(27). This description of Dasein's basic ontological status as a mid-point between its "non-possibility for being thrown" and its "possibility of no-longer being-able-to-be-there" illumines our understanding of Heidegger's description of Dasein's ultimate reality as "Nothing". In the notion of Nothingness the self-disclosure which Heidegger sees being brought to light in the phenomenon of uncanniness is now heightened. The ultimate ontological foundation for Dasein's proximal, everyday mode of being is disclosed in the state of uncanniness as being rooted in "no thing" at all. Before the spectacle of its Nothingness, so defined, Dasein is left suspended in its present moment of existence (its "now") to grasp itself, and to do so *in no other terms* than that of its own Being. This is expressed perhaps most clearly by Heidegger in his essay, "What is Metaphysics?":

> Only in the clear night of dread's Nothingness is what-is as such revealed in all its original overtness (*Offenheit*): that it 'is' and is not Nothing. This verbal appendix 'and not Nothing' is, however, not an a posteriori explanation but an a priori which alone makes possible any revelation of what-is. The essence of Nothing...lies in this: that it alone brings *Da-sein* face to face with what-is as such.(28)

This being brought "face to face with what-is as such" in *Being and Time* is another way of describing Dasein's basic ontological state of *freedom*. Grasping itself between the temporal extremity of its thrownness and its Being-towards-death, Dasein, according to Heidegger, comes into possession of its own destiny. Ontologically, Dasein and Dasein alone is left, or presented, with the possibility of taking hold of and willing the reality of its ownmost Being. What this ultimately means for the call of conscience will become apparent at a later point in our study.

In the foregoing analysis of the call of conscience, it should be remembered that Heidegger has attempted to prepare the way for the final and most important question of its ultimate attestation. In following the course of his analysis in *Being and Time* we have understood Heidegger to have answered the questions as to who it is that is called and who does the calling, to what one is summoned and from whence and in what manner. Now the final question to be taken up is whether or not it is possible for the summons of conscience to be *heeded*, and, if so, *in what way*.

Certainly, in correspondence to a call or summons there must be a "hearing" or "response". But the question rears its head again: Since Dasein's average, everyday being-in-the-world is always fallen or already delivered over to the world of "they", how is it possible for an "authentic hearing" to take place? Indeed, without the possibility for an authentic hearing of the call, there is no way in which Dasein can be summoned from his fallen existence and brought forth to his own original possibility(29). Heidegger meets this question by claiming that it is possible for Dasein to hear the call of conscience in its (Dasein's) very inauthenticity, i.e., even in its fallenness. For Heidegger, such a hearing is that which heeds the call of conscience as a call of "Guilty!"(30) But what does he mean by this?

In the call of conscience, Heidegger states, Dasein is presented with a summons of "Being-guilty" (*Schuldigsein*). This summons of guiltiness, he continues, is generally understood in terms of two significations: it means guilt, in the sense of a "being responsible for" (*schuld sein an*)(31) one's past deeds which are now found wanting, and it means "having debts" (*schulden*)(32) or "owing" in the sense that there is something 'lacking', or positively, that there remains something that is in need of completion. After having analysed the phenomenon at some length in terms of its common-sense character, Heidegger reminds us that it can only be finally attested as it is shown to be constitutive of that kind of Being which is peculiar to Dasein.

The phenomenon of guilt, which is not necessarily related to 'having debts' and law-breaking, can be clarified only if we first inquire in principle into Dasein's *Being*-guilty—in other words, if we conceive the idea of 'Guilty!' in terms of Dasein's kind of Being.

If this is our goal, the idea of 'Guilty!' must be sufficiently formalized so that those ordinary phenomena of "guilt" which are related to our concernful Being with Others, will *drop out*.(33)

Heidegger takes as his clue for this formal ontological interpretation the *not*-character which he sees implied in the general understanding of the phenomenon as "responsibility" and "debt". From a formal-existential standpoint, the call of conscience, as a summons of guilt, presents to Dasein an understanding of itself in terms of *nichtig*, i.e., determined (ontologically) by a "not". Or, as Heidegger puts it, "we define the formally existential idea of the 'Guilty!' as "Being-the-basis for a Being which has been defined by a 'not'"—that is to say, as "*Being-the-basis of a nullity*"(34). The reader will recall the earlier discussion of the state of uncanniness and its disclosure of Dasein's temporal extremity between its condition of thrownness on the one hand, and its Being-towards-death on the other. In this self-disclosure, Dasein, we saw, comes face to face with its own Being as "*Nothingness*". The implications of this earlier analysis are not picked up by Heidegger in his interpretation of the existential-temporal boundaries set earlier: the idea of Dasein's thrownness is carried over and broadened out in the existential interpretation of the idea of "debt" or "owing"; the idea of projection out of Nothingness in the face of Death is elaborated in the interpretation of the idea of "responsibility".

As was indicated in the analysis of the notion of uncanniness, Dasein's "facticity" restricts it from getting back behind its thrownness, as it were, allowing itself to be brought into authentic Being on its own. This self-disclosure emerges, and is given a final significance in the authentic hearing of the call of conscience as an "owing" or "debt". Whereas in its anxiety Dasein is disclosed as "already 'there' as a thrown fact", in its "guiltiness" it is found (in a negative sense) as "*not* as thrown by its *own act*". Implied in this negation is the understanding that Dasein is held in "debt", or as "owing" its being to none other than itself—to itself, that is, as the *basis*, or *ground* of its thrown possibilities.

Now, as we have also seen, just as Dasein's facticity curtails its possibility of getting back behind its thrownness, so does the nature of its *existentiell* projection prevent it from moving beyond its present fallen possibilities into which it is continually being thrown. "The Self", Heidegger writes, "which as such has to lay the basis for itself, can *never* get that basis into its power...."(35). The negation of this power to be *its own* basis resides in Dasein's (everyday) facticity. In its facticity, Heidegger says, "Dasein constantly lags behind its possibilities"(36). He continues, "[Dasein] is never existent *before* its basis, but only *from it* and *as this basis*. Thus 'Being-a-basis' means never to have power over one's ownmost Being from the ground up"(37). What is implied in this negation is that in the call of conscience Dasein is understood as guilty in the sense of "lacking"; it is found wanting in the projection of its ownmost possibilities for being—the projection for which conscience would have it accept full "responsibility", the projection for which it constantly calls us to be "answerable".

An authentic hearing of the call of conscience, therefore, is interpreted here as that understanding which finds its roots in Dasein's ultimate nullity, its being as "*Being-guilty*". Authentic hearing receives its attestation as it arises out of the negation implicit in the understanding presented to Dasein in the call of guiltiness: Dasein, inescapably bound up in its own guiltiness, is forever found "owing" for its failure to project itself forward beyond its last possibilities, and "responsible" for its failure to recover or take over the thrown "fact" of its existence. But, this disclosure is more than the mere laying bare of one's inescapable, and yet responsible *in*authenticity. To the contrary, according to Heidegger:

> Hearing the appeal correctly is... tantamount to having an understanding of oneself in one's ownmost potentiality-for-Being—that is, to projecting oneself upon one's *ownmost authentic* potentiality for becoming guilty.(38)

In putting it this way Heidegger suggests that hearing oneself as "owing" and "responsible" in one's inescapable guilt is in essence the positive disclosure of one's own true potentiality for Being which has been lost. This is a crucial point. Heidegger states that being as "*Being*-guilty" is that kind of being which is an issue for it and for which it must *decide*—or *flee*. If the call is authentically heard (and here it should be added that, for Heidegger, the call is never heard as something general, but always 'concrete', i.e., it occurs always in and with the specific situations of Dasein's every act[s] of being), it is understood as an appeal of the true Self calling Dasein forth out of its inevitable guiltiness to its original potentiality for Being. Heidegger summarizes this clearly at one point:

> The appeal calls back by calling forth: it calls Dasein *forth* to the possibility of taking over, in existing, even that thrown entity which it is; it calls Dasein *back* to its thrownness so as to understand this thrownness as the null basis which it has to take up into existence. This calling-back in which conscience calls forth, gives Dasein to understand that Dasein itself—the null basis for its null projection, standing in the possibility of

its Being—is to bring itself back to itself from its lostness in the "they"; and this means that it is guilty.(39)

In the light of this, I return at this point to the question which Heidegger raises at the start of his inquiry, viz., whether or not Dasein's true potentiality-for-Being could be disclosed in fact as a real ontic (or *existentiell*) possibility for its everyday mode of being. We have indicated Heidegger's answer to this question in the foregoing analysis. The query may be put as to whether Heidegger's interpretation of this phenomenon can bear the weight which he seeks to place upon it. In answering this question several difficulties arise which must be examined briefly.

The first difficulty arises over the nature of the summons as one of "Guilty!" Although Heidegger claims to have overcome the superficial "judgmental" element in the traditional notion of conscience (i.e., the notion which sees the voice of conscience as a bringing man/woman to account for his/her failure to perform certain acts or oughts) through his interpretation of the summons to guilt as a summons which "comes out of the Self, calling Dasein forth from beyond", his stress upon the inevitability of Dasein's state of guiltiness almost seems to contradict him. Is a final judgment not implied in Dasein's being called as "owing" and "responsible" for its own impotency for recovering the thrown fact of its existence and the projection of itself beyond its present possibilities? Is the problem merely a linguistic one, i.e., in the abstruseness of Heidegger's concepts of "Guilty!", "owing", "responsibility", or is it inherent in the very interpretation itself?

Heidegger might answer that a final judgment could be implied in both language and interpretation, but the problem arises through a fundamental misunderstanding on another level. Heidegger would point to his temporal analysis of existence where Dasein's everyday mode of being is interpreted in terms—always—of possibility. Dasein's actions are *never* final, Heidegger would tell us, they are *always* open for the possibility of future projection. This means that any 'judgement' implied in any single projection (which is, inevitably, "thrown") is never conclusive. Because Dasein is always a possibility and never a mere object in itself, it *is* therefore neither guilty nor not-guilty, it "is" neither 'judged' nor 'not-judged' at any given moment.

Everything implied in this last point, however, rests ultimately upon a second difficulty which crops up in Heidegger's analysis, a difficulty which we have already considered in part, viz., just how extreme, or how impossible does it understand Dasein's "fallen" existence to be. More specifically, to what extent is an authentic hearing of the call of conscience taken over and lost in Dasein's fallen, *existentiell* mode of existence? Heidegger claims that it is "possible" for there to be an authentic hearing of the call in and through Dasein's fallenness, and, as we have seen, he presents his interpretation of the hearing of the call as "Guilty!" as its attestation. But, in what sense are we to understand this attestation?

In answer to this I would recall here a quote cited earlier in our study:
> The phenomenon of guilt, which is not necessarily related to 'having debts' and law-breaking, can be clarified only if we first inquire *in principle* into Dasein's Being-guilty—in other words, if we conceive the idea of 'Guilty!' in terms of Dasein's kind of Being.
>
> If this is our goal, the idea of 'Guilty!' must be sufficiently *formalized* so that those ordinary phenomena of "guilt" which are related to our concernful Being with Others, will drop out.(40)

Heidegger points out here that his inquiry is concerned with a clarification "in principle" of Dasein's ontological structure (i.e., "*Being*-guilty") which makes it *possible* for it to heed the call of "guilt". Heidegger is seeking after a "formalized" existential attestation for Dasein's basic mode of "Being-guilty" which would allow for the *existentiell possibility* of an authentic hearing. Some have argued that Heidegger has really sought to go further than this in his phenomenological description. Heidegger's analysis, it is said, is not only concerned to present the *existentiell* possibility of an authentic hearing of conscience "in principle", but also intends to present such an attestation "in fact". In his study on the relationship between Heidegger and Rudolf Bultmann, John Macquarrie(41), for example, raises this question, although he casts the problem in terms of the difference between "ontic" or "ontological" possibilities. He writes, regarding Heidegger's interpretation of Dasein in *Being and Time*:

> Even in his fallen condition, man can still hear the call of the authentic self [i.e., in the phenomenon of conscience], because, so long as he is man, authenticity and inauthenticity are possible ways of being for him. But while authenticity remains an ontological possibility in fallenness, it has ceased to be an ontical possibility. That is to say, it is a bare formal possibility for man, in the sense that he is so constituted in his being that he might exist authentically. It is not, however, a concrete *existentiell* possibility for which he can decide now, because as fallen he has come into a situation in which that possibility is no longer open to him(42).

In turning to Heidegger himself, we will recall an earlier reference, wherein, in regard to the existential situation (i.e., Dasein's fallenness) disclosed by the hearing of the call of conscience as an owing or debt, Heidegger states that the "Self, which as such has to lay the basis for itself, can never get that basis into its power...."(43). His elaboration of this at another point would seem at first sight to coincide with Macquarrie's judgment; Heidegger writes: "In being a basis—that is, in existing as thrown—Dasein constantly lags behinds its possibilities. It is never existent *before* its basis, but only *from it* and as this basis. Thus 'Being-a-basis' means *never* to have power over one's ownmost being from the *ground up*"(44).

For Heidegger, it would seem that in the face of his ultimate thrown *nullity*, man, as everyday Dasein, inescapably finds himself wanting in the *existentiell* power to project his ownmost potentiality for being. In response to such an understanding, certainly it would simply be too easy, if not methodologically dishonest (from the standpoint of Heidegger's further methodological development of this problem), to move immediately from this point to the conclusion that Macquarrie (for one) makes, namely, since conscience "cannot bring man the *existentiell* possibility of authenticity for which he can decide...it now appears that only some Power not fallen as man is fallen, can bring to man this concrete possibility of regaining his authentic being"(45). Several problems are involved in this kind of conclusion.

For one thing, in resting upon his earlier distinction between "ontic" and "ontological" possibilities, Macquarrie's conclusion betrays a definite misunderstanding of the nature and scope of Heidegger's phenomenological interpretation. As Heidegger expresses at several points in his descriptive analysis(46), the question as to whether or not the call of conscience does "in fact" (or "ontically") bring before man the concrete possibility for assuming his authentic existence must be left *open* in the final analysis; in other terms Heidegger has often expressed throughout *Being and Time* that the final *existentiell* (or ontic) attestation of a phenomenon (here, of "fallenness" and the "call of conscience") can never be decided within the formal limits of a phenomenological description, but only "in and with Dasein's being, 'that-it-is'". If this point is missed by Macquarrie, it is caught by Rudolf Bultmann when he states, in response to Karl Jasper's (mis)interpretation of Heidegger: "Certainly, what Jasper calls 'existential clarification' differs from Heidegger's phenomenological analysis of empirical existence in this, that existential clarification [for Heidegger] is effected *only in the act of existing*...."(47). As we shall see, Ebeling's position does not appear to vary from Bultmann on this score.

For another thing, Macquarrie's (mis)understanding of what Heidegger intends by the idea of "hearing" has had the tendency to lead subsequent theological discussion down an unfruitful path, or so it seems to me. In his analysis of Heidegger, Macquarrie admits to the ontological possibility of "hearing" the call of conscience, but, in doing so, he implicitly insists in making a distinction in Heidegger's interpretation of the phenomenon between hearing as "understanding", and hearing (or 'understood-hearing') as "empowered option (or choice)". It is such a distinction that lies behind his statement, for example, that "Conscience, as Heidegger has described the phenomenon, can at best awaken in fallen man the awareness of a lost possibility of authenticity. But it cannot by any means empower him to choose that possibility"(48)—it is this statement, significantly, that immediately precedes his appeal, cited above, for the necessity for an "unfallen Power outside man". The real question which I want to raise here, however, is not so much concerned with the legitimate-illegitimate nature of the distinction itself as it is with the effects that it has had in molding the theological discussion of

Heidegger's thought (in the traditional "inauthentic-authentic" schema) toward the overly-simplified, and misleading question of (1) the "degree" of Dasein's "fallenness" (i.e., theologically, man's/woman's "sinfulness") and (2) the (ontic) "possibility" of authentic "decision" (i.e., theologically, the possibility of man's/woman's natural obedience, [faith] choice without some 'outside' force or power [as "grace"]), overlooking, in the process, the perhaps more viable theological implications in the decisive phenomenon of conscience lying untended between these two points.

Of course, in this same connection, nothing has been said regarding the methodological legitimacy of Macquarrie's desire to move from the question of the impossibility of the power of authentic, *existentiell* choice to the necessity of a "Power" outside (natural) man/woman that *can* effect this choice. By methodological legitimacy here I am concerned not so much with its warrantedness in regard to Heidegger himself as I am with its appropriatness for a viable procedure in our present theological situation. What is really at question here, it seems to me, is the fruitfulness and validity of a procedure which opts for the possibility of "God-language" in the form of an "answer" compelling us toward its necessity in the face of a human "impossibility", as a necessary (or desirable) "Other" which fills up as it were the unbridgeable "gaps" or "voids" of human knowledge and existence. In admitting the necessity of such an "answer" or "Other" as something *ad extra* man's/woman's (natural) situation, what happens then, we might ask, to the status of such a 'man/woman'? What happens to such a man's/woman's "freedom" and "responsibility"? What becomes of man's/woman's "response" (his/her choice and decision) to the call of conscience *qua* man/woman? And furthermore, along the same lines, how then are we to understand such a 'God'? What becomes of God's relationship to the world, to man/woman? What then does "reality" become? Along such methodological lines, do we not, to use Ebeling's apt description, "make reality separate into two strata, or cause an additional reality to be tacked on to that of the world"(49)?

Certainly the questions raised here, along with the problematic nature of the theological method which is under fire, are not to be answered as easily as may be implied; nor should it be implied that Macquarrie himself (and others who work along the same general lines) is unaware of the difficulties entailed in such a criticism, for he is not. Be this as it may, it is my conviction that such a methodological point of departure is ill-conceived: it moves too quickly and silently over a key element in Heidegger's phenomenological interpretation which, upon a second look, may prove to be the more desirable path upon which to tread. In short, I am suggesting that we turn our sights from the question of the "degree" in which Heidegger's interpretation understands man's/woman's "fallenness" to be, and the subsequent question as to the necessity for an 'outside' Power, to the implications of conscience as a mode of "disclosure" of man's/woman's identity, i.e., as that being who *is* as the ever recurring possibility of being opened to him/herself in radical questionableness and challenged to respond. Here, though we are already standing upon that ground where Ebeling has chosen to set his plough. It is Ebeling who would have us fix our gaze upon this particular "defining" and disclosure function of conscience. I believe that, for Ebeling, it is really here that Heidegger's early analysis holds greatest promise of bearing its richest "theological" fruit. And Heidegger? As far as we can still determine, the philosopher would not at all be opposed to such a focal delimitation of his work. As he has often stressed, *Being and Time* is not a presentation of doctrine but a formalized descriptive phenomenology.

Notes

Notes to pages 65–66:
1. Regarding our use of the term "Dasein" in this chapter and elsewhere, cf. the conclusions of John Macquarrie and Edward Robinson, which we follow, as over against William J. Richardson ("Dasein" = "There-being"), Ralph Manheim (= "There-being"), and others: "The word 'Dasein' plays so important a role in this work and is already so familiar to the English-speaking reader who has read about Heidegger, that it seems simpler to leave it untranslated except in the relatively rare passages in which Heidegger himself breaks it up with a hyphen ('Da-sein') to show its etymological construction: literally 'Being-there'. Though in traditional German philosophy it may be used quite generally to stand for almost any kind of Being or 'existence' which we can say that something *has* (the 'existence' of God, for example), in everyday usage it tends to be used more narrowly to stand for the kind of Being that belongs to *persons*. Heidegger follows the everyday usage in this respect, but goes somewhat further in that he often uses it to stand for any *person* who has such Being, and who is thus an 'entity' himself". Heidegger, *BT*, p. 27, n. 1.
2.. "Being-ahead-of-oneself—in Being-already-in...—as Being-alongside"; *ibid.* p. 241. (Ger.: "*Sich-vorweg-sein—im-schon-sein-in...—als Sein-bei...*" in Martin Heidegger, *Sein und Zeit*, 12th ed. [Tübingen: Max Niemeyer, 1972], p. 196.)
3.. Heidegger, *BT*, p. 312.
4.. *Ibid.*, pp. 36ff.
5.. *Ibid.*, p. 313.
6. *Ibid.*, cf. pp. 335ff.
7. *Ibid.*, p. 314.
8. *Ibid.*, cf., pp. 172ff.
9. *Ibid.*, cf., pp. 179ff., 391f.
10. *Ibid.*, p. 182. (To avoid any possible confusion it should be noted that

Notes to pages 66–69:
whereas Walter Lowrie renders Kierkegaard's concept of "*Angst*" by "dread", Macquarrie and Robinson use "dread" for Heidegger's "*Grauen*", reserving "anxiety" for his concept "*Angst*". For the latter, see Heidegger, *BT*, pp. 226-35, 309f., 392ff.; in relation to conscience, see pp. 320-323, 342f.)

11. *Ibid.*, pp. 181f.
12. *Ibid.*, p. 182.
13. Actually, the state of "uncanniness" (*Unheimlichkeit*) is, strictly speaking, the more fundamental concept, as Heidegger develops it in connection with the basic existential-ontological mood of "anxiety" (Angst). See Heidegger, *BT*, pp. 228-36, especially 332-34.
14. Heidegger describes it: "in the tendency to disclosure which belongs to the call, lies the momentum of a push—or an abrupt arousal". *Ibid.*, p. 316. One important aspect of the call mentioned only in passing here is its "silent" character: "The call dispenses with any kind of utterance. It does not put itself into words at all; yet it remains nothing less than obscure and indefinite. *Conscience discourses solely and constantly in the mode of keeping silent.* In this way it not only loses none of its perceptibility, but forces the Dasein which has been appealed to and summoned, into the reticence of itself". *Ibid.*, p. 318.
15. *Ibid.* , p. 317.
16. *Ibid.*, p. 318.
17. *Ibid.*
18. *Ibid.*, p. 320 (emphasis is mine). Regarding Heidegger's critique of a 'theological' interpretation see criticism of H. G. Stoker's work, *ibid.*, p. 495, n. vi.
19. *Ibid.*, p. 322. (Cf. *ibid.*, pp. 232ff.)
20. *Ibid.*, pp. 328ff.
21. Heidegger designates this mode of 'radical questionableness' by means of such terms as "summons" (*aufrufen*), or "summoning" (*Aufruf*), "appeal" (*Anruf*), and "call" (*Ruf*). Cf. the key statement, *ibid.*, p. 314: "if we analyse conscience more penetratingly, it is revealed as a call [Ruf]. Calling is a mode of discourse. The call of conscience has a character of an *appeal [Anrufs]* to Dasein by calling it to its ownmost potentiality-for-Being-its-Self; and this is done by way of *summoning [Aufrufs]* it to its ownmost Being-guilty".
22. See the above note.
23. *Ibid.*, p. 233.
24. *Ibid.*
25. *Ibid.*
27. See Heidegger's definition of "projection" (*Entwurf*), *ibid.*, pp. 184ff.
27. *Ibid.*, p. 294 ("*Nicht-mehr-dasein-konnens*").

Notes to pages 70–76:
28. Martin Heidegger, *Existence and Being*, trans. and ed. Werner Brock (Chicago: Henry Regnery Company, 1949), p. 399.
29. Even more important for Heidegger, from another perspective than that broached here, is the fact that without the possibility of an authentic hearing there is also no way in which Dasein can arrive at an actual *existentiell* understanding of its true Being, the consequence of which being that, apparently, the question of an understanding of the "meaning of Being as such" (the fundamental question of Heidegger's philosophical concern) is left hanging.
30. Heidegger, *BT*, pp. 325ff.
31. *Ibid.*, p. 327.
32. *Ibid.*
33. *Ibid.*, p. 328.
34. *Ibid.*, p. 329.
35. *Ibid.*, p. 330
36. *Ibid.*
37. *Ibid.*
38. *Ibid.*, p. 333.
39. *Ibid.*
40. *Ibid.*, p. 328 (emphasis is mine).
41. John Macquarrie, *An Existentialist Theology* (London: SCM Press, 1955).
42. *Ibid.*, p. 148.
43. See above, chapter I.
44. Heidegger, *BT*, p. 330 (emphasis is mine).
45. Macquarrie, *An Existentialist Theology*, p. 148; cf., also, pp. 149f.
46. See, e.g., Heidegger, *BT*, pp. 313f.
47. Bultmann, *Kerygma and Myth*, II:187f. (emphasis is mine).
48. Macquarrie, p. 148.
49. Ebeling, *WF*, p. 410.

Chapter IV

Ebeling's interpretation
of the phenomenon of conscience

The reader will recall my statement at the beginning of the second chapter that the concept of conscience was the "prismal plane through which all the multi-faceted elements of [Ebeling's] thought achieve their final distinctive focus and illuminative power"(1). This contention, which I attempted to establish in a preliminary fashion through key passages drawn from various points throughout Ebeling's work, needs to be confirmed in a more complete manner through an analysis of Ebeling's "Theological Reflexions on Conscience"(2). Actually, in the first part of this important essay, Ebeling as much as expresses our contention for us. In this section Ebeling is concerned to shed light on the material significance of the phenomenon of conscience, "existentially interpreted", and its importance as a methodological starting point for systematic theological reflection. Consider the following four theses which comprise this section:

1. Reflecting on the concept of conscience should help towards a clearer grasp of the *connexion between theology and language.*
2. Reflecting on the concept of conscience should help towards the understanding of a basic characteristic of the Reformers' theology, viz. that salvation is communicated (in the full sense of appropriation) solely by word(4).
3. Reflecting on the concept of conscience should allow us to perceive rightly the *connexion between man, the world and God*(5).
4. Reflecting on the concept of conscience should lead us to consider the *relation of morality and faith* as a fundamental theological problem(6).

Taken together, could we have a more complete structural outline for systematic theological reflection? Surely our supposition is not mistaken: The prismal point of refraction for reflection on the the "subject-matter" of theology is to be the phenomena of man as "conscience", i.e., that "mathematical point where everything meets"(7), where it is decided what man/woman truly is(8), "where the world is encountered as world" and "time is received as time"(9), that place "where we experience what 'God' means"(10).

Utilizing basic insights reflected in the above theses, both as they are elaborated in this essay and as they are enlarged upon at other points in his work, we shall seek to establish in the following the contribution of Ebeling's thought to the constructive thesis underlying our study, namely, that "in the experience given to man/woman as 'conscience' we have a qualitatively unique ontological grounding for understanding the reality deemed 'God'"(11).

We must emphasize the importance of having Heidegger's phenomenological description before us as we proceed with this phase of our analysis. In its compact form, comprising a mere four pages of his essay on conscience, Ebeling's interpretation would present insurmountable difficulties for understanding in our present intellectual-cultural situation (especially in the United States) without the definitive backdrop of Heidegger's analysis. Ebeling's "existential analysis" of the significance of the etymological roots of the phenomenon of conscience in the original Greek term *syneidēsis*, has already been set forth at an earlier point in our study(12). In recovering the root meaning of the phenomenon of conscience in one's relation to oneself as "joint cognizance", Ebeling is in keeping with Heidegger's fundamental insight that "man does not 'have' a conscience, but he *is* conscience"(13). If, then, "conscience is a matter of *the coming to expression of man himself*", the subject-object distinction mentioned in our second chapter is simply not an appropriate interpretation of this phenomenon. Together with Heidegger, Ebeling stresses that the essential aspect of this phenomenon, more so than any of the other existential characters, or *Existenzialen*, constituent of man and his self-understanding, is its provision for the concrete possibility for man's *transcending* the subject-object distinction within which his usual "everyday" self-understanding is ensnared.

But exactly what does Ebeling mean by this? What is the precise nature and import of this disclosure of "selfhood" as "identity of subject and object"? Adhering closely to the phenomenal indications of the compound *syneidēsis*, i.e., "self-awareness(understanding)", or better, "awareness(understanding)-with-oneself (in Being with others)"(14), Ebeling emphasizes the peculiar "witnessing"(15) or "confrontation" character of this intra-personal process. The first thing to observe concerning the formal structure of this phenomenon, Ebeling states, is "that the structure of human nature itself *is* confrontation". Philosophical, clinical and biographical data often speak superficially of conscience as "accusing" and of the "pangs" of conscience. Ontologically interpreted (i.e., with an eye to the true existential roots of these metaphors), such expressions actually disclose the dialectical-confrontation mode of conscience: As conscience man experiences himself as both 'accuser' and the 'one who is accused'; as conscience man becomes aware of himself—"his true nature"— as *both* the one who gives the 'pangs' *and* as the one who receive 'them'. It is on this basis that Ebeling rejects as "inappropriate" those interpretations which depict the phenomenon as an external "authority over against man"(16). Such interpretations, as in Freudian analysis, for example, if left standing in their present, literal form, must be deemed as *post*-ontological.

Heidegger makes this same point, we should add, regarding Kant's representation of conscience as an authoritative "court of justice"(17). According to Heidegger, the "basic guiding idea in [Kant's] Interpretation" of this phenomenon was simply "the idea of moral law". Left as it stands, i.e., as an "objectivized" element within Kant's metaphysics of morals, it becomes highly doubtful, if not impossible, he writes, "whether the conscience can ever become authentically accessible here at all"(18). Like Heidegger, Ebeling attempts to penetrate these descriptions when possible, to provide an interpretation which "is [ontologically] *prior* to any description and classification of *Experiences* of conscience..."(19). Hence, regarding those varied experiences of an external "authoritative" conscience, Ebeling concludes: "Instead of speaking of an authority (*Instanz*), it would therefore be more appropriate to speak of the 'dissociation' (*Distanz*) which is given with conscience in human nature itself". Ontologically conceived, "Man [as conscience] experiences himself as one who is not identical with himself, *but whose essence it is to be questioned about his identity with himself. Only in being thus questioned in his identity given*"(20). This leads, Ebeling notes, in close parallel to Heidegger's description, to the important "temporal" aspect of this phenomenon. Before turning to this dimension of conscience, however, Ebeling takes up one further problem regarding an exact description of the nature of conscience's call. This problem has to do with the distinction made in both ordinary and scientific discourse between the so-called "good" and "bad" conscience. Is such a distinction valid? What, after all, is a "good" conscience? Is such a designation appropriate to the actual evidence at hand, as adduced in existential analysis? Ebeling's answer to these question is best seen, I believe, against Heidegger's detailed reply in *Being and Time*.

Against a recent interpretation of this idea of a "good" conscience by Max Scheler, which defines this purported phenomenon as "'an Experienced lack of bad conscience'", Heidegger asks, "...how is such a 'lack' Experienced"(21)? His reply:

This supposed Experience is by no means the experiencing of a call; it is rather a making-certain [*Sichvergewissen*] that a deed attributed to Dasein has not been perpetrated by it and that Dasein is *therefore* not guilty. Becoming certain [*Gewisswerden*] that one has not done something, has *by no means* the character of a conscience-phenomenon...."(22).

As we have seen, for Heidegger, conscience is a phenomenon which appears (in its genuine form) as an uncanny call in the wake of Dasein's "acts" (ontologically conceived). In conscience's voice the reference is always to one's completed acts, to one's authentic "potentiality-for-Being" which *has already been* "delivered over" through one's decisions. In this sense, in following Heidegger's deliberate play on words (i.e., his dissociation of "Gewissen" from the above derivatives), "conscience" ("*Gewissen*") does not "make certain" ("*Sichvergewissen*") at all. To the contrary, in "conscience" ("*Gewissen*") one's "certainty" ("*Gewissheit*") is "shattered"! In conscience as "shattered certainty" we are "summoned" not *to be released from*, but rather, *to be held "accountable for"* the fundamental "questionableness" of our everyday existence.

Now at first sight, Heidegger says, the idea of a conscience-type voice "which points forward and warns", a second form of the so-called "good" conscience, might appear to come very close to what he has described as conscience's "summoning" character. This apparent agreement, however, "is just an illusion"(23). "When we experience a warning conscience", Heidegger states, "the voice is regarded in turn as merely oriented towards the deed which *has been willed*, from which it seeks to preserve us"(24). And this warning, he adds, "as a check on what we have willed, is possible only because the 'warning' call is aimed at Dasein's potentiality-for-Being—that is, at its understanding of itself in *Being-guilty*; not until we have such understanding does 'what we have willed' get shattered"(25). Hence, for Heidegger, the so-called "warning" (good) conscience, in the last analysis, is no more than a manifestation of Dasein's "everyday" attempt "from moment to moment" to keep itself "free from indebtednesses". Existentially interpreted, it aims ultimately at keeping one free from a true understanding of one's ownmost "potentiality-for-Being"—as "Being-*guilty*". In this sense its "summoning" character is really a summons to *un*truth. The "good" conscience as a "warning", or even a "cautioning" or "prescribing" phenomenon (as it is often described) is nothing more than another mode of "fleeing"(26). "In the 'certainty' here mentioned in the so-called 'good' conscience", Heidegger writes, "lurks the tranquillizing suppression of one's wanting to have a conscience—that is, of understanding one's ownmost and constant Being-guilty. The 'good' conscience is neither a self-subsistent form of conscience, nor a founded form of conscience; in short, it is not a conscience-phenomenon at all"(27).

Ebeling sides squarely with Heidegger's position in denying that, from the perspective of a genuine ontological-existential description of this phenomenon, there is such a thing as a "good" conscience. Giving an interesting twist to Heidegger's interpretation, Ebeling observes that the only kind of "good" *conscience* we can speak of is a "bad" conscience which is "good at its job"! A "bad" conscience is "good at its job", he adds, when it in itself brings one to "*truth*", i.e., when it holds one fast in "radical questionableness" (a term which is synonymous with "conscience" through Ebeling's work) concerning one's "real nature", or "reality" ("who", and "where" one really is), and thereby calls for a genuine, non-illusory decision(22).

So far we have observed Ebeling's interpretation of conscience as "bad" conscience, and we have sketched out his understanding of this phenomenon as the fundamental disclosure of man's ontological non-identity with oneself. This "identity" of man/woman (as "questioned identity") must now be understood in terms of its fundamental grounding in "time". In Heidegger's analysis, the primordial roots of the phenomenon of conscience lie in the structure of Dasein's "temporal being", i.e., Dasein's basic ontological situation (its being-in-the-world as "Care") characterized as a continual project between its "thrownness", on the one hand, and its "being-towards-death", on the other. These two extremity modes of Dasein's temporal way of being must surely be presupposed by Ebeling when he defines man's ontological structure as essentially, and always, a present relation to his past and future: "The diastasis in temporal being as the present relation to past and future is the ground of the fact that man's identity is questionable, and consequently of the appearance of conscience"(29). This is to say that the basic structure of man's temporal being, that mid-point status *between* (= his continual "present") his "thrownness" (= his "past") on the one hand, and his "Being-toward-death", or simply the impossibility of authentic projection "beyond" or "ahead of" his thrownness" (= his "future") on the other hand, is not only the foundation for the *essential nature ("identity") of man as "questionable"*, but also the basis for the *phenomenon of conscience wherein* this peculiar understanding of man's nature is "given a hearing".

I believe that only from the standpoint of such an expanded Heideggerian interpretation can Ebeling now meaningfully assert that, as conscience, "man exists as one who is continually questioned as to what attitude he takes to himself is his own past and future, whether he identifies himself with himself, confesses to his past and decides for his future, and thus (though this of course is a secondary mode of the identification in question) whether he identifies himself with his deeds and his potentialities"(30). For Ebeling, it is here where we are called to "make a decision" to "identify ourselves with our future possibilities" and in this manner "to answer for them", that man's absolute, fundamental "*responsibility*" is constituted. As "conscience", therefore, one comes to know oneself as inescapably "responsible for" one's "past" deeds, or, at the "primary level" of identification, as ever responsible for his "thrown 'potentiality-for-Being'" (Heidegger). In this state of utmost "radical questionableness" man is not only called to "answer for" one's past Self, but one is also summoned, *in* one's "answerability", to "make a decision" with respect to one's "future" (authentic) possibilities(31).

At this point in his discussion Ebeling makes the observation that this basic temporal "identity" which is brought to question, and, hence, to decision, in man/woman as conscience, is one, he says, "which is never finally given and yet always demanded"(32). How are we to understand his statement? Again, I suggest, Ebeling surely must presuppose a familiarity with Heidegger's interpretation(33), in this case his description of Dasein's fundamental "lacking", or "owing", with respect to its "being a 'basis' for" its thrown possibilities(34). In the mood of "uncanniness", the very heart of "conscience's" anxious call, Dasein's "thrownness" is made manifest in a heightened sense as Dasein's being summoned to take responsibility for itself as "*not* as thrown by its own act"(35). In the mood of anxiety we are presented simply with the "fact" of our "finitude" as "thrown"; uncanniness presents us with the charge of being responsible for this "fact" as our "own", hence, the charge of "*guilty*". In this latter disclosure, Dasein comes to understand itself (and to project its Self upon this "guilty" understanding of itself) as "owing" or "lacking" its being to itself as the "null basis" or "ground" of its thrown "potentiality-for-Being". We recall Heidegger's words: "[Dasein] is never existent *before* its basis, but only *from it* and *as this basis*. Thus 'Being-a-basis' means never to have power over one's ownmost Being *from the ground up*"(36).

From the standpoint of this analysis, therefore, a dual distinction can indeed be made: As existing, one's basic identity with oneself is "*always demanded*" of one, in the sense that one is continually called to "take over" the "basis" of one's Being (as one's original, authentic "potentiality-for-Being"). But, in spite of this incessant "being appealed to", a genuine grasp of this identity (as authentic "*Being*-a-basis") is really "*never finally given*". Why? Because that fundamental "basis" which one is called upon to "take over: is *always already* a "*null* basis"(37). This character of human existence as "never finally given" *and yet* "always demanded" in conscience is summed up by Heidegger in one crucial sentence: "The Self, which as such *has* to lay the basis for itself, can *never* get that basis into its power; and yet, as existing, it *must* take over Being-a-basis"(38). At one place in his analysis Ebeling does raise the very pregnant question as to what the implications might be for our understanding of "god" in light of the curious fact that in this particular disclosure of conscience "man can find himself asking how *in spite of* his constant non-identity with himself *he yet* remains upheld in that identity, in remaining questioned about it and summoned to it"(39). Unfortunately, Ebeling does not really pursue this momentary query until a later essay wherein he begins to reflect upon the implications of Lombard's and Aquinas' doctrine of God. We shall, however, reserve further comment on this observation for a later section of our analysis.

At this point in his study Ebeling emphasizes the fact that conscience can do no more than "*define*" man/woman in this insoluble dialectical "confrontation", between the knowledge of one's ontological "guilt", on the one hand, and the glimpse of one's authentic "potentiality-for-Being", on the other hand(40). It is upon this peculiar "defining" function of conscience that Ebeling would have us fix our attention; it is here that we find its real meaning for a basic theological anthropology. "Conscience", he states, "can do no more than define man as a divided being, hold him fast in his dividedness, his self-contradiction..."(41). Heidegger, in methodological agreement with this delimitation of the function of conscience, has, in fact, provided us with a rich, detailed description of what is potentially involved in this "holding [man] fast". We recall, for example, his interpretation of the appeal of conscience as that which

> calls back by calling *forth*: it calls Dasein forth to the possibility of taking over, in existing, even that thrown entity which it is; it calls Dasein *back* to its thrownness so as to understand this thrownness as the null basis which it has to take up into existence. This calling-back in

which conscience calls forth, gives Dasein to understand that Dasein itself—the null basis for its null projection, standing in the possibility of its Being—is to bring itself back to itself from its lostness in the 'they'..."(42).

As we can see, this "defining" function of conscience is not to be belittled, for, indeed, there is an authentic form of "freedom" and "truthfulness" bestowed upon man/woman in this back-forth "holding" action: Only as one allows oneself to be thus appealed to in conscience does one have the possibility of understanding "who" and "where" one *really* is, i.e., with respect to his total being. In Ebeling's words:

> Man is neither an object of experience to himself nor to others. Human nature is respected as personal being only when it is respected as a mystery that is out of reach of experience, incalculable, not at our disposal, i.e., when man is respected as man by being granted freedom, allowed a future, given a hearing, regarded with trust. This characteristic of mystery in human nature becomes all the greater in the relation of man to himself. As the being which has relations with itself, man in his selfhood, questions and is questioned about his selfhood, has to account for his selfhood. *Only as conscience* can man be seen as *totus homo*, as *persona*. But he can be seen as such *only in the word-event*. For conscience is the event of being questioned and being challenged to respond and thus the act of being responsible.(43)

However, as both Ebeling and Heidegger stress, our "everyday" tendency is to "flee from" this disclosure of the real nature of our (everyday) being. Rather than (Heidegger) projecting one's Self in the "freedom" of what conscience has to say, one, "for the most part", chooses to remain "behind-Himself" (contrary to one's Being as "Care") in the "tranquillizing" world of the "they"(44). As Ebeling puts it, rather than standing in the cold, defining light of conscience, man "hounded by conscience and therefore fleeing from conscience", chooses to "veil it behind religions and world-views that are supposed to justify man and soothe his conscience"(45).

So far, Ebeling, in line with Heidegger's analysis, has presented an interpretation of conscience as the supreme "*principium individuationis*". The voice of conscience, he holds, "is of course indisputably and inscrutably the conscience of the individual...and only the individual as such can appeal to it"(46). This does not mean, however, that such an interpretation "by any means leave[s] the world out of account"(47). As we have seen with Heidegger, man/woman, as human being, is in essence "being-in-the-world"(48). Man/woman is primordially an intentional being who can never be defined apart from his/her essential, active relationship to the world in all its various dimensions. It is of the utmost importance to keep in mind that it is by means of conscience, above all other "states-of-mind"(49), that the "wholeness" of one's Being-in-the-world (one's Being as "Care"), and hence, the "whole" structure of the "world" itself, comes into view for understanding (and decision), both for existing man/woman (that place where Dasein's Being-in-the-world "becomes an issue") and for man's/woman's formal existential interpretation(50). Not only does the familiar subject-object distinction between oneself and the world collapse in the phenomenon of conscience (here, "*Distanz*"), but, as a consequence of this collapse, one (to be sure as individual) also finds oneself responsible for the world which one now knows as one's "own". "The questionable nature of man's identity in time", Ebeling states, "takes concrete form in the question as to his identification of himself with his being in the world and therefore in the question as to his responsibility for the world"(51).

Up to this point Ebeling has been speaking about conscience "in an entirely formal way", as he says. He now addresses himself to the question of the material "content" or "nature" of the call of conscience. We have already observed how Ebeling rejects those views which would understand the content of conscience"s call as a "codex of general truths and commands"(52). It is important, he says, "to free ourselves entirely from the usual view of conscience as a law written in the heart, which is conceived as a sum of inborn ideas that by nature form part of the content of human consciousness". He adds: "The law written in the heart is nothing else but the pure call and question of conscience, so to speak the question mark branded ineradicably upon man"(53). Incidentally, we should not miss Ebeling's thoroughgoing "existential" interpretation of Luther here, with the idea of conscience as a "law written in the heart" being a fundamental concept of the latter's thought(54). "But", Ebeling asks, "*what* is conscience's call, what does it ask about?" His answer: "It calls man himself, it asks about himself, it demands himself. Conscience makes no speeches"(55).

To elaborate this brief response Ebeling relies upon an extended quote from Heidegger, who, he says, "gives a wholly proper interpretation" of this matter.

The call [*Ruf*] dispenses with any kind of utterance [*Verlautbarung*]. It does not put itself into words at all; yet it remains nothing less than obscure and indefinite. *Conscience discourses [redet] solely and constantly in the mode of keeping silent [im Modus des Schweigen]*. In this way it not only loses none of its perceptibility, but forces the Dasein which has been appealed to and summoned, into the reticence [*Verschweigenheit*] of itself. The fact that what is called in the call has not been formulated in words, does not give this phenomenon the indefiniteness of a mysterious voice, but merely indicates that our understanding of what is 'called' is not to be tied up with an expectation of anything like a communication [*Mitteilung*](56).

In order to understand the full implications of Heidegger's passage it is important to make brief reference to his fundamental distinction between "Articulation" ("*Articulation*"), "communication" ("*Mitteilung*"), "Assertion"

("*Aussage*"), "utterance" (*Verlautbarung*"), and "Word" ("*Wort*"), on the one hand, and "articulatedness" (or "capacity for Articulation"), "call" ("*Ruf*"), and "discourse" or "talk ("*Rede*") on the other hand. Here we also have our eye on the subsequent discussion of Ebeling's key term, "word-event" ("*Wortgeschehen*") (Ebeling makes the important point that "existence is fundamentally word-event" and that it can be "answered for", i.e., in conscience, "only in word-event")(57), and his conception of the emergence of "reality" (the unitary meaning of "human being", "world", and "God") in that fundamental "passivity" which is given with conscience.

These key terms are clarified in the important hermeneutical section of *Being and Time* (sections 28 through 34)(58). Because of the length and general systematic difficulty of this section I have laid out the following diagrammatic sketch to facilitate our analysis (overleaf).

The Emergence of Language in the "Disclosedness of the 'There,'" and the "Grounding of the Totality of the Structural Whole of Existence"

A. "State-of-Mind," B. "Understanding," and C. "Discourse," below, represent the fundamental equiprimordial "structures of Being," or "existentials" (*existentialia*) of Dasein's "Being-in-the-world as a whole":

I

A. "STATE-OF-MIND" (*Befindlichkeit*), (*BT*, pp. 172ff.)
(= "bare-mood," "how one is...")
—together with "Being-there" (*Da-sein*) or "Situation"
&
"Projecting" or "Sketching Out" (*entwerfen*) "possibilities"

B. "UNDERSTANDING" (*Verständnis*), (*BT*, pp. 188-195)
(= The pre-articulate "comprehension," or "intelligibility" given in and with the "there," regarding "possibility")

As "authentic," understanding demands:
(a.) "keeping silent," (*Schweigen*)
(b.) "reticence," (*Verschweigenheit*)
(c.) "hearing," (*hören*)

C. "DISCOURSE" (*Rede*), (*BT*, pp. 203f.)
("λόγος," "discursive speech," "talk," or "articulate-ness")
(= The "capacity for articulation of the 'there' of intelligibility as ...")
(a.) "That which can be Articulated in interpretation..."
(b.) "That which gets articulated as such in discursive Articulation..."
(c.) That which is "dissolved or broken up into separate significations..."

II

"INTERPRETATION" (*Auslegung*)
&
"Meaning" (*Sinn*)

(The "appropriation" of articulated intelligibility"), (*BT*, pp. 192-195)

"ARTICULATION" (or "articulate"), (*Artikulation/artikulieren* or *Gegliederte/gliedern*), (*BT*, p. 195)

IV

"LANGUAGE" (*Sprache*)
as a
"totality of word(s)"
(*Wort / Worten*)
(*BT*, pp 203f.)

"SAYING" (*sagen*)
&
"SPEAKING" or "UTTERANCE"
(*Verlautbarung*)
(*BT*, pp. 206.)

III

"ASSERTION" (or "JUDGMENT") (*Aussage*), (*BT*, pp. 196f.)
as
"Derivative Mode of Interpretation"

Its Three "Significations":

(1.) "Pointing Out" (*Aufzeigen*)
("In this we adhere to the primordial meaning of λόγος as ἀπόφανσις —letting an entity be seen from itself...not a 'meaning,' but an entity in the way that it is ready-to-hand (*zuhanden*)", (*BT*, p. 196; cf. p. 196)

(2.) "Predicate," "Predication" (*Prädikat*) ("...the 'subject' is given a definite character"), (*BT*, p. 196)

(3.)* "COMMUNICATION" (*Mitteilung*) ("Speaking-forth as Being-with"), (*BT*, p. 197)

* (Note: For Heidegger, "Understanding" as "Being-with" is also founded in "Discourse" (*Rede*), and "significant articulation" emerges always as *"something shared"*—the existential-ontological foundation of "Communication" is "Discourse")

The basic circular character of human understanding is shown clearly in the unbroken relationship between "I.", the fundamental modes of disclosure which constitute Dasein's essential being as "Care", and "V.", the emergence of "word(s)" and "language" through which some discursively interpreted understanding (of the world) gets expressed. In so describing the process of understanding (hermeneutics, which is concerned with the art or method of interpretation, is also, for Heidegger, a theory of understanding) with, as he puts it, "a full view of Dasein's circular Being"(59). Heidegger purposely eschews both (1.) the Cartesian model of the subject, which (as he describes it) takes its point of departure "from a worldless 'I' in order to provide this 'I' with an Object and an ontologically baseless relation to that Object"(60), and (2.) the equally "worldless" Kantian "theoretical subject", which (in Heidegger's terms) attempts in the end to "round [the subject] out 'on the practical side' by tacking on an 'ethic'"(61). Heidegger's existential analytic presents human being from the start as essentially "being-in-the-world"(62). The self, or primordial "I", for Heidegger, is always and already part of a world (which, of course, includes being-with other Daseins); such 'worldly being' entails in every case a pre-reflective understanding of itself (and of entities in the world) together with a language as an articulated vehicle for the latter's interpreted meaning. Human being as speaker (that worldly being who "points out", "Predicates", and "speaks forth" to others, and to itself) is such only on the basis of a prior discursive interpretation of the world, and yet the latter never appears without an attendant verbal, or conceptual structure (63). A helpful model for understanding the hermeneutic circle set forth diagrammatically above is that of a dialogue between persons. Prior to the emergence of a verbal expression ("language" as a "word" event, or as "utterance" in word form) is (for both hearer and speaker) a definite pre-linguistic understanding of the world. This understanding is given shape and substance, according to Heidegger, by three equiprimordial "structures of being", or "existentials" (*existentialia*)(64): "state-of-mind" (*Befindlichkeit*), "understanding" (*Verständnis*), and "discourse" or "talk" (*Rede*).

Ontically, for Heidegger, Dasein is always "in a mood"; neither personally nor inter-personally communicated disclosure of the world occurs meaningfully apart from specific moods. Speaking ontologically, however, "state-of-mind" does not stand for "moods" or "feelings" as such, but for that constitutive structure of being on the basis of which Dasein "has" its moods or feelings. Specifically, "state-of-mind" is that basic existential through which the meaning of Dasein's being "there" (or "here", ["*Da*"]) in the world comes to light(65). Keeping in mind the above diagram, at "I./A.", what comes to light on the basis of "state-of-mind" is essentially the "how", or "that-it-is" of Dasein's "situation", or what Heidegger calls technically Dasein's "Facticity" (*Faktizität*)(66).

Whereas with "state-of-mind" Dasein is disclosed to itself primarily with regard to the how-it-is of its situation, with "understanding" it is disclosed to itself in terms of its essential being as "possibility" (or its essential "potentiality-for-Being" [*Seinkönnen*]). "Dasein", according to Heidegger, "is such that in every case it has understood (or alternatively, not understood) that it is to be thus or thus. As such understanding it 'knows' what it is capable of—that is, what its potentiality-for-Being is capable of". He adds: "This 'knowing' does not first arise from an immanent self-perception, but belongs to the Being of the "there"..."(67). That aspect of Dasein's "being-there" which grounds such 'knowing' is, as my diagram indicates, the modality of "projecting" or of "sketching out" possibilities which is explicit or implicit in every "Being-there". As a fundamental existential, equiprimordial with "state-of-mind", "understanding" has its primary roots, according to Heidegger, in the everyday, worldly phenomenon of "projecting" (*entwerfen*), literally a 'throwing forward', or 'sketching forth' something which is to be accomplished or carried out. It should be remembered, as we indicated earlier regarding the distinctive function of conscience in relation to understanding(68), authentic understanding depends, or demands a genuine "hearing" (*hören*) of Dasein's ownmost potentiality-for-Being in the "there", which in turn calls for "reticence" (*Verschweigenheit*) and "keeping silent" (*Schweigen*)(69).

The third, and, for our purposes, the most important existential is "discourse"(70). We should take careful note of the fact that in Dasein's everyday being (one's projective possibilities in *existentiell* situations) the primordial, existential-ontological foundation of "language" (*Sprache*) is "discourse" (*Rede*). Strictly speaking, then, "discourse" is neither "saying" (or "speaking" or "utterance") nor the latter's expressed structural emergence, "language". "Discourse" represents that tacit capacity of intelligibility, always equiprimordial with "state-of-mind" and "understanding", which provides the possibility for spoken (or written) "assertion".

With the foregoing terminological clarification the ambiguity we might have sensed in the above quotation from Heidegger regarding the peculiar "silent" mode of speaking which is appropriate to the "call" of conscience should be dispelled. The key terms can now be understood as follows. The "call" of conscience, which "dispenses with any kind of utterance" or "communication", is *that center-most "discursive locus"* whereby one's understanding of oneself as being-in-the-world as a whole (and, hence, the understanding and meaning of the "world" itself, for one) is given a "hearing", and prepared, as it were, to "Articulate" itself "interpretatively". To this we should add that spoken (or written) "language" which emerges at the tertiary(71) level of "Articulation" always carries with it (and appeals to, in "communication") this primary "discursive-articulate" dimension of one's (*existentiell*, or "existential", if clarified formally) self-understanding(72).

It is in the light of the above distinctions that Ebeling's key concept of "word-event" (*Wortgeschehen*) comes into meaningful focus. On the one hand, for Ebeling, "word-event" manifests itself on the level of "*Sprache*", i.e., as "assertion", "utterance", and "communication". Here this linguistic event encounters us in, or through, such "Articulated-Interpreted" historical and interpersonal forms as spoken words, expressive non-verbal symbols and acts, and as written documents, artifacts and works of art. On the other hand, from the standpoint of its internal, existential-ontological genesis and goal, "word-event" manifests itself fundamentally as "discourse" (*Rede*). In the act of communication, for instance, word-event as "language" (*Sprache*) is both a vehicle for, and a bridge between the "discursive loci" (*Rede*) of each individual: *Although manifestly "spoken word", (Sprache), word-event, in essence, begins with and aims toward itself as "discourse" (Rede), that primordial, existential center of human "understanding" and "interpretation"*.

It might be noted here that the evocative character of language and the foundational status of inner "discourse", or pre-reflective, "discursive" understanding (73), in communication is touched upon, both indirectly and directly, by recent works in both the British-American and Continental philosophical traditions. Although lacking the descriptive precision and refinement of Heidegger's interpretation, Eugene Gendlin's phenomenological description of what he terms "the interaction of symbols with pre-conceptual 'felt-experiencing'" in his book, *Experiencing and the Creation of Meaning*, is, in my opinion, an exemplary, corraborative description of this phenomenon. "Meaning", Gendlin writes, "is *formed* in the interaction of experiencing and something that functions symbolically. Feeling without symbolization is blind; symbolization without feeling is empty"(74). With regard to interpreted meaning and understanding, language and situations are described by Gendlin as fundamentally evocative, or actional in nature. They take on "meaning", he argues, to the extent to which "they function to *call forth* in us the felt meaning"(75). There is, however, a definite priority which must be given to inner discourse, or, what Gendlin calls, "pre-thematic, felt-experience", especially in a hermeneutic of interpersonal communication. In such a context, Gendlin writes,

> we cannot...know what a concept "means," or use it meaningfully without the "feel," of its meaning. No amount of symbols, definitions, and the like can be used in the place of the *felt* meaning. If we do not have the felt meaning of the concept, we haven't got the concept at all—only a verbal noise.(76)

But Gendlin as a phenomenologist is not alone in emphasizing the unique function of discourse, or discursive speech in a fundamental theory of understanding; voices from the side of Anglo-American linguistic philosophy can also be heard echoing (albeit in a different pitch) this same theme. Stanley Cavell's torturously brilliant musings about the puzzling interrelationship of particular "language games" to certain "forms of life" are in my view some of the best to emerge from the philosophers in this tradition, and most illuminative for our particular purposes(77). Although, in the following remarks, Cavell is concerned primarily with non-verbal communication in music and the plastic arts, his grasp of the presence, and necessity of a tacit, discursive principle of intelligibility, i.e., for communicable self-understanding, could well apply to a wider hermeneutic of verbal acts: "'Knowing by feeling'", Cavell writes,

is not like 'knowing by touching'; that is, it is not a case of providing the *basis* for a claim to know. But one could say that feeling functions as a touchstone: the mark left on the stone is out of sight to others, but the result is one of knowledge, or has the form of knowledge—it is directed to an object, the object has been tested, the result is one of conviction. This seems to me to suggest why one is anxious to communicate the experience of such objects.(78)

Cavell explores the texture of this elusive form of discursive (and affective) knowledge as follows:

It is not merely that I want to tell you how it is with me, how I feel, in order to find sympathy or to be left alone, or for any other of the reasons for which one reveals one's feelings. It's rather that I want to tell you *something I've seen, or heard, or realized, or come to understand,* for the reasons for which such things are communicated (because it is news, about a world we share, or could). Only I find that I can't *tell* you; and that makes it all the more urgent to tell you. I want to tell you because the knowledge, unshared, is a burden—not, perhaps, the way having a secret can be a burden, or being misunderstood; a little more like the way, perhaps, not being believed is a burden, or not being trusted. It matters that others know what I see, in a way it does not matter whether they know my tastes. It matters, there is a suggestion (and to myself as well) that I do not know. But I do—what I see is that (pointing to the object). But for that to communicate, you have to see it too. Describing one's experience of art is itself a form of art; the burden of describing it is like the burden of producing it.(79)

In returning to our own object of concern we must emphasize that for Heidegger and Ebeling the phenomenon of conscience is (1) not only the most intimate *intra*-personal phenomenon of *self*-communication (and understanding), but (2) more significantly, it "discourses" (*redet*), as Heidegger puts it, "solely and constantly in the mode of *keeping silent*". Further, in this peculiarly "silent" mode of expression conscience, according to Heidegger, "not only loses none of its perceptibility, but *forces* the Dasein which has been appealed to and summoned, into the reticence [*Verschweigenheit*] of itself"(80). Thus, just as "discourse" is constitutive of "Language" and "saying" or "speaking", so "keeping silent" (*Schweigen*) is a fundamental existential-ontological constituent of "hearing" (*Hören*)(81). In order for Dasein to "discourse" and, hence, "speak" understandingly (about himself, to himself; and from himself, to others) he must "hear" truthfully, and this in turn depends upon whether he is able, or rather, *enabled* to "keep silent" before the "summoning" of his real situation in the world of his concerns and projects. Heidegger illuminates the relationship of "hearing" to "discursive" speech and understanding as follows:

We can make clear the connection of discourse with understanding and intelligibility by considering an existential possibility which belongs to talking itself—hearing. If we have not heard 'aright,' it is not by accident that we say we have not 'understood,' Hearing is constitutive for discourse, so is acoustic perception on hearing. Listening to...is Dasein's existential way of Being-open as Being-with for Others. Indeed, hearing constitutes the primary and authentic way in which Dasein is open for its ownmost potentiality-for-Being—as in hearing the voice of the friend whom every Dasein carries with it.(82)

Heidegger further analyzes the nature of the relationship between "hearing" and "keeping silent" as an expansion upon, and extension of, the technical terminological distinctions delineated above. It reads in full:

Keeping silent is another essential possibility of discourse, and it has the same existential foundation. In talking with one another, the person who keeps silent can 'make one understand' (that is, he can develop an understanding), and he can do so more authentically than the person who is never short of words. Speaking at length...about something does not offer the slightest guarantee that thereby understanding is advanced. On the contrary, talking extensively about something, covers it up and brings what is understood to a sham clarity—the unintelligibility of the trivial. But to keep silent does not mean to be dumb. On the contrary, if a man is dumb, he still has a tendency to 'speak.' Such a person has not proved that he can keep silence; indeed, he entirely lacks the possibility of proving anything of the sort. And the person who is accustomed by Nature to speak little is no better able to show that he is keeping silent or that he is the sort of person who can do so. He who never says anything cannot keep silent at any given moment. *Keeping silent authentically is possible only in genuine discoursing. To be able to keep silent, Dasein must have something to say—that is, it must have at its disposal an authentic and rich disclosedness of itself. In that case one's reticence [Verschwiegenheit] makes something manifest, and does away with 'idle talk' [Gerede]. As a mode of discoursing, reticence Articulates the intelligibility of Dasein in so primordial a manner that it gives rise to a potentiality-for-hearing which is genuine...*(83).

Now we know from Heidegger's earlier analysis that man, "for the most part", flees from "genuine discoursing", and hence from "keeping silent authentically". Conscience, it would appear, is that dimension of existing-man, that silent, summoning "friend whom every Dasein carries with him", which lopes along beside him and at times succeeds in catching him in flight, casting before him that "authentic and rich disclosedness" of himself. As we have seen, though(84), this "rich disclosedness" is essentially a revelation of man's existential-ontological state of "Being-guilty": as conscience man comes to know himself as the ultimate *nullity* of his possibility of "Being-a-basis". And what is it that Dasein "has to say" in the light of this disclosure? "Nothing", Heidegger states" In conscience man is *brought to silence*—in spite of himself. In the silent gaze which conscience effects, man is *opened to* the possibility of authentic "reticence" and "hearing", again, in spite of himself. In his 1966 Bampton Lecture, entitled, "Religion, Atheism, and Faith"(85), Paul Ricoeur catches the glint of the important reflexive, or passive dimension of this phenomenon as described by Heidegger. "To keep silent", he writes, "is to let things be said by others. Silence opens a space for hearing...". In such an event, he states, "I find that ultimately I dispose of nothing, I do not impose myself. I am no longer master...In this situation of nonmastery lies the origin of both obedience and freedom..."(86). This disclosure of human reality in terms of open, silent "passivity" is, as we shall see, a key element in Ebeling's interpretation of the divine-human relationship. Ebeling for his part, speaks not only of the origin of "obedience" and "freedom" in this experience, but of genuine "responsibility" as well.

Before turning to this development in the latter's thought, we must mention one final observation regarding Ebeling's interpretation, a point which, although presupposed, is nevertheless easily missed in understanding Heidegger's highly formalized interpretation of conscience. The phenomenon of conscience, Ebeling reminds us, *always has a definite context*. To be sure, "The call of conscience receives its content by being heard, i.e., by man's taking up the challenge", but this "hearing" and "taking up" can become truly living and real only in *actual lived experience and historical participation*. Hence, we have really two contextual modes of conscience which must always be kept in view: "First, the concrete situation in which the call of conscience takes place and to which it is related...". The call of conscience, for Ebeling, "takes place only in relation to concrete situations, never in a general way."(87). And the second contextual mode: "Everything in the way of training in understanding concrete situations which exists as a result of education in the widest sense and thus of participation in the history of language"(88).

The second contextual mode is of the greatest importance not only because it indicates the central place which language holds in both Ebeling's (and Heidegger's) understanding of reality—here, for Ebeling, "historical reality" can be deemed "the history of language"—but also it evidences the decisive point of departure between the "theologian" on the one hand, and the "philosopher" on the other. In an important essay which Ebeling prepared in conjunction with his joint seminar with Heidegger in 1961(89), he states that theology and philosophy do participate together in the Western "history of language", considered in the widest educational, or intellectual sense. There is an important distinction to be made, however, regarding the *specific* linguistic paths which these two disciplines(90) have followed. Heidegger's linguistic path winds its way within the close confines of the history of Western "philosophical thinking" and "poetic composition" concerning "the question of Being". Christian theology, as Ebeling sees it, although beginning with the question of man/woman, strikes out upon a quite different trail. Ebeling's theological linguistic path is attuned, ultimately, not to the history of philosophical ontology and poetic discourse, but rather to the history of the language of Christian faith, both in its beginnings, with the appearance of Jesus and his word, and in its development, through various key interpretations of his word throughout the history of the community of faith(91). To be sure, Ebeling avers, these two pathways have crossed, and still continue to cross one another from time to time. Ebeling's encyclopedia article on "Theology and Philosophy"(92) presents, in fact, a masterful summary of these critical points of encounter in the history of the Western linguistic tradition.

As for theology's encounter with Heidegger's own particular pathway, Ebeling cites two positive areas of contact. The first, and most important for our purposes, is Heidegger's early "existential-hermeneutical" clarification of the structure and dynamics of "human being"(93). Ebeling indicates that theology, as with all other sciences concerned with the interpretation of (human) reality stands in debt to Heidegger for having so rigorously described the fundamental structure of human being in terms of its fundamental "historicality" (*Geschichtlichkeit*). It should welcome such a helpful, philosophical clarification of key anthropological and epistemological concepts, especially vis à vis those objectivizing substantialist interpretations which have laid claim to our modern intellectual tradition. It is important to point out here that Ebeling does not, either in the two studies mentioned immediately above, or elsewhere in his historical and constructive work, explicitly state (as his mentor, Bultmann, has done) that Heidegger's early work is to be regarded as "the right philosophy"(94) for theological interpretation. But I would argue that this lack of explicit recognition does not indicate a rejection of the corroborative function of Heidegger's "philosophical" hermeneutic in "theological" work. Although we shall have more to say concerning Ebeling's ultimately successful, or unsuccessful, handling of this point in the final critical and constructive chapter, the following observations serve to clarify Ebeling's "post-Bultmannian" position with regard to its methodological *intention*.

For Ebeling, it is a misleading and, hence, an unnecessary "abstraction" to speak of "philosophical" conceptions distinct and apart from "theological" conceptions: "The difference between theology...on the one hand", he writes, "and philosophy, on the other hand, is not a question of single terms, single vocables, or single thoughts and ideas, but much more a question of *total horizons*". "The meaning of a vocable", he states, "is dependent on its use, and therefore the distinction between philosophy and theology is, in any case, an abstraction, since theology is a historic phenomenon only on the ground of the encounter between Christian faith and philosophy"(95). Two things are implied here. First of all, with regard to their respective "standpoints", calling for different ultimate "horizons" in the light of their respective concerns(96), and historic-linguistic traditions(97), the "theologian" does maintain a stance qualitatively distinct from the "philosopher". Secondly, such historical and existential 'positioning' within the ultimate perspective of a "total horizon"(98) does not, however, present the "theologian" from, as Ebeling puts it, "*thinking philosophically*"(99). This would indicate, in contradistinction to Bultmann's manner of putting it(100), that the "theologian", in his/her own reflection, is free to utilize critically the hermeneutical assistance of Heidegger's philosophical analysis (especially with regard to anthropological concepts)(101) without this indicating any kind of "dependence". Conversely, the theologian's "thinking philosophically" does not entail his/her acceptance of the "philosopher's" ultimate linguistic horizon.

Theology's second positive meeting point with Heidegger's philosophy relates to the latter's attempt at "overcoming", or "passing beyond" metaphysics, both with respect to man, as *animal metaphysicum* (the theoretically conceived "*animal rationale*")(102), and with respect to God, that is, the "God" which has entered the history of Western metaphysics both internally, from within the philosophical tradition itself(103), and externally, from outside religious and theological thrusts. Ebeling bids us to take quite seriously, and indeed to consider as one of theology's methodological starting points, Heidegger's judgment concerning the utter prostration of this tradition today. In the final section of his essay, "Verantworten des Glaubens in Begegnung mit dem Denken M. Heideggers", devoted to the question of what "the encounter with Heidegger's thought gives theology to think above all", Ebeling states:

> Indeed, theology always has had a presentiment that metaphysical talk of God is unsuitable for Christian faith; but only now is its great task beginning to become clear, namely, to talk of God unmetaphysically, i.e., according to the dominant theological tradition: godlessly.(104)

By this latter reference to "the dominant theological tradition" Ebeling has in view those theologians, of which he himself is one, who would attempt to pursue Dietrich Bonhoeffer's program of a "non-religious interpretation of biblical concepts", in a "world come of age"(105). In his study, "Reflexions on Speaking Responsibly of God", Ebeling writes, "We must surely...consider Heidegger's deeply penetrating interpretation of Nietzsche's saying, 'God is dead', according to which nihilism heralds the end of Western metaphysics.... A doctrine of God today...is abstract speculation if it does not have the phenomenon of modern atheism before it from the start"(106). Here, as elsewhere, Ebeling reflects a position akin to Bultmann, Fuchs, Helmut Franz, and others which takes quite seriously Heidegger's thoroughgoing exclusion of the idea of God (God as "Creator", man as "creature") in his philosophy. This position also accepts as unambiguous Heidegger's various statements which imply a fundamental distinction between the world-god or gods of a philosophy of finitude and the "divine God" of a theology of faith(107). Ebeling agrees explicitly with the view Heidegger expresses in his later work *What Is Called Thinking?*, and in *An Introduction to Metaphysics*, that a whole "world", or "chasm", separates a "philosophy of thinking" with its unending concern with the questionableness of the word, from a "theology of faith" with its stake in the recognition of a proclamation of a final unquestionable word(108). *But* we must take careful note of the precise place at which Ebeling understands this rent to occur:

> Philosophy and theology encounter each other as different ways of the word. Philosophical talk is itself the word in order for it to do philosophy: which is to make the question questionable. Theological talk is directed to serving the word of preaching: which makes the *conscience* certain.(109)

This difference rests upon an even more fundamental distinction:

> [The] radical *explication* of linguisticality...is not identical with the radical fulfillment of linguisticality. The responsibility for which man is held accountable is not to be realized in thinking [*Denken*], but only in the word-event which emerges in the linguisticality which meets him in *conscience*.(110)

Here Ebeling not only stands in criticism of Heidegger's later position, but also, it seems to me, clearly calls the philosopher back to recognize the full significance of that point of departure which he established so firmly in *Being and Time*.

Notes

Notes to page 81:
1. See above, chapter II.
2. Ebeling, *WF*, pp. 407-23.
3. *Ibid.*, pp. 407-08.
4. *Ibid.*, p. 409.
5. *Ibid.*, p. 410.
6. *Ibid.*, p. 414.
7. Ebeling, *NF*, p. 180.
8. Ebeling, *WF*, p. 384 (emphasis is mine).
9. Ebeling, *NF*, pp. 160-61.
10. Ebeling, *WF*, p. 349 (emphasis is mine).
11. See above, chapter I.
12. See above, chapter II.

Notes to pages 82–83:
13. See Ebeling, *WF*, p. 417 (emphasis is mine). For Heidegger, see above chapter II. We recall that Heidegger's analysis draws primarily upon the work of Kähler and Stoker. The reader may wish to consult these sources directly. If so, see Martin Kähler, *Das Gewissen; die Entwickelung seiner Ramen und seines Begriffes (Geschichtliche Untersuchung zur Lehre von der Begründung der sittlichen Erkenntniss)* (Halle: Julius Frike, 1878), pp. 23-33; H. G. Stoker, *Das Gewissen, Erscheinungformen und Theorien*, Vol. 2 of the series *Schriften zur Philosophie und Soziologie*, ed. Max Scheler (Bonn: Friedrich Cohen Verlag, 1925), pp. 5-15.
14. In designating the phenomenon of conscience as an interpersonal process it is easy to misread it as happening apart from its essential social context. The fact cannot be over-emphasized that for both Heidegger and Ebeling conscience is rooted in man's "Being-with others" ("*Mitmenschlichkeit*", or Heidegger: "*Mitsein*"). For example, Heidegger, *BT*, pp. 153-68, and pp. 307ff. in connection with conscience.
15. Professor Paul Ricoeur has drawn my attention to the importance of this feature of conscience and its relevance for Christian theology. See his essay, "L'Hermeneutique du Temoignage", *Archivio di Filosofia* (La Testimonianza), 42 (1972): 35-61. (Eng. trans. by David Stewart and Charles E. Reagan, "The Hermeneutics of Testimony", in Paul Ricoeur, *Essays on Biblical Interpretation*, ed. Lewis S. Mudge [Philadelphia: Fortress Press, 1980], pp. 119-54.) Through this essay and in subsequent discussion Ricoeur has made clear the significance of Jean Nabert's work for our undertaking which seeks to ground the meaning of God in the structure of man/woman as conscience. Although beyond the scope of this particular study it would be fruitful to examine Nabert's important works, *Essai sur Le Mal* (Paris: Presses Universitaires de France, 1955) and *Le Desir de Dieu* (Paris: Aubier, 1966).

Along these lines Karl Rahner's work on the phenomenon of "witness" is also relevant and useful. See his essay, "Theological Observations on the Concept of Witness" in his *Theological Investigations*, Volume XIII trans. David Bourke (New York: Crossroad, 1983), pp. 152-68. See also in the same volume Rahner's important, related essay, "Experience of Self and Experience of God", p. 122-32.
16. See above, chapter II.
17. See Heidegger, *BT*, p. 339.
18. *Ibid.*
19. *Ibid.*, p. 313.
20. Ebeling, *WF*, p. 417 (emphasis is mine).
21. Heidegger, *BT*, p. 338. For Scheler's account, see *Formalism in Ethics and Non-Formal Ethics of Values*, trans. Manfred S. Frings and Roger

Notes to pages 83–87:
L. Funk (Evanston: Northwestern University Press, 1973), p. 322.
22. Heidegger, *BT*, p. 338. Concerning Heidegger's treatment (or non-treatment) of the term "*Gewissen*", see our observation above, chapter II.
23. *Ibid.*, p. 339.
24. *Ibid.* (emphasis is mine).
25. *Ibid.*, pp. 338-39.
26. That is, Dasein's call to itself to "flee from" an authentic "reckoning" with its everyday being as fundamentally and always a "Being-guilty". See *ibid.*, p. 184.
27. Heidegger, *BT*, p. 338.
28. There is one other way in which Ebeling would accept the term "good conscience": "*bona conscientia*' as '*fides*'", (*WF*, p. 419. Here, though, Ebeling is not concerned with "*conscientia*" as strictly a "conscience-phenomenon". We must await another stage of our analysis, however, before elaborating this point.
29. Ebeling, *WF*, pp. 417-18.
30. *Ibid.*, p. 418.
31. *Ibid.*
32. *Ibid.* (emphasis is mine).
33. Or, if not, a familiarity ought to be presupposed.
34. See Heidegger's duscussion, above, chapter II.
35. See above, chapter II.
36. Heidegger, *BT*, p. 330 (emphasis is mine); cf., above, chapter II.
37. See above, chapter II.
38. Heidegger, *BT*, p. 330.
39. Ebeling, *WF*, p. 419.
40. Here, especially, Ebeling would insist upon the purely "formalized" character of Heidegger's phenomenological description. See our discussion above, chapter III.
41. Ebeling, *WF*, p. 422.
42. Heidegger, *BT*, p. 333.
43. Ebeling, *WF*, p. 414. Cf. Heidegger, *BT*, pp. 340-41: "The call [of conscience] discloses nothing which could be either positive or negative as something with which we *can concern ourselves*; for what it has in view is a Being which is ontologically quite different—namely, *existence*. On the other hand, when the call is rightly understood, it gives us that which in the existential sense is the 'most positive' of all—namely, the ownmost possibility which Dasein can present to itself, as a calling-back which calls it forth into its factical potentiality-for-being-its-Self at the time. To hear the call authentically, signifies bringing oneself into a factical taking-action". Cf., also, p. 322.
   Although I agree firmly with the late Professor Carl Michalson in his

Notes to page 87:
> critique of the "later" Heidegger, for whom "poetic calm and rational ineffability supplant existential anguish and the quest for a concrete historical articulation of meaning", I must equally object to his contention that, for the young Heidegger (the Heidegger of *Being and Time*), it is man's/woman's self-understanding as "being-toward-*death*", rather than being as "*conscience*", which constitutes the most important "rudimentary *aporia* of historical existence". See Michalson's discussion in Robinson and Cobb, eds., *New Frontiers in Theology, I*, pp. 138ff. Michalson is not alone in his emphasis on the theme of "death" in Heidegger's existential analysis; this interpretation of *Being and Time* is to be heard in almost every study with which this writer is familiar. The centrality of "conscience" as a basic mode of disclosure over all other affective "states-of-mind" ("falling", "thrownness", *and* "being-toward-death", etc.) should be obvious with even a cursory reading of Heidegger's study. Ebeling surely surpasses Michalson and others in discernment on this point of Heidegger's interpretaion. In contrast to Michalson's view, cf. Ebeling's critique of the "later" Heidegger in the essay utilized in a joint seminar with the philosopher entitled, "Verantworten des Glaubens in Begegnung mit dem Denken M. Heideggers," *Zeitschrift für Theologie und Kirche*, Beiheft 2 (1961):134f.

44. Cf. Heidegger, *BT*, p. 222 ("Since the way in which things have been publicly interpreted has already become a temptation to itself in this manner, it holds Dasein fast in its fallenness. Idle talk and ambiguity, having seen everything, having understood everything, develop the supposition that Dasein's disclosedness, which is so available and so prevalent, can guarantee to Dasein that all the possibilities of its Being will be secure, genuine, and full. Through the self-certainty and decidedness of the 'they', it gets spread abroad increasingly that there is no need of authentic understanding or the state-of-mind that goes with it. The supposition of the 'they' that one is leading and sustaining a full and genuine 'life', brings Dasein a *tranquillity*, for which everything is 'in the best of order' and all doors are open. Falling Being-in-the-world, which tempts itself, is at the time time *tranquillizing [beruhigend]*".); cf. also, p. 334 ("The common sense of the 'they' knows only the satisfying of manipulable rules and public norms and the failure to satisfy them. It reckons up infractions of them and tries to balance them off. It has *slunk away* from its ownmost Being-guilty of the Self".)(emphasis is mine).
45. Ebeling, *WF*, p. 422.
46. *Ibid.*, p. 420. Cf. Heidegger, *BT*, pp. 325ff. ("ownmost possibility"), also pp. 307-09 with reference to "Being-towards-death".
47. Ebeling, *WF*, p. 418.
48. See above, chapter III. Cf. Heidegger, *BT*, p. 78ff., and *passim*.

Notes to pages 87–88:
49. *Ibid.*, p. 203.
50. Cf. *ibid.*, p. 318 ("The appeal to the Self in the they-self does not force it inwards upon itself, so that it can close itself off from the 'external world'. The call passes over everything like this and disperses it, so as to appeal solely to that Self which, notwithstanding, is in no other way than Being-in-the-world"), and pp. 312-15.
51. Ebeling, *WF*, p. 418.
52. See above, chapter II.
53. Ebeling, *WF*, p. 420. Cf. pp. 287-79, in the context of the essay, "Reflexions on the Doctrine of the Law": "Hence even the so-called 'man without the law' is not outside the real event of the law. '*Omnium quidem ist lex, sed non est omnium sensus legis*'. From that point of view the law written in the heart cannot be interpreted as a detailed legal codex, but only as the state of being utterly open to question. The law written in the heart is so to speak the question mark that is branded upon man: Where art thou? It would then be the task of a detailed doctrine of the law to show how this question mark that is branded upon man sets in motion the whole reality that concerns man and brings it to expression, thereby summons to the interpretation of reality, and then crystallizes also in positive laws".
54. Cf., e.g., Ebeling's interpretation in *ibid.*, pp. 276-81: "The theology of the reformers derived from this its justification for the extension of the Pauline concept of law, which it took to mean, transposed into universal terms, *the law written in every man's heart*. This was supported firstly by the traditional doctrine of the *lex naturalis*, secondly by the reduction of the Mosaic Law (as a result of the *abrogatio legis* that took place in Christ) to the moral precepts of the Decalogue, and finally by the identification of the *lex naturalis* and the Decalogue. In the tangle of problems which confront us here, the following necessarily brief points may perhaps bring some clarification...It is an undeniably correct criterion when Luther allows validity as 'law' in the theological sense only to what touches and binds the conscience, *what does not concern him unconditionally as charge and commitment, is not law as it must be understood in interpreting the Pauline doctrine of the law*". (p. 276) (final emphasis is mine).

Again, cf. the following passage (pp. 277f.) where Ebeling calls for a proper "grounding" of Luther's (= "the Pauline") doctrine of conscience via "existentialist [Ger: "existential"] interpretation", making reference to Günther Jacob's study of the idea of conscience in Luther's theology: "For the elucidation of this view of the law written in the heart Luther made use of the traditional view of the lex naturalis, which in the form of definite notitiae communes is supposed to belong to man inalienably

Notes to pages 88–91:

from birth...We have become aware today of the flaws in this method of arguing from natural law. But that does not by any means do away with the reformers' doctrine of the law written in the heart. It merely requires a different grounding and elucidation. And a basis for that is provided precisely by Luther's doctrine of conscience, in which it is not a case of registering what we know but of pointing to a claim made on us. Luther knows very well that conscience is no infallible source of information about the ideal contents of the law. Even—and precisely—when it is led astray, the conscience still functions as conscience. The decisive question put to the conscience is concerned not with its knowing but with its hearing. For conscience is the question 'Where?' knocking at man's door, and by conscience that question is decided to the effect: in prison or in freedom". For a more detailed interpretation by Ebeling, see his study, Luther; An Introduction to His Thought, trans. R. A. Wilson (Philadelphia: Fortress Press, 1970) pp. 147, 261-62, and passim. (Hereafter this work shall be cited as Luther.)

55. Ebeling, WF, p. 420.
56. Ibid., p. 420 (we have chosen, however, to use the translation by John Macquarrie and Edward Robinson in Heidegger, BT, p. 318).
57. Ibid., p. 418.
58. Heidegger, BT, pp. 169-211. See also section 68 (in Division Two) where the ontological grounding (in temporality) of the phenomena presented in sections 29-34 is set forth.
59. Ibid., p. 363.
60. Ibid.; cf. also sections 18(b) through 24, pp. 116-148.
61. Ibid., p. 364.
62. Sometime after writing this analysis the following interpretation by Paul Ricoeur came to my attention. His reading of this important hermeneutic section of *Being and Time* is very insightful and, happily, at certain key points corroborates the approach which I have taken here. For example, on this particular point Ricoeur elaborates: "Heidegger who [in contrast to Dilthey] has read Nietzsche...knew that the other [person], just as much as myself, is more unknown to me than any phenomenon of nature can be...If there is a region of being where inauthenticity reigns, it is within the relation of each person to every other possible person. This is why the great chapter on being-with is a debate with the 'they', as the home and privileged location for all dissimulation. It is thus not surprising that it is not by a reflection on being-with, but on being-in that the ontology of understanding begins. Not being-with another—which would duplicate our subjectivity—but being-in-the-world. This placement of the philosophical locus is just as important as the transfer from the problem of method to the problem of being. The question about the

Notes to pages 91–93:
'world' replaces the question about 'others'. In making understanding 'worldly', Heidegger 'de-psychologizes' it." "The Task of Hermeneutics", trans. David Pellauer, *Philosophy Today*, 17 (1973):321.

63. Unmentioned here, of course, is the crucial role of the "fore-structures", particularly "fore-conception" (*Vorgriff*), in interpretative understanding, and the primordial grounding of "language" (via "saying") therein. See Heidegger, *BT*, pp. 190ff. A helpful elaboration of this point can be found in Richard Schmitt, *Martin Heidegger on Being Human; An Introduction to "Sein und Zeit"* (New York: Random House, 1969), pp. 91ff.

64. See initially Heidegger, *BT*, p. 70. Macquarrie and Robinson have translated "*die Seinscharaktere*" as "characters of Being". Either "characters" or "structures" is legitimate here, but, as Heidegger points out, not "categories".

65. *Ibid.*, p. 171.

66. *Ibid.*, p. 174.

67. *Ibid.*, p. 184.

68. See above, chapter III.

69. Note "I./B." of the above diagram.

70. Note "I./C.' of the above diagram.

71. It is important to observe, it seems to me, that while "language" (as an articulation of interpretation in "statements" or "totality of words") emerges at a tertiary level of articulation, it is "saying", for Heidegger, which emerges at the secondary level. And, significantly, "saying" does not have its primary determination in "uttering", or "speaking", but in the triple, unified phenomena "reticence", "keeping silent" and "hearing". See Heidegger, *BT*, pp. 206f.

72. The necessity of recognizing the absolute priority of the dimension of "discourse" (*Rede*) in any theory of understanding and interpretation is one of the most important, and characteristic aspects of the so-called Bultmannian, existential hermeneutic (here, in its emphasis upon the notion of "prior-understanding"). In this connection, it seems to me that above all others it is Ebeling who is in keeping with the original insights of the early Heidegger through his insistence upon the centrality of the phenomenon of *conscience* in the *complete* hermeneutic process.

73. In order to avoid confusion we should point out that we are using the term "discursive" in its qualified, technical sense as an adjectival form of "discourse" (*Rede*), as defined in Heidegger's analysis. "Discursive" speech is not to be taken (unless so indicated) in the sense intended by traditional philosophical and theological parlance.

74. Eugene Gendlin, *Experiencing and the Creation of Meaning; a Philosophical and Psychological Approach to the Subjective* (New York: The Free Press of Glencoe, 1962), p. 5.

Notes to pages 93–97:
75. *Ibid.*, p. 101.
76. *Ibid.*, pp. 5-6.
77. Stanley Cavell, *Must We Mean What We Say?* (New York: Charles Scribner's Sons, 1969).
78. *Ibid.*, p. 192. Heidegger (and Ebeling) would make a distinction here between "knowing", in a strict perceptual-cognitive sense, and "understanding", in the wider and more fundamental sense of the "knower's" historical being-in-the-world.
79. *Ibid.*, pp. 192-93 (emphasis in the second sentence is mine).
80. See reference, above, (emphasis is mine). The reference is, again, by Ebeling, *WF*, p. 420, from Heidegger, *BT*, p. 318.
81. See diagram above.
82. Heidegger, *BT*, p. 206.
83. *Ibid.*, p. 208 (final emphasis is mine).
84. See above, chapter II.
85. Alasdair MacIntyre and Paul Ricoeur, *The Religious Significance of Atheism* (New York: Columbia University Press, 1969), pp. 57-98.
86. *Ibid.*, pp. 72-74. It is interesting to observe in the following passage (p. 73) how *close* Ricoeur comes (in his joint reflections with Heidegger) to pin-pointing the phenomenon of conscience as that "mode of being" wherein God-language becomes intelligible. An even *closer* look at the relationship of "*conscience*" to "hearing" and "hearkening" in *Being and Time*, however, would have enabled Ricoeur to move from the frustrating aporia of "still far" to the more helpful anticipation of "not far at all": "The 'hearing which understands', [Heidegger] such is the knot of our problem. Of course, nothing has yet been said about the word as Word of God. The philosopher is still far from being able to point toward a word which would truly deserve to be called the Word of God, although he may designate the mode of being which makes the Word of God existentially possible—as we have read: 'It is on the basis of this potentiality for hearing, which is existentially primary, that anything like hearkening [*Horchen*] becomes possible'".
87. Ebeling, *WF*, p. 420.
88. *Ibid.*
89. Gerhard Ebeling, "Verantworten des Glaubens in Begegnung mit dem Denken M. Heideggers", *ZThK*, Beiheft 2 (1961):119-124.
90. "Disciplines" perhaps misses Ebeling's true understanding of these two "ways". For Ebeling, although he has not sufficiently clarified this point, "philosophy" and "theology" are disciplined activities which take place in specific, historically continuous *communities*.
91. Actually, the issue is much more involved, and profound, than this. In order to grasp fully the significance of this conception in Ebeling's

Notes to page 97:
thought, I think it must be understood (and elaborated) in the light of what we have said above concerning Ebeling's notion of the peculiar "linguistic-historical" character of our Western intellectual tradition. Ebeling's chosen pathway, although beginning, as Heidegger does, with man considered simply as finite man, finds itself attuned ultimately to a specific directional-reading of the "linguistic history" of Western thought. (Regarding the "non-arbitrary" nature of this reading, see Ebeling, *WF*, pp. 251f.) For Ebeling, the "linguistic event" which occurred in the work of Luther, with the reformer's retrieval and articulation of the authentic "subject matter" of that decisive word-event which appeared with Jesus and his word, not only commands our utmost attention, but also must determine—if we take seriously our concrete historicity, not by happenstance, but by responsible decision: as "theologians"—the character and directionality of our theological method. A comparison might be made here with Heidegger's own "attunement" to the West's linguistic history, with the decisive "word-event" occurring in the thought (language) of the early pre-Socratics. Heidegger's "Luther" might well be the poets of our post-Christian and post-metaphysical era, above all, Hölderlin (cf. Ebeling's discussion in *WF*, pp. 340-42). Hölderlin's "Melanchthon", to carry out the analogy, would be none other than Heidegger himself. It would not be at all inappropriate to put to Heidegger, as Ebeling actually does, the question as to whether the philosopher—and especially a "German" philosopher—can really act in an arbitrary fashion toward that linguistic event which occurred, as Heidegger himself has put it, in that "subject matter" of "the Christian life that existed for a brief moment before the writing of the Gospels..." (see Heidegger, *Holzwege*, p. 202), and again, definitively, in the "language of Luther", (cf. Ebeling, *WF*, pp. 336, 337; 338-39). Of course, as Ebeling recognizes, Heidegger has actually made a "decision" regarding this matter; he has opted for "unbelief" (as Heidegger himself makes clear). Heidegger is important, for Ebeling, in that he not only speaks for himself, but that, through his responsible decision for "unbelief", he also speaks, in synoptic fashion, for the secular cast of our age. Furthermore, Ebeling points out that where "truth" and "reality" are concerned (and here, I think, is the real issue between the later Heidegger and the fundamental problematic in the doctrine of conscience at the heart of *Being and Time*)—there can be no such thing as "neutral ground", no "third element", no "half-way", no "'both-and'" (Ebeling, *WF*, p. 375).
92. Gerhard Ebeling, "Theologie und Philosophie", *Die Religion in Geschichte und Gegenwart*, 6 volumes. (3rd ed.; 1957), 6:782-830.
93. *Ibid.*, pp. 816-17. Also, observe the *operation* of this principle of encounter in Ebeling's "Dogmatic" section, pp., 820-30. Cf. Ebeling's dis-

Notes to pages 97–98:
cussion in "Verantworten des Glaubens", pp. 122f.
94. See, e.g., Bultmann, *Kerygma and Myth*, 1:193; cf. his statement in "The Historicity of Man and Faith", *Existence and Faith*, p. 102.
95. This quote is taken from a statement by Ebeling in his essay, "Schleiermacher's Doctrine of the Divine Attributes", trans. James W. Leitch, *JThC*, 7 (1970):175 (emphasis is mine). Significantly, it was made in direct response to a question by Van Harvey (and indirectly to earlier queries by Schubert Ogden and Langdon Gilkey) as to whether or not theological concepts were actually, in both Schleiermacher's and Ebeling's thought, "under the control of philosophical conceptions". Cf. Ebeling's expanded analysis in "Theologie und Philosophie", pp. 782-89.
96. For example, Heidegger: "Being"; Ebeling: "man before 'God'".
97. For example, Heidegger: "Western, philosophical ontology"; Ebeling: "biblical-Christian theology".
98. Regarding the notion of "total horizon", see Ebeling's discussion in "Theologie und Philosophie", pp. 782-89, 819-29, and in "Verantworten des Glaubens", pp. 119-121.
99. Ebeling, "Schleiermacher's Doctrine of the Divine Attributes", p. 169.
100. It can be argued that this really represents a more careful re-statement of, rather than a departure from, Bultmann's basic position. (Cf., Bultmann, *Kerygma and Myth*, 1:193: "...it would be a fallacy to suppose that exegesis can ever be pursued independently of profane terminology. Every exegete is dependent upon terminology which has come down to him by tradition, though it is accepted uncritically and without reflection, and every traditional terminology is in one way or another dependent upon a particular philosophy. But it is vital that we should proceed neither uncritically nor without reflection. It is imperative that we should consider the nature and the source of the terminology which directs our exposition". Cf. Bultmann, *Faith and Understanding, Vol. I*, p. 330.
101. See the discussion which follows regarding what Ebeling sees as the uniquely problematic character of the concept of "God" as it emerges via its origin and development in its respective "philosophical" and "theological" linguistic traditions. This analysis justifies, I believe, our singling out "anthropological" concepts in this manner as being more congenial to philosophical-theological 'collaboration'. It is important to note that, as with Bultmann, Ebeling utlizes Luther's principle of the distinction between "law and gospel" to indicate the appropriate point of encounter between (Heidegger's) philosophical anthropology and theology (see, "Theologie und Philosophie", pp. 827-28). Heidegger's interpretation of the structures of human existence in his early work, for Ebeling, applies to theology's understanding of "man [before God]

Notes to pages 98–99:
under law" ("man qua man", "natural man"). Actually, it does not seem to me that Ebeling's specification of theology's "philosophical thinking" here departs significantly, if at all, from Bultmann's. The strengths and weaknesses of Ebeling's position as it applies to his interpretation of "man as conscience" will be taken up in the final chapter of this study.

102. This point relates, of course, to the area of encounter just cited, above. Heidegger's phenomenological description of Dasein represents his attempt to "pass beyond" the traditional metaphysical conception of the being of man.
103. See Ebeling, "Verantworten des Glaubens", pp. 119-20, and "Theologie und Philosophie", pp. 789-817 for a historical description of these developments.
104. Ebeling, "Verantworten des Glaubens", p. 124 (my translation).
105. See "The Non-religious Interpretation of Biblical Concepts", and "Dietrich Bonhoeffer", in Ebeling, *WF*, pp. 98-161 and 282-87. Note, especially, Ebeling's criticism and correction of Bonhoeffer, pp. 130ff., n. 4.
106. *Ibid.*, p. 344.
107. See, e.g., Martin Heidegger, *Essays in Metaphysics: Identity and Difference*, trans. Kurt F. Leidecker (New York: Philosophical Library, 1960), pp. 64f.: "God entered philosophy through the issue which we think first of all as being the advance point in the essence of the differences between Being and Existence. Difference represents the ground plan in the essential structure of metaphysics. The issue yields and cedes Being as the pro-duc-tive ground, which ground in itself requires an appropriate understanding on the part of what it helped found. The appropriate understanding is equivalent to causation by the ultimate and original reality. This is the Cause as *causa sui*, and this is the just and proper name for God in philosophy. Man may neither pray to this God, nor may he sacrifice to him. Confronted by *causa sui* man may neither sink onto his knees nor could he sing and dance". See also Heidegger's discussion pp. 47-53.
108. See, e.g., Martin Heidegger, *What Is Called Thinking?*, trans. Fred D. Wieck and J. Glenn Gray (New York: Harper and Row, 1968), p. 177: "Absolutely valid can at the very most be only the sphere of ideas within which we beforehand place the text to be interpreted. And the validity of the presupposed sphere of ideas can be absolute only if the absoluteness rests on something unconditional—on a faith.

"The unconditional character of faith, and the problematic character of thinking, are two spheres separated by an abyss". See also, Heidegger, *An Introduction to Metaphysics*, p. 6: "Anyone for whom the Bible is divine revelation and truth has the answer to the question 'Why are there essents

110 *Ebeling's interpretation*

Notes to page 99:

rather than nothing?' even before it is asked: everything that is, except God himself, has been created by Him. God himself, the increate creator, 'is'. One who holds to such faith can in a way participate in the asking of our question, but he cannot really question without ceasing to be a believer and taking all the consequences of such a step. He will only be able to act 'as if'...On the other hand, a faith that does not perpetually expose itself to the possibility of unfaith is no faith but merely a convenience: the believer simply makes up his mind to adhere to the traditional doctrine. This is neither faith nor questioning, but the indifference of those who can busy themselves with everything, sometimes even displaying a keen interest in faith as well as questioning.

"What we have said about security in faith as one position in regard to the truth does not imply that the biblical 'In the beginning God created heaven and earth' is an answer to our question. Quite aside from whether these words from the bible are true or false for faith, they can supply no answer to our question because they are in no way related to it. Indeed, they cannot even be brought into relation with our question. From the standpoint of faith our question is 'foolishness'. Philosophy is this very foolishness. A 'Christian philosophy' is a round square and a misunderstanding. There is, to be sure, a thinking and questioning elaboration of the world of Christian experience, i.e., of faith. That is theology. Only epochs which no longer fully believe in the true greatness of the task of theology arrive at the disastrous notion that philosophy can help to provide a refurbished theology if not a substitute for theology, which will satisfy the needs and tastes of the time".

109. Ebeling, "Verantworten des Glaubens", p. 121 (translation and emphasis is mine).

110. Ebeling, "Theologie und Philosophie", p. 882 (translation and final emphasis is mine). Incidentally, Ebeling also considers this to be the key issue upon which a genuine "*Gesprach*" between theology and Heidegger's *later* philosophy might get started. Ebeling ventures a proposition which could form the basis for such a dialogue, and, again, the issue emerges once more as the phenomenon of man as "*conscience*": "Wird der Bann des metaphysischen Sprachverständnisses durchbrochen und das 'Wesen der Sprache' als die 'Sprache des Wesens,' das menschliche Sprechen als Ent-sprechen gedacht, *so bleibt doch zu fragen, wie von daher der konkrete Ort der Sprache, die Mitmenschlichkeit, erhellt wird und worin die eigentliche Notwendigkeit und damit die wahre Macht des Wortes als des das Gewissen angehenden Wortes besteht*". Ebeling, "Verantworten des Glaubens", p. 124 (emphasis is mine). Cf. the same proposition in summary form in the article, "Theologie und Philosophie", pp. 829-30.

Chapter V

Man as conscience and the reality of "God"

With Ebeling's interpretation before us, we now turn from the experience of the reality of "man as conscience" to ask how the reality "God" comes into view. In what way does Ebeling's position contribute to the development of the constructive thesis proposed at the start of our study, namely, that in the phenomenon of conscience we have a qualitatively unique ontological grounding for understanding the reality deemed "God"(1). We know from our earlier quotations of Ebeling's work that conscience is not only "the place where it is decided what man truly is"(2), that locus where "the whole reality that concerns man" becomes manifest(3), where "the world is encountered as the world", and "where time presses upon us and is received as time, abused or gained"(4), but it is also "the place where we experience what 'God' means"(5). At this stage of our study we should have a reasonably clear idea of what Ebeling intends in the first part of this dual claim. I believe the concept "man as conscience" is in fact Ebeling's contribution to what was asked for in the beginning of our inquiry: a new "theological anthropology" which takes its stand solely within the horizon of one's everyday being. But what about the second part of Ebeling's claim? Precisely in what way does he understand the relation between "man as conscience" and "God"? Is there justification for stating that it is basically "as conscience" that man has the possibility of understanding what the reality deemed "God" means?

Ebeling's answer to these questions unfolds on two levels. The clue which distinguishes these two levels is given in Ebeling's methodological thesis referred to earlier, namely, that the formation of theological concepts proceeds through an open attentiveness to the "linguistic tradition", on the one hand, and the "reality that confronts us", on the other hand(6). In his essay, "Rudimentary Reflexions on Speaking Responsibly of God", where he directly takes up the problem of a modern reformulation of the concept of God, Ebeling observes that in accordance with the methodological procedure followed in recent Protestant theology it would appear that an interpretation of the doctrine of God ought to begin at the level of Christianity's ongoing "linguistic tradition"(7). Certainly, there are good reasons for justifying such a procedural starting point. First, there is the recognition on the part of all "scientific work" that in the formulation of its central concepts it cannot escape the fact that it already operates within a specific linguistic tradition upon which it is dependent and with which it must enter into conversation. As Ebeling explains in an earlier essay, "jurisprudence", "natural science", and "theology" are all "sciences" which are concerned with the concept of "law". In spite of the common use of this term, however, each discipline remains dependent, as a first order of business, upon the peculiar emergent development of this concept within its own specific language tradition(8). In the case of the concept of "God" the necessary methodological dependency becomes even more pronounced than with concepts utilized in non-theological disciplines, for

> God is no phenomenon immediately confronting us, no ascertainable object of direct investigation. Had we not heard of God, had we not been taught about him, were he not announced to us, what resources would we then really have for contesting a doctrine of God—indeed, how would the idea of a doctrine of God ever occur to us at all?(9)

He concludes: "The givenness of God means his existence *in history*". Hence, "in order to encounter God" we must "become involved in a *definite* tradition...*a concrete religious tradition*"(10)—and, for Ebeling, in acceptance of his own personal "historicity", this means the concrete "Christian" tradition(11). This latter tradition is, of course, not to be identified at its primary level with its "intellectual, dogmatic" development. For, "in, beside, and behind" the Christian religion's intellectual and dogmatic language concerning God there is an originative linguistic tradition, a fundamental word-event "which springs from entirely different depths and sweeps through the ages with overwhelming breadth and power"(12). Here, according to Ebeling, we have to do with the "*biblical* Christian tradition". So important is this particular "linguistic event", Ebeling states, that "even the man who finds himself only under the more distant influence of this stream of biblical tradition cannot possibly develop a doctrine of God which would not be determined by it, even if only by way of antithesis"(13). It is with a certain degree of justification then, Ebeling concludes, that Protestant theologians for the past several decades have attempted to formulate a doctrine of God in close attunement to this original "biblical tradition", and, in pursuit of the authentic course of this "primeval river", in close adherence to this tradition it was recovered in the "theology of the Reformers"(14). But, he asks, even if we do grant the fundamental importance of this principle concerning the connection between God and our historical linguistic tradition (a principle which, as we shall note, Ebeling works out on his own terms), are we really able to take it as a prime *starting* point for the formulation of a doctrine of God in our own time? We cannot, Ebeling answers(15), and for several reasons.

First of all, to assume such a methodological starting point would presuppose that the original "linguistic *situation*" from which this tradition sprung (considered in a wider religious-cultural sense) and to which it wants to relate is the same in our modern period as it was in the past. But this is simply not the case, and, indeed, in a most critical way(16). Beginning with Jesus and the early disciples, it was simply taken for granted that the hearers of the 'Christian' proclamation "already [had] some sort of knowledge of God and faith in God if they [were] to understand such preaching"(17). This supposition maintained itself throughout the history of Christian preaching and theological reflection up to our modern era. It was on this basis, for example, that Luther and his age could so easily work out their main theological concepts within the exclusive sphere of the "biblical usage"(18). The Reformation and post-Reformation period was to all effects no different with its particular "biblical norm" than the age of Scholasticism with its respective "metaphysical", or "rational" norms. In the case of Aquinas, for instance, "dogmatics [could] begin with God, because man", so it was assumed, "by virtue of his rational knowledge of reality, [was] already in proximity to the subject 'God'"(19). For Aquinas, "the comprehensibility of *sacred doctrina*, of Christian talk of God, [was] grounded in the fact that even prior to *sacra doctrina* and apart from it, God [was] already under discussion. 'God' [was] not a specifically Christian word. And by the same token, the substance which this word express[ed] [was] not first discovered through Christian talk about God and then made into a subject for discussion"(20). Now, Ebeling points out, whereas it was Aquinas' coniviction "that *sacra doctrina* [could]—indeed, must!—speak about God,...because God [was] already under discussion anyway", our modern situation is exactly the opposite. Although our situation is identical to Aquinas' as reflected in *quaestro I.* of his *Summa*, in that we too must concern ourselves with the meaning of "God" as a first order of business, we must do so precisely because it is *not* under discussion. We must "bring up God first", Ebeling urges, because we "live in a world which knows nothing about God"(21).

But what is it about our age that causes the theologian to assume such a different posture, such a radical methodological stance concerning his talk of "God"? "Our place in the history of religion", Ebeling states, "is marked by the fact that polytheism is for us a thing of the past(22), *while atheism is the possibility attaching to our own situation and as such determines our reality*"(23). It is with this situation of "secularistic godlessness" that the theologian must begin today in broaching the question of "God". Here we want to recall a statement of Ebeling's quoted earlier: "A doctrine of God today...is abstract speculation if it does not have the phenomenon of modern atheism before it from the start"(24). Let us now add the remarks which immediately follow this assertion:

When I [say] that atheism is the possibility attaching to our own situation and as such determines our reality...I am concerned with the inner grasp of something which is far more complex than short-winded apologists suspect, and which does not by any means threaten Christianity only from without, *but has already also penetrated as it were through the walls of the heart into our inmost being as a sort of atmosphere whose influence no one can evade.*(25)

According to Ebeling, it has become a truism in recent Protestant "revelational" theology to stress the fact that while 'genuine' "biblical monotheism sets God over against our reality as a whole", ancient polytheism, with its modern counterpart in certain "post-Christian" philosophies and so-called "secular theologies", "lets the divine merge in our reality and our reality in the divine..."(26). Now while this view might well carry within it a "very true observation", there is reason to believe that, even when elaborated in a systematic way instead of merely being brandished about as a slogan, it creates more misunderstanding than clarity. The reason for this, Ebeling feels, is inherent in the conclusion which is usually drawn from such a distinction—by theologians and non-theologians alike—namely, that "it is peculiar to paganism to think of and experience the divine when it looks at this reality of ours, whereas it is the mark of Christianity to think in terms of *two separate spheres of reality*"(27). For Ebeling, the idea that Christianity speaks of "God", or proclaims "the word of 'God'", as a sphere of reality separate from that of the world, or our secular experience in this world, is intolerable, not only from the standpoint of modern "pagan" man/woman, but from the standpoint of the meaning of the word "God" itself.

It is not without significance then that the essay to which we have been referring in *Word and Faith* is followed by three studies entitled "Worldly Talk of God", "The World as History", and "Faith and Unbelief in Conflict about Reality". It is in this latter study especially that he attempts to set right the kind of misunderstanding cited above, first, by clarifying once and for all what the real issue is between "faith" and "unbelief", and secondly, by demonstrating where in one's everyday experience this issue ought to be, or, in fact, actually *is* settled. Many would want to say, Ebeling states, that "faith...is concerned with God, with the Beyond, with eternal salvation, etc.", whereas unbelief, "is concerned only with man, with this world, with temporal life"(28). Nevertheless, he replies, "this characterization is a wholly inadmissible caricature.... In [this] case the conflict between faith and unbelief could [seemingly] be settled by a peace of partition: the Beyond for faith, this world for unbelief. But this suggestion has so far been made only by cynical politicians, not by conscientious men"(29). However, Ebeling adds: "It would not by any means...be correcting the mistake to say: naturally faith is not concerned *only* with God, the Beyond and eternal life. For that still abides by the idea of two spheres bordering on each other"(30).

In order to overcome this dilemma of the "two spheres", we must recognize to begin with that the so-called modern conflict between faith and unbelief is not, from the standpoint of the latter, about the peculiar nature of the former, i.e., as if the real issue were whether, in a trivial sense, "a particular sector of reality", with which "faith" has to do can be "everyone's cup of tea"(31), or if, in a more serious vein, a "secret reality which is accessible only to the believer" can be recognized or justified before the "non-believer". No, for Ebeling, the real issue between the man/woman of faith and the man/woman of unbelief is about *the true nature of the one single reality which should concern them both—simply as human beings.* "Rightly understood", then, faith is concerned with the world, with human nature; and what it says of God, of the Beyond and of eternal life has no other point at all than to bring man and the world to expression as what they truly are. That does not amount in the end, as is so often feared, to shifting the centre—to putting man in the centre instead of God, to thinking anthropocentrically instead of theocentrically. It would certainly be a foolish way of speaking to say that faith is concerned with God only for the sake of man. But the very fact of its certainly having to do with God alone is the way in which it has to do with real men. We cannot here make separations and play off one against the other. *Otherwise we turn God into a supernatural ghost that has still to be added on to reality, yet stands in competition with it and is therefore after all only a part of reality as a whole.* What the conflict between faith and unbelief is about comes to light in greatest clearness only when the antithesis is sharpened to the point of saying: *reality itself* is what the conflict is about between faith and unbelief(32).

Now if the theologian is going to take his or her stand concerning the question of God within the sphere of that "one single reality" which concerns one as simply human, it must be made clear from the start exactly what is entailed by this term "reality". A preliminary clarificaton of this concept is particularly important especially in view of the present dominant tendency to equate "reality" automatically with the "physical view" of the world as determined by the objective-empirical method appropriate to the natural sciences. And, lest the theologian utterly exclude himself at the beginning from having anything at all to say concerning "the true nature of reality"(33), Ebeling warns that we (that is as "secularly" attuned theologians) must "beware of a one-sided adherence...to the physical concept of reality...." "Strictly and indisputably valid as the physical view of reality is within its limits", he states, "it is yet precisely because of the method of objectification a most violent abstraction from *reality as a whole*"(34).

For Ebeling, the issue concerning "reality as a whole" comes to a head primarily over the question of the true nature of "man/woman". "Reality" is defined, in its primoridal sense, as that "*indivisible complex of all that concerns me*" as a living, historical being(35). This definition does not by any means exclude that 'world' which is the object of the natural sciences. To the contrary, not only does it recognize the existence of this 'world' (i.e., as one of several perspectival 'worlds'), but it also raises it to a higher order of intelligibility, as it were, by placing it within the yet more fundamental sphere of the human being's personal, intentioned, historical existence(36). Like Heidegger, Ebeling asserts that we can determine the true nature of that 'world' constructed by the natural sciences (or rather, by the common methodological presuppositions shared by the physical sciences, and by those philosophies which take the latter as their model), only when it is understood "for what it truly is", namely, as fundamentally a human phenomenon, a

116 *Man as conscience and the reality of "God"*

human project "for the sake of" something which arises out of the human being's concernful existence in time. Hence, the true locus or horizon for determining the final meaning and truth of the "world" is man's/woman's everyday "worldly being"(37) viewed in terms of its primordial existential-historical character. And the appropriate epistemological mode involved in such a determination is neither "action" nor "knowledge" (or "perception"), strictly defined, but "understanding".

In his discussion concerning the question of the "conflict" about reality Ebeling makes an important observation. Drawing upon the etymological root and usage of the German word for "reality", "*die Wirklichkeit*", he contends that (the notion of) "the real" ("*das Wirkliche*"), is to be interpreted in its primordial linguistic sense as "something which is effective (*wirksam*)", as that which is "active, mighty, which has the capacity to impress as real (was als *wirklich* zu beeindrucken)", i.e., in being "effective" it "contains possibilities and hence the capabilities, has a reference to the future"(38). Now it would seem that here Ebeling is taking a different tack from his earlier definition of "reality", defined as that "indivisible complex of all that concerns me" as a living, historical being. The apparent disconnectedness can be resolved if we recognize that in the earlier definition we have an existential-ontological rendering which is equivalent to "world", or 'world-experience', (i.e., "reality" = "world", as that "'indivisible complex of all that concerns me' as a living, historical being")(39). In his second interpretation ("reality" as "that which is effective", etc.) we have what might be termed the "truth" of the "world" (or world-experience). "Reality", for Ebeling, can be either "real" (= effective, capacity to bring about the future) or "unreal" (= inactive, impotent, incapacity for bringing about the future); hence, the conflict between "faith" and "unbelief" is, in essence, a dispute concerning the ultimate "truth" (= "effectiveness") or "untruth" (= "impotence") of the "world" (or world-experience).

Now, according to Ebeling, this dispute concerning the truth or untruth of reality can be carried on at three different levels: at the level of "action", of "knowledge", and of "understanding". He puts it this way:

> If 'conflict about something' means that in one respect or another the right is in dispute in point of reality, then the possible causes of conflict can be grouped under three heads. For the right can be in dispute in point of reality in three ways. The most immediate one is the conflict about the claiming and possessing of reality, about the right way of dealing with it, and thus about the command over reality and the moulding of it. Another kind is the conflict about the correct perception of reality, about the establishing of facts and of links between events. A third kind is the conflict about the true understanding of reality, about the grasping and conferring of meaning. These three forms of the conflict about who is in the right where reality is concerned, are interconnected in manifold ways and condition each other; *but they are different spheres that are subject*

to different laws(40).

The conflict involved in the sphere where the question of "action" is raised can be resolved, according to Ebeling, "on occasion by *force*"(41). Here, the question as to the "truth" ("real" as effective, etc.) or "untruth" of reality is settled simply by the application of autonomous power, by human beings "taking command over reality" coercing and "moulding" it to their own purposes, to their own personal tastes, desires, schemes, programs. In the realm of action one "does justice" to reality with power solely in the name of man/woman. And we might add that the question of "God" does not emerge at this level as such. The phenomenon "God" comes into view only when one passes out of this sphere at the point of "doing justice", or rather, at that point when one's forceful "doing justice" to reality in the name of man/woman becomes "questionable". Here we become involved neither with "action" nor "knowledge" but with "understanding".

Settling the issue concerning the truth of reality by force is "senseless", Ebeling states, at the levels of "knowledge" and "understanding". As for the sphere of "knowing" the conflict over the question of the truth of reality finds its resolution solely within the horizon of that which is "scientifically ascertainable"(42). The truth of reality within this sphere is determined *in toto* by "what man as such with his rational and empirical faculties can know, perceive, prove and control"(43). As we have seen, the thoroughgoing, systematic application of the objective-empirical method to traditional "self-evident assumptions" concerning nature, history, and even human beings (considered as an objects of nature) marks the dawn of our modern "secular" age(44).

The ascendancy of the sphere of "knowledge" in deciding the question of the truth of reality has brought about two fundamental changes in our intellectual-cultural landscape, according to Ebeling, "which can never again be unmade". The first concerns a basic "restriction" of what was hitherto understood as knowledge, viz., "the elimination of all metaphysical statements from the realm of the self-evident"(45). The second involves a certain "extension" of the claim of "knowledge", in the establishment of "the relative autonomy of science and of social life"(46). As for the first "restriction", Ebeling bids modern theology to beware of presupposing, methodologically and materially, a "metaphysical" starting point with its unspoken assumption of the self-evident rationality, or coherence of the natural world process. In the sphere of "knowledge" as it is understood today, this "assumption" is simply, and perhaps irreversibly, "*non*-self-evident". In fact, as Ebeling sees it, the modern scientific method, manifested in various forms in the natural and humane sciences, is predicated on the assumption of the *non*-self-evidentness of the previously considered evident. Accordingly, the determination of "certitude" ("calculable knowledge") regarding the problematical non-evidence of the world has been taken out of the hands of common sense and direct intuition and placed within the separate regional spheres of scientific research in accordance with their respective methodological techniques. Whether we like it or not, in our time the latter enjoys a definite "relative autonomy" which, he adds, can only be encroached upon in the name of "pseudo-knowledge". Ebeling elaborates upon the character of this "relative autonomy":

'Relative autonomy' is intended to mean that here, while respecting the proximity of the problematical and refraining from absolutism, i.e., refraining from taking the non-self-evident as self-evident—or we could also say, in a state of aporia where metaphysics is concerned—men can after all attain to [a knowledge] that is universally binding. Or to put it more concretely: it is a legitimate self-evident assumption of the modern age, never again to be unmade, that neither the church nor any worldview that supposes itself absolute may impugn the relative autonomy of science and of social life. That the modern age is in actual fact full of repeated attempts to do that after all in one form or another, that in the modern age the self-evident assumption in question is thus not everywhere recognized and treated as self-evident, merely makes clear that in the so-called self-evident assumptions we have not to do with automatisms but with claims to validity.(47)

Now, according to Ebeling, "faith" and "theology" make their "claim to validity" (i.e., concerning the truth of reality) not within the sphere of "knowledge" but in the sphere of "understanding," i.e., that "understanding" which is given in and with one's personal existence in time. Does this mean that faith does not grant the scientific examination of the world its due? Far from it, Ebeling cautions. To fail to do so can only mean a failure to grasp the proper meaning of faith and of that epistemological sphere wherein it finds its true home. Hence Ebeling states quite flatly:

If faith comes into conflict with what is *knowable* and what stands conscientious testing as an indisputable item of *knowledge*, then that so-called faith proves itself to be pseudo-faith. *For faith is not a matter of knowledge (in the sense of what is scientifically ascertainable) and can therefore never enter into competition with such knowledge either* (unless the latter can be shown *scientifically* to be pseudo-knowledge).(48)

This does not mean either that faith (and understanding), properly considered, is indifferent to the scientifico-mathematical perception of the world. As he says: "...faith is never by any means indifferent towards scientific examination of reality. For faith actually demands and promotes the right and proper use of reason. That is what distinguishes it from superstition"(49). The most obvious examples of this encouragement of the right use of reason, for Ebeling, can be seen in theology's use of the modern "historical-critical method". As an interpreter of Scripture, and of Christianity's intellectual tradition, the systematic theologian (among other things) operates from the perspective of a "modern historian". As such he cannot help but be "convinced that he *knows* certain things better" than his spiritual predecessors(50).

For instance,
> the fact that for the modern age all that is metaphysical and metahistorical has entered the dimension of the problematical is...a thing that the modern historian cannot simply put out of his mind when reading sources which presuppose the self-evident validity of statements which introduce metaphysical beings in the sense of the older picture of the world as internal factors in the world and its history—just as of course he himself also oversteps the bounderies of scientific method if for his own part he tries to explain something historically problematical by means of metaphysical statements, i.e., to render it self-evident.(51)

With this recognition we turn to that sphere where faith and theology lay legitimate "claim to validity" concerning their proper object, the reality termed "God". "Faith", Ebeling states, "has its proper place where it is a case of understanding reality. And indeed, *understanding reality as a whole*". "This wholeness", he adds, "is not a sum of individual parts, but *the experience that at one particular point everything stands or falls together*"(52). What does Ebeling mean by this? First of all, there must be no misunderstanding concerning the impossibility of laying claim to an understanding of the truth of "reality as a whole" within the sphere of "knowledge". As Ebeling observes, if anything, the "objective world" projected by "natural science is a supreme degree of abstraction from reality as a whole. It presents the world, not as it is 'in itself', but as it appears to the man who is capable of this abstraction"(53). A prime example of this can be seen in the area of modern atomic physics where "the limits of what can be unequivocally objectified" is reached in the recognition that "the decision on the appearance of corpuscle or wave is made with the choice of the method of experiment"(54). This is not to say, however, that modern proponents(55) of the 'world' of "scientific realism" have, even in the face of such methodological relativity, refrained from laying claim to a knowledge of something like "reality as a whole". To the contrary, this "secularistic"(56) tendency is the hallmark of our age; it determines not only the outlook of the 'professional' (i.e., the scientific and philosophical naturalist) but the 'layman' as well. Given reflective and systematic treatment, this tendency achieves "wholeness", according to Ebeling, either by the lumping together of "limited wholes, such as outer world, inner world, world of nature, world of history", and other objective constructs as has been the usual case, or, by opting for a natural or physical view of the world *in toto* as essentially a "matter of conviction", or a "*Weltanschauung*, as it has been called since the beginning of the nineteenth century..."(57). As for the first attempt to attain wholeness through the stringing together of "limited wholes", one has only to attend to the pronouncements of the physical sciences themselves regarding the illegitimacy—and even at times the absurdity—of such a procedure. It is true that theology has in the course of its history been tempted to work alongside such constructs as these, representing God, for example "as *ens perfectissimum* crowning...reality conceived in pyramid form"(58). But even here, even as "*ens perfectissimum*", God is still no more than a mere part of reality as a whole(59). As for the second tendency to construct a positivistic *Weltanschauung*, we have already observed at length in our first chapter, with close attention to Heidegger's analysis of the rise of "the spirit of subjectity (*Subjectität*)," the ultimate "nihilistic" implications involved in these attempts to attain wholeness. In contrast to Bultmann, however, it is important to note that Ebeling, although he is in firm agreement with Heidegger's reading of history, especially in its "spiritual development" from Descartes to Nietzsche, does not lead us to "nihilism" as a point of departure for faith and for a constructive reformulation of the understanding of God(60). Ebeling prefers that we dwell thoughtfully and constructively upon that one crucial area demarcated above wherein the meaning of one's being in the world as a whole—its why, whither, and wherefore—comes to expression for self-understanding and decision(61).

Before moving to consider how the reality of "God" emerges within this sphere, we must pause parenthetically for the following observations. Although it has been indicated all along in our comparison of Ebeling's and Heidegger's interpretations of conscience, it must now be stated explicitly, particularly in light of Ebeling's treatment of the concept of "reality", just how much he is actually committed to an *existentialist ontology*, with all that this implies with respect to its rejection of the presuppositions of the dominant intellectualistic and cognitivistic philosophical tradition regarding the epistemological status of experience, the nature of truth, and the verification of religious knowledge. Ebeling's important distinction between "knowledge" (*Erkenntnis*) and "understanding" (*Verstehen*), clearly indicates his commitment to the kind of epistemological claims put forth by an existentialist or "voluntarist"(62) position, for which *Being and Time* stands as a seminal, and in many ways a definitive expression(63). "Knowledge", for Ebeling, stands terminologically for that mode of cognition appropriate to "things", or to entities considered as objects within the realm of "nature". In *Being and Time* Heidegger uses the term "theoretical reason" (*theoretische Vernunft*) to designate this kind of knowing in contrast to "understanding" (*Verstehen*). The "world" posited in this realm is, according to Heidegger, the Cartesian world of *res extensae*, and it is important to remember, he adds, that the vocabulary of cognition evinced here is not unlike that manifested in the context of everyday perceptual experience(64). In this respect both Heidegger and Ebeling would be in agreement with Husserl's observation: "Daily practical living is naive. It is immersion in the already-given world, whether it be experiencing, or thinking, or valuing, or acting.... Nor is it otherwise in the positive sciences. They are naivetés of a higher level. They are the products of an ingenious theoretical technique; *but the intentional performances from which everything ultimately originates remain unexplicated*"(65). This latter, "already-given world" pertains, for Heidegger and Ebeling, to that which is interpreted in and through our everyday, personal existence, or being. The nature of our apprehension of reality at this level can be understood with the help of a conceptuality which is appropriately derived from those existential structures inherent in everyday being as such, and presumably, Heidegger's "phenomenological hermeneutics" (or "existential Interpretation") of Dasein in *Being and Time* presents us with just such a conceptual reconstruction. Hence, if "knowledge" pertains to that kind of knowing which we can have of *things qua nature* (i.e., at a secondary level of cognitive knowing) in keeping with Heidegger's terminological distinction, then, as Ebeling puts it, "understanding" must be reserved for that kind of knowing which we have of *man/woman qua historical being* (i.e., at the primary level of cognitive knowing). To be sure, man/woman may be looked at (and, hence, "known") objectively as a mere "natural entity", but for both philosopher and theologian this would not be to know man/woman as a "human being"(66)! Actually, we should recognize that Ebeling does not refer to the realm of understanding as a mode of "knowing" *per se*. I, for one, would not want to sacrifice this designation with respect to the existentialist (Heidegger) category of "*Verstehen*"(67). It seems to me that Ebeling's position, when considered critically, is quite vulnerable at precisely this point. This vulnerability is symptomatic, I believe, of Ebeling's general failure to acknowledge in *practice* the scope and depth of the "philosophical" task which he apparently recognizes in theory(68). And here it is important to remind Ebeling of a crucial programmatic statement formulated in an early essay and not as yet brought to fruition in his work:

> Theology must clarify the concept of reality and consequently take upon itself the ontological task. In place of merely contrasting personal and ontological thinking, the aims of personalism must be turned to good account for *fundamental ontology*. The result will then be a concept of reality which takes its bearings not on objectification but on historic encounter, not on the availability of reality but on its linguisticality, not on the existing present but on the future that is still to come. An ontology of this kind will certainly be nourished by theological insights and intended for theological use, yet it will be no *theological* but a *fundamental ontology* open to general discussion, and one in which the derivative modes of reality, such as natural science's concept of reality, will also have their place.(69)

It may be that Ebeling's later interest in the development of what he now terms "fundamental theology"(70) represents the beginnings of this programmatic project, and this expressed intention would then encourage us to proceed in the kind of constructive exploration proposed. Indeed, in lieu of a developed fundamental theology (which, presumably, would include an articulated general, or philosophical, ontology) we are obliged to follow through the implications of a clearly recognizable, if tacitly assumed and only indirectly expressed, "fundamental ontology" within Ebeling's present position. Now Ebeling may protest that such a treatment of his thought forces him prematurely into a philosophical (or "ontological") position for which he may not want to assume reponsibility. To this we could only respond that until more explicit guideposts are erected we must, in view of the urgent necessity of our present theological situation, run this kind of risk. That Ebeling presents us with one of the most potentially fruitful positions from which to build is, of course, the underlying presupposition of our study.

Ebeling's commitment to what I have termed an existentialist-voluntarist ontology can be illustrated by one other important example, namely, his view regarding the ultimate "perspectival" character of scientific knowledge and the primary, constituitive function of the will. This view, so basic to Heidegger's epistemological orientation in *Being and Time*, is expressed clearly in the above quotation ("a fundamental ontology...in which the derivative modes of reality, such as natural science's concept of reality, will have their place"). In the final analysis, Ebeling is arguing that "everyday" and "scientific" perception are activities "which appear within the intentional framework of human subjectivity"(71). This is not to say, of course, that the being of things grasped within the former two realms is by this means made identical with the original intentional act which founds them, or, for that matter, reduced to the status of mere intentional objects. Ebeling, I believe, agrees completely with the position Heidegger develops in *Being and Time* over against the Husserlian phenomenological reduction which in attempting to isolate the sphere of "pure consciousness" together with its intentional correlates for methodological purposes, tends in the end of assimilate the intentional referents to itself in a thoroughgoing idealistic sense. In fact, we can go so far as to say, I believe, that only because Ebeling stands so closely to Heidegger on this point is he justified in his claim that when he speaks of "understanding reality as a whole" within the sphere of man's personal, historical being, he is not at the same time denying the "relative autonomy" and legitimacy of claims to knowledge within the sphere of objectifying reason.

We return now to complete the analysis of the way in which Ebeling conceives the relationship between God and conscience. Our basic understanding of the reality "God" is grounded, Ebeling claims, in that place wherein the meaning of one's being in the world as a whole comes to decisive expression—in conscience. With an eye to the development of my own constructive thesis, the task before us at this point is twofold: on the one hand, to discern what Ebeling takes to be the most distinctive characteristics of this experience as they point to an understanding of the meaning of "God", and, on the other hand, to determine precisely what kind of status Ebeling gives this experience as knowledge or understanding.

In the important essay, "Rudimentary Reflexions on Speaking Responsibly of God", Ebeling singles out three essential aspects of the experience of reality in conscience: "radical questionableness" (*radikaler Fraglichkeit*), "passivity" (*Passivität*), and "linguisticality" (*Sprachlichkeit*)(72). It is the notion of radical questionableness which forms the primary experiential-ontological basis for a prior understanding of the term "God". The phenomena "passivity" and "linguisticality" represent two further extensions of this primal experience. As for the basic notion, Ebeling asserts, "The question how God is actually experienced, how it can actually become clear what God means in the context of the reality that encounters me, can be answered in the first instance...by the pointer: God is experienced as a question. In the context of the reality that encounters me God encounters me as the questionableness of that encountering reality"(73). Now by "questionableness of that encountering reality", Ebeling does not mean a questionableness for which reality at some point will eventually provide an answer. Rather, radical questionableness pertains to (1) "a questionableness to which reality does *not* contain the answer"(74), and (2) a questionableness which "seeks to be answered by me myself"(75). "The radicality of the questionableness comes", Ebeling stresses, "only when I become questionable in my own eyes, when the questionableness of the reality that concerns me and my own questionableness are identical"(76). To be sure, Ebeling observes, the latter is not unrelated to those critical moments in everyday experience, when the question of meaning, of anxiety, guilt, and communication arise. Yet in exhibiting the reality of radical questionableness Ebeling does not rely upon a common sense or scientific description of these experiences as such(77), but rather upon an ontological-existential interpretation of the phenomenon "man as conscience"(78)

In this instance he is concerned with the special phenomenon of "dissociation" (*Distanz*) which, as we have seen, is that aspect of conscience's "call" wherein man experiences himself "as one who is not identical with himself, but whose essence it is to be questioned about his identity with himself"(79). The "radical questionableness" of reality as a whole arises under the impress of that "being questioned about" one's non-identity, coupled with that "being summoned to" a responsibility for one's true identity (one's ownmost potentiality for being). Here is a form of questionableness which does not contain its own answer as it were, for it is the very nature of the phenomenon that one (Dasein) finds oneself being questioned about an identity which is always *already* shattered or lost, *while yet at the same instant* being summoned to attain that unity between self (as "thrown") and self (as "authentic factical potentiality-for-Being") by means of a projection (*being* one's authentic "Being-a-basis") lying 'outside' one's apparent finite possibility of being(80).

Now in what sense does this form of radical questionableness provide an understanding of "God", for Ebeling? Most precisely, what becomes manifest here is man's experience of himself in his "existence between 'God' and 'world'", or, as expressed elsewhere, drawing upon the suggestive terminology of Luther: it is man "*coram seipso*" ("before himself"), stripped of his identity "*coram mundi*" ("before the world"), in the determination of his true identity "*coram Deo*" ("before God")(81).

This way of putting the issue suggests that we can identify the radical questionableness experienced "*coram seipso*" with that forum phenomenon "*coram Deo*", and thereby lay claim, if not to a knowledge of God, at least to an awareness, or prior understanding of a reality in experience to which the term "God" refers. Ebeling himself at points does seem to support such an identity and the implications we have drawn from it. For example, in his essay on conscience, Ebeling writes: "Conscience is the condition on which it becomes possible to understand what is meant by the word 'God'. In the interpretation of conscience it must become clear what we mean when we say 'God'"(82). And he adds this pregnant insight: "...the striking fact that man in his selfhood always faces towards something over against him, and even in his most private things has a certain tendency towards openness, raises the question what that may mean"(83). Again, regarding the forum experience in conscience, he says: "The fact of man's identity being open to question opens also the question of God. And indeed not least also in the sense that man can find himself asking how in spite of his constant non-identity with himself he yet remains upheld in that identity, in remaining questioned about it and summoned to it"(84). But, alas, these insights remain only suggestive. In the end Ebeling fails to draw the positive conclusions towards which the preceding analysis points. For example, in the same essay on conscience we confront the surprising demurrer: "Certainly, the relation of '*coram seipso*' which characterizes man as conscience is not simply already the '*coram Deo*'..."(85). He concludes: "God and conscience will not be related to each other in the right way by means of such reflections, but rather by the fact that God is spoken to the conscience(86). Only so do the locative statements '*in conscientia*' and '*coram Deo*' coincide"(87).

Why does Ebeling bring us to the threshold of understanding the phenomenon of conscience as some kind of primary locus for apprehending the reality deemed "God", only to turn us back so abruptly? Clearly such a contradictory delimitation imposes unnecessary restrictions on the fruitfulness of his interpretation of conscience for a theological prolegomenon. Unfortunately, Ebeling does not address himself to this issue, and it is perhaps only possible to point out critical tendencies in his thinking which help to explain, if not justify, this puzzling retraction.

We should note first the general predilection of his Lutheran orientation which at crucial points leads Ebeling to cast the problem of God solely in terms of soteriological interests. A striking example of this is found in his opening statement concerning the nature of "theology" in his essay on conscience: "...to ask what speaking of conscience contributes towards interpreting the salutariness of speaking of God...means asking about the significance of the concept of conscience for the exposition of soteriology)"(88). Again: "Since my intention[!] is not to reduce theology to soteriology...but to recall the real point of everything theology says, I shall use the word 'theology' always in view of the soteriological aim of the theological linguistic event and understand the term 'soteriology' in turn as a pointer to the specifically linguistic character of theology. For teaching about God and teaching about salvation are identical"(89). As with his beloved Luther, the getting at the real point of what theology has to say, which is the theologian's task, betrays a tendency to move all too quickly to the necessity and meaning of the gospel and faith, while leaving unexamined what might well be necessary for an understanding of the gospel—as precisely the "Word of '*God*'". This overriding concern for the soteriological dimension of the problem of God explains, I believe, why in his reinterpretation of conscience Ebeling does not address himself directly to the question which is of primary concern to us, namely, in what sense that experience and understanding of reality given in conscience is *itself* (i.e., prior to the question of salvation, and to revelation and faith) a meaningful basis for "God" language. His central concern, which is the fundamental concern of theology as Luther conceives it, is to show what it means for man/woman to be necessarily open to and receptive of the saving word-event in the kerygma(90). But this of course does not mean that Ebeling's interpretation of conscience is thereby restricted from being extended to our question. As I shall try to show, it can indeed be directed toward our question with more positive results than Ebeling is seemingly willing to recognize.

A second restrictive tendency in Ebeling's thought resides in his desire to ultimately uphold the view that God can never be made an object of conceptual thinking. He expresses this in a number of ways, although it is most typical of him to lay claim to the classical theological tradition with its axiomatic recognition that God, as opposed to worldly being, can never appear as a direct object to thought and, hence, must remain "indefinable"(91). On the other hand, we should observe that in his call for the development of a "fundamental ontology" (which, in having "personal reality" as its subject, would attempt to work out a systematic "concept of reality which takes its bearing not from objectification but on historic encounter")(92) it appears that Ebeling does indeed, at least in principle, recognize an appropriate way in which man/woman can be made the object of conceptual thought. Nevertheless, in practice (93) Ebeling does deny the further possibility of developing a clear idea of God "analogically" on the basis of such existential-ontological concepts(94). This resistance to an indirect knowledge of God in the usual analogical sense is illustrated clearly at one point when he states that the theological function of such an ontology "is not to *derive* the being of God from the being of man, but to *direct* man towards the situation in which he can understand what is said of God"(95). It appears that in the word-event of conscience, for Ebeling, we are presented with the being of man/woman in relation to 'God', whereas in the word-event of the kerygma we are presented with the being of God (proclaimed as such) in relation to man/woman. But what sense are we to make of that reality to, or before which, we understand ourselves to be related in conscience? Surely some sense must be made of this reality precisely so that the kerygmatic address can be recognized as word of "God"!

The above limitation which Ebeling places upon the knowledge of God is both a direct and indirect sense finds its real source, I believe, in Ebeling's conception of language. We miss entirely the essential character of "God" language, he claims, if we remain confined to the "prevailing view of language" which is oriented almost exclusively toward the "descriptive" or "significatory" function of words(96). God-language, as it functions from the standpoint of faith in such doctrinal or confessional statements as "maker of heaven and earth", "Father of Our Lord Jesus Christ", even Jesus' talk of "God the 'Father'", is only apparently representational in function, Ebeling avers. Such "representations...give expression to that which is meant by the word 'God' only to the extent that they *present man to God*..."(97). That is to say, only as they awaken in man and point him to the awareness and 'utterability' of that which hitherto lies hidden in his experience of reality(98).

Now surely this last hermeneutical point implies that that language which is spoken or addressed to us from the standpoint of faith aims towards—indeed, I would say depends necessarily upon for its meaningful functioning—a prior, 'hidden' understanding of a transcendent or unconditional reality which may be deemed "God", in our experience outside of faith and special revelation. It is a weakness in Ebeling's thought that he never develops this point beyond a few brief, suggestive reflections scattered here and there in his work. Among these reflections those which appear in the essay "Theology and the Evidentness of the Ethical"(99), appear to be more fruitful than others for the purposes of theological prolegomenon. Attending in this work to the defining function of the "call" of conscience which in the experience of "radical questionableness" brings before one the possibility of understanding oneself as a whole, Ebeling first considers the point which we have earlier touched upon. The word "God", he says, "points in the direction" of this situational apprehension of the "radical questionableness of reality as a whole". He continues with the important statement that here we have a meaningful locus for speaking of the "absent God", the *deus absconditus* "whose absence is precisely the troublesome thing...present as radical questionableness"(100). Man, torn between the summons to be himself an answer for his own reality, which is his true potentiality, and the inability to be such an answer in fact, apprehends his need for an unconditioned, or transcendent response or word which will enable him to yet answer for himself and the world. Ebeling observes that at times such an apprehension may emerge in the utterance of the word "God" itself, spoken as an "interjection", or a "'catcall' of existence", expressive of one's overwhelming sense of 'god-lessness'(101).

Thus, although Ebeling appears earlier to have restricted that forum phenomenon *"coram Deo"* to our encounter with God in and through the word of salvation which comes to expression in Jesus and the kerygma, it now appears that this "revealed" forum indeed does have a "hidden" or "veiled" counterpart in the structure and experience of man as conscience. With this in mind I would now venture a necessary revision of Ebeling's position which, for the purposes of our constructive thesis, will allow us to state the following: The relation of *"coram seipso"* which characterizes man as conscience is, *in a hidden sense, already* the *"coram Deo"*(102). I am not parting here from Ebeling's epistemological claim that as conscience man cannot know or experience God "in himself", but I am affirming that as conscience we are presented with the possibility of experiencing and understanding ourselves in relation to the hidden presence of God. The experience of reality in conscience can be seen to provide a basis for understanding ourselves before the hidden, or indirect presence of God as the unconditional, or transcendent ground of our personal being(103). Let me state this more precisely from the standpoint of a prolegomenous theological anthropology: *that reality before which we understand ourselves to be standing as the ground of our personal being is what is meant by the term "God"*. Going beyond the untenable restrictiveness of Ebeling's position, I contend that the experience of reality as conscience provides a meaningful basis (within the context of "Christian" experience and reflection) not only for talk of "God" as "limiting judge" and "savior", but also, and more fundamentally, as "personal creator" and "preserver". Very briefly we can make this dual claim explicit by drawing out the full implications of two distinguishable aspects in the phenomenon of conscience, one which Ebeling has developed by ambiguous implication, and another which he has not developed at all. I shall set forth these two aspects in the form of two concluding theses:

1. If we focus prolegomenously upon the aspect of *questionableness* manifested *within* conscience's call, we are able to see this: In the joint-cognizance of one's identity being open to radical question one stands "before oneself" stripped of one's identity (as thrown), and called to responsibly take over the impossible possibility of becoming one's own "Being-a-basis". This questionableness of one's being, if ascertained in its fundamental radicality, provides a primal awareness of a transcendent, or unconditioned power or word outside of itself, hence raising the question of "God", as that saving power which one needs to be truly whole. Here in one's awareness of one's (and the world's) radical questionableness such talk of "God" as "judge" and "savior", and of "man/woman" as "sinner" and responsibly "free" (as spoken of in "Christian" and non-Christian "theistic" communities) has its meaningful ontological-experiential grounding. It should be noted that the two forum phenomena *coram seipso* and *coram Deo* coincide here in a negative way:

"God" is discerned as a void, or absent reality which makes its necessity (as need) felt in and through one's responsible non-identity.

2. Going beyond the implications of the questionableness manifested within conscience's call and summons and focusing upon the *irrepressible questioning process itself* (actually, the most direct, or obvious phenomenal mark of conscience), we are able to see this: As one stands before the *questioning power* of conscience, *one stands literally before the unconditional ground of one's personal being*. The questioning of conscience alone—that incessant and inescapable pressure of being, which imposes itself ever upon me so long as I exist, this questioning is that which *enables* me to be open to who and what I am to be. And this questioning power does not only enable, let us note, it also *upholds* me—strange as it may seem—in and through the radical questionableness which is the content of its summons. In this *coram* phenomenon the term "God" (again, as named in Christian and non-Christian theistic communities) refers not, as in the above instance, to a power which stands outside of me, whose mere necessity is disclosed in its absence. It refers instead to a reality apprehended *in* its indirect presence in the experience of conscience itself—that mysterious(104) source, or 'whence' of the questioning power of conscience through whose call I am awakened to, enabled, and sustained in my personal being. Herein, I contend, resides the more fundamental and positive basis for talk of "God" (in the historic religious community) as "personal creator" and "preserver"(105). As with Adam in the second Genesis myth(106), who finds himself ever stalked by a 'verbal presence' calling, "Adam, Where art thou?", we too "in conscience" know ourselves as ultimately defined, or determined by a transcendent reality to whom we owe the possibility of being what and who we are to be(107).

We have clear indication, I believe, in these final constructive theses, as to how the phenomenon of conscience is to be understood in a positive sense as itself an ontological-experiential locus for understanding the term "God". A few additional words of clarification are needed, however, before concluding our investigation. In order to avoid any misunderstanding, I should stress that this prolegomenous interpretation of conscience does not of itself serve as a *direct* basis for God-language in a Christian doctrinal system. In keeping with the prolegomenous character of our study, which we set forth in Chapter I, we have attempted to show only (although most importantly) that outside the specific context of the historic community of faith we as human beings are not closed to, but rather are positively open to an understanding of an unconditioned or transcendent reality which may appropriately be termed "God". *That* as such we do necessarily call the reality experienced in conscience "God" is, of course, not a claim of our investigation. We recognize that amidst specific ontic contexts, and within varied linguistic horizons, we come to name or refer to this reality by a variety of terms. Having said this, however, we should be quick to press the point that *ontologically* speaking (and, hence in a *potentially* ontic-experiential sense), among these various terms, those which pass over or fail to recognize the unconditional or divine dimension of this phenomenon, as we have just delineated it in its two-fold character, must be judged as inadequate. Their inadequacy resides not in a certain myopia which could be corrected through the acquired spectacles of special revelation and faith, but rather in a non-attendance to the actual phenomenal facts of the matter! Disputes concerning the presence or absence of a transcendent or divine dimension in conscience are to be settled on philosophical-descriptive grounds, and it is upon these grounds, and these alone, that I have argued for the presence of such a dimension.

We now need only to clarify the implications of our investigation for the task of Christian theology *per se*. As Schleiermacher has taught us, systematic theology is a reflective enterprise which takes its rise not on neutral ground, but from within a specific historical community of faith with its array of symbols and terms for God and man/woman. As theologians our critical articulation of the meaning of the reality of God and man/woman emerges from, and speaks to, this positive symbolic realm. Nevertheless, we must stress the point (108), which was made earlier in this study, that the term "God" is not a specifically "Christian" term, despite the unique nuance and concrete specificity it receives in the context of this tradition. In criticism of Ebeling we have said that the notion "Word of God" (even that Word of God which addresses us in Jesus), far from presenting us *ab ovo* with the category of deity, actually presupposes a prior understanding of this reality. Although such a prolegomenous study as we have presented does not decide the issue of the *validity* of Christian language concerning God, it does attempt to specify and illuminate that ontological-experiential locus where such language *arises to start with*, and where historic Christian God-language (as, e.g., "savior" and "personal creator") can *fit meaningfully*(109). The difference between the position which I have taken here and that of Ebeling should be clear. Whereas Ebeling in the end understands the function of a theological prolegomenon as providing the mere point of encounter, as it were, between the Christian word-event and "secular" experience, I understand it to provide a logically prior, and necessary, hermeneutic grounding for Christian God-language explicated theologically. What the Christian is capable of experiencing and what he or she is capable of saying reflectively concerning "God" *depends* for its *meaningful* functioning upon a prior, hidden understanding of the category of the divine in our everyday being as conscience.

Notes

Notes to page 111:
1. See above, chapter I, p. 24.
2. See above, chapter II, pp. 44, 45. (Quoted from Ebeling, *WF*, p. 384.)

Notes to pages 111–113:
3. See above, chapter II, p. 43. (Quoted from Ebeling, *WF*, p. 279.)
4. See above, chapter II, pp. 40–41. (Quoted from Ebeling, *NF*, p. 161.)
5. See above, chapter II, p.43. (Quoted from Ebeling, *WF*, p. 349.)
6. *Ibid.*, pp. 248-53.
7. Cf. Ebeling's discussion, *ibid.*, p. 335.
8. *Ibid.*, p. 249. See also the analogy regarding legal hermeneutics, pp. 330f.
9. *Ibid.*, p. 338.
10. *Ibid.*, pp. 338-39 (emphasis is mine).
11. *Ibid.*, p. 338.
12. *Ibid.*, p. 335.
13. *Ibid.*, p. 336.
14. *Ibid.*, pp. 338f.
15. *Ibid.*, pp. 335-47. Cf., also, Ebeling's position in *NF*, pp. 81f., and in his *God and Word*, trans. James Leitch (Philadelphia: Fortress Press, 1967), pp. 33ff.
16. Ebeling, *TP*, p. 137, n. 2: "What I have in mind here is not in the first place mere changes in world-views (which is, regrettably, the point of view which governs most discussions of the situation in which we have to make ourselves understood) but in a fundamental sense *a change in our understanding of reality. What has changed is the sort of things which immediately strike us as self-evident, which impress us, which make a claim on us and bind us, which have authority, that is to say, the things we experience and the way we experience them, the things we will and the way we will them, the things for which we take responsibility and the way we take this responsibility*". (Emphasis is mine.)
17. Ebeling, *WF*, p. 334.
18. *Ibid.*, p. 250; see also, Ebeling, *Luther*, pp. 242ff.
19. Gerhard Ebeling, "The Hermeneutical Locus of the Doctrine of God in Peter Lombard and Thomas Aquinas", trans. David C. Steinmetz, *JThC*, 3 (1967):92.
20. *Ibid.*
21. *Ibid.*
22. Ebeling refers here to Ephesians 2.12 and to the early Christian apologists.
23. Ebeling, *WF*, p. 340 (emphasis is mine). See also, the discussion by Ebeling in "The Message of God to the Age of Atheism", *Graduate School of Theology Bulletin* (Oberlin College, Oberlin, Ohio), 9 (1964):11 and *passim*.
24. Ebeling, *WF*, p. 342.
25. *Ibid.*, pp. 342-43 (emphasis is mine). At this point in his essay Ebeling presents a brief sketch of this phenomenon of "godlessness", that

Notes to pages 114–119:
> thoroughgoing secularization of our modern self-understanding. Ebeling's analysis, incidentally, follows the general lines of interpretation which we ourselves sketched out in our first chapter in reference to Bultmann's essay, "The Idea of God and Modern Man". The reader may recall that Ebeling's more extended work was a principal source for Bultmann's analysis.)

26. *Ibid.*, pp. 340ff.
27. *Ibid.*, p. 340 (emphasis is mine).
28. *Ibid.*, p. 377.
29. *Ibid.*
30. *Ibid.* (emphasis is mine).
31. See, e.g., Alasdair MacIntyre's argument concerning the issue between belief and unbelief in his lecture published in *The Religious Significance of Atheism* (New York: Columbia University Press, 1966), pp. 1-55.
32. Ebeling *WF*, pp. 377-78 (emphasis is mine).
33. Cf. the same point in Ogden, *The Reality of God*, pp. 14ff.
34. Ebeling, *WF*, p. 379 (emphasis is mine).
35. Ebeling, *WF*, p. 113 (emphasis is mine); cf., also, Ebeling, *TP*, pp. 28-29 and Ebeling, *NF*, pp. 190-91.
36. See Ebeling, *WF*, p. 199.
37. Cf. Ebeling's essay, "Worldly Talk of God", *WF*, pp. 354-61. Cf. Martin Heidegger, *The Essence of Reasons*, trans. Terrence Malick (Evanston: Northwestern University Press, 1969), pp. 81-91.
38. *Ibid.*, p. 379.
39. In Heideggerian terminology, human/reality as "Care".
40. *Ibid.*, pp. 379-80 (emphasis is mine).
41. *Ibid.*, p. 380 (emphasis is mine).
42. *Ibid.*, p. 383.
43. *Ibid.*, p. 43.
44. See our discussion above in chapter I. Cf. Ebeling's analysis in *WF*, pp. 17-61, 363-73.
45. Ebeling, *WF*, p. 45.
46. *Ibid.*
47. *Ibid.*, p. 45.
48. *Ibid.*, p. 383 (emphasis is mine).
49. *Ibid.*
50. *Ibid.*, p. 47.
51. *Ibid.* Ebeling makes the further interesting observation: "And the most amazing thing about the history of theology in modern times is, that it was above all the theologians themselves who dauntlessly and inexorably employed the critical historical method and in the field of research into Old and New Testament, Church History and the History of Dogma

Notes to pages 119-120:
made way for startlingly new and unforsakable insights, yet—with few exceptions—did not feel that gave them reason to turn their backs on the business of theology proper" (pp. 47-48).
52. *Ibid.*, pp. 384f.
53. *Ibid.*, p. 366.
54. *Ibid.*
55. And, we could add, this includes all modern "secular" men as unconscious proponents.
56. For the special meaning of this term, see above, chapter I, p.3.
57. Ebeling, *WF*, pp. 366-67. See also Heidegger's earlier treatment of the same theme in his essay, "The Age of the World View",. trans. Marjorie Grene, *Measure*, 2(1951):269-284, and especially 276ff.
58. Ebeling, *WF*, p. 194.
59. *Ibid.*
60. See, for example, Ebeling's analysis, *ibid.*, pp. 343ff., 396f. This is expressed clearly by Ebeling in the more recent essay, "The Message of God to the Age of Atheism", p. 13: "We as Christians should not arrogantly accuse atheism of nihilism without realizing that Nietzsche accused Christianity itself of nihilism, that is, he accused it of negating all real values. And to that extent he was, in his way, interested in overcoming nihilism. We are likewise at cross-purposes with the serious atheistic thinkers if we do not realize how passionately they deal with such subjects as morality, responsibility, and the obligation to the conscience. Nietzsche, Sartre and Camus provide impressive substantiation for this. The question remains, however, where an atheistic ethics gets its orientation. *Yet we must avoid introducing God too quickly as a necessary postulate of the ethical.* Apart from other misgivings, we might be in danger of destroying the very understanding of God. It was precisely the ethical God whom Nietzsche declared to be dead. And the God of morality is only a variation of the metaphysical understanding of God because God is here considered likewise to be the first cause of the realm of morality". (Emphasis is mine.)

It should be clear in the above quote that in response to Nietzsche's challenge, as Ebeling understands it, the phenomenon of conscience must be understood and reinterpreted in more fundamental terms than its usual "ethical" sense. That Ebeling understands his own interpretation of the God-conscience relationship to be a definitive departure from the Kantian(-Ritschlian) tradition is unmistakably clear. But that this point is so easily overlooked, or misinterpreted, is due more than anything to Ebeling's failure to clarify fully the philosophical (ontological) grounding of his reinterpretation of conscience vis à vis the nineteenth century tradition. Without this clarification I believe Ebeling is in a weak posi-

Notes to page 120:
tion to respond to the kind of criticism made, for example, by Jürgen Moltmann in his book, *Theology of Hope*, trans. James W. Leitch (New York: Harper and Row, 1967), p. 273: "When G. Ebeling says that the radical questionableness 'seems to arise at a totally different point from where the usual so-called proofs of God placed it', then this alternative merely shows how strong the tendency is today to understand by the 'proofs of God' only the theoretic reason's cosmological proofs of God, and then to confine oneself to the proof of God from existence—an extended and deepened form of Kant's moral proof of God".

61. Cf., Ebeling, "The Message of God to the Age of Atheism", pp. 13-14: "The significance of the message of God for the question of morality is grasped correctly only when the question concerns itself with the subject of actions. This brings us to the decisive point of the encounter between the message of God and the message of atheism. We could say that *the definition of man is in dispute.* In the western philosophical tradition man has been defined as *animal rationale*, as rational being. The atheistic position in its sharpest manifestation did not replace this traditional definition with another one, but negates any definition of man as static and of an invariable nature. Nietzsche paradoxically defines man as 'the not-yet-determined animal'. What distinguishes man from the animal is precisely his indefinable being. And Sartre writes: 'Atheistic existentialism...declares that if God does not exist, then there is at least one being in whom existence precedes essence; i.e., one being which exists before it can be defined by any concept whatsoever...Man, as the existentialist understands him, cannot be defined, because he is nothing at all in the beginning. He will only become subsequently, and he will be as he will be as he will have created himself. Thus, there is no human nature; for there is no God who would design it. Man is only as he conceives himself to be...'. Thus man defines himself. In a critical resistance against traditional metaphysical thinking, these words, which may sound blasphemous, are notable for the radical seriousness with which they assert man as freedom, man's 'being condemned to freedom' as Sartre puts it. However, what does it mean that man's freedom is conceived here in a way which characterizes it as fundamentally passive? And, in a manner which is noteworthy, existence is thereby preceded by an opinion, a word". (Emphasis is mine.)

Unfortunately, with these last pregnant questions Ebeling moves (in the next and final paragraph) much too quickly to Luther's idea of man (freedom vis à vis the gospel) and faith! To what extent such a methodological move typifies Ebeling's constructive position, and, hence, brings him within range of the same kind of criticism we directed towards Bultmann will be discussed below.

Notes to pages 120–121:
62. Cf. Frederick A. Olafson, *Principles and Persons; An Ethical Interpretation of Existentialism* (Baltimore: The Johns Hopkins University Press, 1967), pp. 14, n. 14; 59ff. *passim*. Although cast as a study of the "ethical" dimensions of contemporary existential philosophy, Olafson's book is in reality an analysis of key ontological and epistemological themes running throughout this tradition as a whole—and an excellent analysis at that. Most illuminating is his sketch of the roots of (the early) Heidegger's, and Sartre's epistemological position in the "theological voluntarism" of Ockham and others (Chapter II), and in "philosophical voluntarism" from Kant to Nietzsche (Chapter III).
63. This terminological distinction does of course have its roots in Dilthey. For Ebeling, however, as for existentialist theologians who employ the same terminology (e.g., Bultmann, Gogarten, Buri, Fuchs, Marquarrie:) it is surely Heidegger's insights as developed in the all-important sections 31-32, 67-68, 72-77 of *Being and Time* which provide the background for this methodological-epistemological position. See Richard E. Palmer, *Hermeneutics; Interpretation Theory in Schleiermacher, Dilthey, Heidegger, and Gadamer* (Evanston: Northwestern University Press, 1969):, pp. 103-23, and especially 130-32. See also, Hans-Georg Gadamer, *Wahrheit und Methode*, 2nd ed. (Tübingen: J.C.B. Mohr [Paul Siebeck] 1960), pp. 245-90.
64. See, e.g., Heidegger, *BT*, pp. 122-34.
65. Edmund Husserl, *Cartesian Mediations*, trans. Dorian Cairns (The Hague: Martinus Nijhoff, 1960), pp. 152-53 (emphasis is mine). Cf. Heidegger, *BT*, p. 490, n. 10 (H. 50): "Edmund Husserl has not only enabled us to understand once more the meaning of any genuine philosophical empiricism; he has also given us the necessary tools. 'A-priorism' is the method of every scientific philosophy which understands itself. There is nothing constructivistic about it. But for this very reason a priori research requires that the phenomenal basis be properly prepared. *The horizon which is closest to us, and which must be made ready for the analytic of Dasein, lies in its average everydayness*". (Emphasis is mine.) Cf. Ebeling, *WF*, pp. 42-49.
66. For an excellent discussion of this distinction as developed in the work of the early Heidegger, Sartre, Merleau-Ponty, F. J. J. Buytendijk, and others, over against modern empirical psychology, see Joseph J. Kockelmans, *Edmund Husserl's Phenomenological Psychology, A Historical-Critical Study*, trans. Bernd Jager (Pittsburg: Duquesne University Press, 1967), pp. 332-51. Cf. Heidegger, *BT*, pp. 71-77.

In "The Message of God to the Age of Atheism", p. 14 (I have corrected the translation in conjunction with the original text in Gerhard Ebeling, *Word und Glaube II, Beiträge zur Fundamentaltheologie und*

Notes to page 121:
Zur Lelre von Gott (Tübingen: J. C. B. Mohn [Paul Siebeck], 1969, p. 394. Ebeling attempts to link a theological conception of man with that developed by such existentialists as Sartre and Camus by means of an interpretation of Luther(!): "We do not have to defend against an atheist like Sartre the traditional philosophical definition of man, furnished with a theological substructure. On the contrary, we have to remember that Luther, in his Disputation of Man...subjected this philosophical definition [i.e., man as *animal rationale*] to a radical critique and opposed to it a theological definition of man, but a definition the form of which is very curious. It defines man with respect to his history". What Ebeling does not mention in this particular essay is that such an "existential" interpretation of Luther's idea of human being has become a legitimate possibility today (as for Bultmann, Gogarten, and others before him) primarily because of the early hermeneutic position staked out by Heidegger. (As for Heidegger's own expressed indebtedness to Luther, cf., e.g., *BT*, p. 10; 492, n. 4 (H. 190)! As for the important 'influence' of the Augustinian-Lutheran tradition in general upon Heidegger's anthropological hermeneutic, see the important footnote, *BT*, p. 492, n. 7 (H. 199): "The way in which 'care' is viewed in the foregoing existential analytic of Dasein, is one which has grown upon the author in connection with his attempts to Interpret the Augustinian (i.e., Helleno-Christian) anthropology with regard to the foundational principles reached in the ontology of Aristotle".

67. Here we need only to affirm the position which Heidegger quite explicitly presents in *Being and Time*. In contrast to Ebeling, Heidegger is very clear on this point: "Understanding is the Being of potentiality-for-Being...As such understanding [Dasein] 'knows' what it is capable of— that is, what its potentiality-for-Being is capable of. This 'knowing' does not first arise from an immanent self-perception, but belongs to the Being of the "there"..." (pp. 184-85) (emphasis is mine). See also the important sections of *Being and Time* where Heidegger argues (vis à vis the traditional epistemological tradition) for the ontological priority— and fundamental epistemological significance—of *verstehen* as non-theoretical, existential "*knowing*": pp. 84-86 (Section 12), 86-90 (Section 13), 182-88 (Section 31), 214-17 (Section 36), 408-15 (Section 69, b.), and 415-23 (Section 69, c) through Section 71). A very cogent elaboration and defense of the position I would affirm here with Heidegger can be found in Richard Schmitt, *Martin Heidegger on Being Human*, pp. 119-48 and 149-80. See also Schmitt's argument in his essay, "Two Sense of Knowing", *The Review of Metaphysics*, 18 (1965):657-677.

68. On this point the problem, as I see it, becomes merely verbal as to

Notes to page 121:
whether the theologian assumes this task "qua theologian" (as Ebeling argues) or "qua philosopher".
69. Ebeling, *WF*, p. 199 (emphasis is mine). A close look at this statement indicates that the late Carl Michalson seriously misunderstood the nature of this undertaking proposed by Ebeling. I have in mind here the criticism cited by Michalson in his book, *The Rationality of Faith* (New York: Charles Scribner's Sons, 1963), p. 127: "Merleau-Ponty has outflanked the ontological being/non-being duality by giving priority to the thoroughly historical meaning/non-meaning (*sens et non-sens*) duality. Martin Werner, the Swiss church historian, is convinced that the issue facing the primitive church was precisely that between the being-question and the question of eschatological meaning. The question of being came to prevail in Christendom, through the influence of Greek philosophy, until the Protestant reformers restored the question of eschatological meaning to the center. The being-question has continued to over-shadow the historical question even in Protestantism, however, and Werner believes 'the Protestant way' for the future is to gain acceptance of its dominantly historical reading of primitive Christianity. In this context it is misleading for Gerhard Ebeling to say that because theology deals with 'all reality', it must undertake ontology. If the reality of the world man lives in is historical, there is no way of going deeper than this reality without slighting the world man lives in".

In a personal conversation Ebeling indicated to me that he was unaware of this criticism. He expressed surprise that Michalson had taken this programmatic statement in the way in which he did. To me, this only confirms the peculiarly vulnerable character of Ebeling's position when it is developed in tacit detachment from its real philosophical context. This is unfortunate, because Ebeling's position is (with Heidegger) potentially capable of overcoming the intolerable separation upon which Michalson insists between "nature" and "history". I might add parenthetically that Ronald Gregor Smith, in his posthumously published work, *The Doctrine of God*, ed. K. Gregor Smith and A. D. Galloway (Philadelphia: The Westminster Press, 1970), represents a position somewhere ambiguously between Ebeling and Michalson (see Chapters 3 and 4, but then compare what he has to say about the rethinking of "natural theology" in response to the "crisis about God" in Chapter 2).
70. See Ebeling's essay, "Erwägungen zu einer evangelischen Fundmentaltheologie", *ZThK*, 67 (1970):479-524. This essay comprises the guest lectures which Ebeling gave June 2-4, 1970 in Innsbruck in response to a special invitation by the faculty of the Institute for Dogmatic and Fundamental Theology, Leopold-Franzens University, in conjunction with a convocation commemorating the three hundredth anniversary of the

Notes to pages 121–123:
    founding of the university. Although informally Ebeling has expressed reservations about the possibility of carrying out such a far-reaching program at this stage in his career, indications are, both from this essay and from an experimental "Integrations-kursus" planned by Ebeling in the summer of 1971 at the University fo Zürich, he will at least begin to meet the challenge with the high level of competence that has characterized his previous work. Ebeling's book, *The Study of Theology*, trans. Duane A. Priebe (Philadelphia: Fortress Press, 1978), while disclaiming to be a "fundamental theology", nonetheless represents a worthy approach which suggestively "invite[s] the reader to further thought" (p. 160). See especially his discussion, pp. 153-65.

71. Olafson, *Principles and Persons*, p. 68.
72. See especially the three theses in the essay, *WF*, pp. 3476ff.: "1. The understanding of what the word 'God' means has its place within the sphere of radical questionableness". "2. The nature of the radical questionableness which affects man can be further defined as experience of passivity". "3. Knowledge of God is a linguistic event, in accordance with the wordliness of reality". (The "linguisticality" of reality and human being which comes to expression in the phenomenon of man as conscience is used synonymously by Ebeling with what he terms the "wordliness" (*Worthaftigkeit*) of reality, and man as "word-event" (*Wortgeschechen*).)
73. *Ibid.*, p. 347. Although there is food for thought in Jürgen Moltmann's observation that Ebeling's position here is for all effects a cosmological proof in the disguise of "an extended and deepened form of Kant's moral proof of God", I believe he is basically mistaken. See *Theology of Hope*, p. 273, and my remarks above, pp. 132–33, n. 60. Ebeling admits that one might think here of those cosmological proofs of God which develop the implications of the idea of questionableness in terms of the notion of radical "contingency" as exhibited in a comprehensive empirical (or, rather, metaphysical) description of experience and the structures of the natural order. But he asserts clearly that his particular concept of radical questionableness arises on different ground: not with the "question of the *primum movens* or such like" but with the questionableness which concerns "personal being as a whole". *WF*, p. 349.
74. *Ibid.*, p. 348 (emphasis is mine).
75. *Ibid.*
76. *Ibid.* See also Ebeling, *NF*, pp. 9-11, 75, 80-83.
77. As Ebeling understands it, this is a task reserved for the special sciences of man, although they are ultimately limited by the fact that their respective horizons do not permit this reality as a whole to come into view.

Notes to pages 123–124:
78. Ebeling here is in keeping with the distinctions Heidgegger makes in *BT*, pp. 31f., 358-64, *passim*. Heidegger, although stressing the descriptive priority of an "ontological" hermeneutic, nevertheless understands the relationships between the two types of description (ontological-existential and ontic-*existentiell*) non-sequentially and as involving mutual dependence. For Heidegger, "ontological" analysis ("Fundamental ontology" or "ontological-existential description") entails the recommendation of new concepts whose purpose it is to provide descriptive criteria for illuminating the fundamental structures of personal being made manifest in our pre-ontological (ontic/*existentiell*) understanding. It is true that these new concepts, along with their descriptive criteria, demand corroboration in an ontic/*existentiell* sense (e.g., in relation to one's own pre-ontological understanding). But, for Heidegger (and Ebeling), one does not need to await the explication of the latter in terms of some separate ontic (common sense or scientific) analysis before going on to develop new ontological-descriptive concepts. On the contrary, an ontic explication of everyday experience (attested in pre-ontological understanding in its various expressions) is not only presupposed by, but also unfolds (albeit in a limited fashion within the context of *Being and Time*) along with the descriptive development of the categories of existence in ontological-existential analysis. Richard Schmitt makes the same point we have attempted regarding Heidegger's notion of ontological-existential description in *Martin Heidegger on Being Human*, pp. 16-30.
79. See above, pp. 83ff.
80. See above, p. 83.
81. See especially Ebeling's disucssion *WF*, pp. 401ff. See also the important analysis of the *coram* structure of existence in Ebeling, *Luther*, pp. 193-201, and the relation of this structure to the phenomenon of conscience, pp. 201-04, 267.

In regard to our question it should be noted parenthetically that, although it might appear otherwise, a close look at Ebeling's constructive statements indicates that he eschews the implication that such questionableness entails some kind of religious a priori, or natural knowledge of God. The following conclusion is typical: "This is not a matter of some kind of natural knowledge of God in the sense of a positive consciousness of God. We could perhaps say it is a question of the condition on which it is possible for the problem of a natural knowledge of God to arise". And again: "It would be premature to designate that [radical questionableness] an inborn, original knowledge of God. It would likewise be premature to characterize it as the quest for God that is native to man as man, if indeed the quest for God already presupposes some kind of knowledge of what it seeks". Ebeling, *WF*, pp. 347-48.

Notes to page 124–125:
83. *Ibid.*
84. *Ibid.*, pp. 418-19.
85. *Ibid.*, p. 418.
86. I have amended James Leitch's translation here in *Word and Faith* where we find the peculiar rendering: "...but rather by *God's being [?] spoken to the conscience*". The passage in question is: "...vielmehr dadurch, dass *Gott dem Gewissen zugesprochen wird*" (*Wort und Glaube*, 3rd. ed. [Tübingen, J. C. B. Mohr (Paul Siebeck), 1967], p. 442). My translation avoids the confusion in Leitch's as to whether "being" functions as a gerund or a noun (as Leitch has it, the latter must be the meaning). Even with this correction it is nevertheless true that Ebeling's notion that "God is spoken to..." (or "God being spoken to...") the conscience is a difficult one as it stands. Here we have Ebeling's sharp distinction between the revelation of the being of God in the special "word-event" of Christian proclamation (the being of God presented directly in his historical "Word"), and the general word-event in man's self-understanding (e.g., as conscience) which has to do, strictly speaking, with the being of man. As Ebeling sees it, the being of God himself in relation to the world has come to expression in Jesus as the "witness of faith" (cf., Ebeling, *NF*, Chapters IV and V; Ebeling, *WF*, pp. 201ff., 288ff.), and through its historical destiny within the on-going "language tradition" of the community of faith (cf. Ebeling *NF*, Chapters XII and XIII; Ebeling, *WF*, pp. 162ff., 386ff.; Ebeling, *The Word of God and Tradition; The Problem of Historicity, in the Church and Its Proclamation*; his essays on Luther, Lombard, Aquinas, and Schleiermacher) it gets expressed (represented) concretely in the Christian proclamation today (cf., Ebeling, *NF*, Chapters IV-VIII; Ebeling, *WF*, pp. 305ff., and especially the studies on the distinction between the "doctrine of the two kingdoms", "law and gospel", and the "hidden and revealed God" in Ebeling, *WF*, pp. 247ff., 386, and in Ebeling, *Luther, passim.*)

To trace out Ebeling's full position as summarized in the above is not, of course, a necessary concern of this study. The difference, e.g., between our work and that of Peter Knauer, S.J., which seeks a systematic exposition and analysis of the major themes in Ebeling's thought, should be clear. Cf. his monograph, *Verantwortung des Glaubens (Ein Gesprach mit Gerhard Ebeling aus katholicher Sicht)* (Frankfurt am Main: Josef Knecht, 1969).
87. Ebeling, *WF*, p. 419.
88. *Ibid.*, p. 407.
89. *Ibid.* See the later statement in Gerhard Ebeling, *Introduction to a Theological Theory of Language*, trans. R. A. Wilson (Philadelphia: Fortress Press, 1973), pp. 47-48.

Notes to page 125-127:
90. In this, of course, Ebeling is also in methodological agreement with his mentor Bultmann. See, e.g., his statement in conjunction with Bultmann's position in Ebeling, *TP*, pp. 151-52, nn. 13, 15.
91. See Ebeling, *WF*, pp. 335-37. Cf., Ebeling's *NF*, pp. 81f.; *Theology and Proclamation*, pp. 84f.; *Introduction to a Theological Theory of Language*, pp. 45f. See especially Ebeling's discussion in *God and Word*, trans. James Leitch (Philadelphia: Fortress Press, 1967), p. 27, n. 4.
92. Ebeling, *WF*, pp. 199-200.
93. Although not unambiguously, Ebeling at times does not deny the possibility of an extended existential form of an *analogia entis* in principle. But, as with Bultmann before him, he denies the usefulness of such an extension; i.e., one grasps (for Ebeling) the reality of God here only negatively and indirectly, where as because God can only be truly grasped positively in the act of faith in encounter with Jesus and the Word, the latter is what is most worth talking about.
94. See Ebeling, *TP*, pp. 84f. and Ebeling, *God and Word*, pp. 42f.
95. Ebeling, *Luther*, p. 253.
96. See Ebeling, *God and Word*, pp. 16ff. and *Introduction to a Theological Theory of Language*, pp. 100ff.
97. Ebeling, *God and Word*, p. 31
98. See Ebeling, *God and Word*, pp. 40-42, 46f.; *Introduction to a Theological Theory of Language*, pp. 101f. See also his discussion in the essay, "Theology and the Evidentness of the Ethical", trans. James Leitch, *JThC*, 2 (1960):112f.
99. Ebeling, "Theology and the Evidentness of the Ethical", pp. 96-129. See also Ebeling, "The Hermeneutical Locus of the Doctrine of God", pp. 102-11 and "Existence between God and God: A Contribution to the Question of the Existence of God", trans. James P. Carse, *JThC*, 5 (1968): 130, 140f., 147-54.
100. Ebeling, "Theology and the Evidentness of the Ethical", p. 124 (emphasis is mine).
101. *Ibid.*, p. 125. Cf., the discussion of 'godlessness' in Ebeling's essay "Existence between God and God", p. 154, and in Chapter I of *God and Word*.
102. Ebeling has said (WF, p. 353) that "the personal being of God and the personal being of man...are not so to speak two separate things, but are to be grasped only in relation to each other". Having affirmed this, however, he is wrong to hold that our awareness of this living relationship is restricted to the interaction between hearer and kerygmatic word-event. Over against Ebeling I contend that *the being of God is already manifest in its most intimate relation to the being of man via that disclosive word-event of conscience, which stands prior to the kerygmatic*

Notes to page 128-129:

summons of faith. And let me also emphasize the fact that such a criticism of Ebeling is not made on a priori theological or epistemological grounds, but rather on the basis of what "appears" in and through a complete phenomenological description of conscience. (Regarding this last point, and as a definitive clarification of how I take Heidegger's [and Ebeling's] mode of "phenomenological description", see the very helpful discussion in Gilkey, *Naming the Whirlwind*, pp. 279-81, especially 280, n. 21.)

103. It is here and in the manner which follows that our study would want to relate to the work of Eberhard Jüngel in *God as the Mystery of the World*, pp. 15-42, and esp. 57-63. Such an anthropological possibility as this would have to 'precede' a description of God through the mystery of the Cross of Christ.

104. By "mysterious" here I do not mean simply 'that which is enigmatic'. On the distinction which we are making between genuine "mystery" and mere "puzzle", see e.g., Gabriel Marcel's discussion in his essay "The Ontological Mystery" in the *The Philosophy of Existentialism*, trans. Manya Harari (New York: The Citadel Press, 1968), pp. 9-46.

105. Note that "God" language related ontologically and experientially here entails an *historic* and *personal* conception of being as "created" and "preserved". This, I believe, provides the correct hermeneutic link to the normative biblical doctrine of God as Creator and Preserver which operates within the fundamental horizon of an historic ontology.

106. Genesis 2-3 is most genuinely grasped when its mythical expression is exhibited in its true hermeneutic grounding in the experience of reality in conscience as we have interpreted it.

107. Although standing outside the limits of our study, we should note in passing that perhaps the most important mode of "God" talk in Christian religious experience having a direct relationship to the experience of the divine in conscience is that of prayer. A comparative phenomenological treatment of the twin phenomena of "prayer" and "conscience" is an undertaking which could produce some very valuable, and surprising, results for our theological situation.

108. We scarcely need to add, of course, that this is a point which Schleiermacher also argued in his own manner and time.

109. That the phenomenon of conscience is a decisive locus for such talk is, of course, the fundamental assumption of this undertaking. I would not, however, want to leave the impression that conscience is the sole locus for God-language, given the obvious multi-dimensional character of man's/woman's being and the manifold richness of our experience. Hence, I have consistently described this study as a "*contribution to*" (a more fully developed) theological prolegomenon.

Bibliography

Works by Ebeling and Heidegger
(Listed chronologically according to original German publication.)

Ebeling, Gerhard. *Word and Faith*. Translated by James W. Leitch. Philadelphia: Fortress Press, 1963. (Ger. ed.: *Word und Glaube*. Tübingen: J.C.B. Mohr [Paul Siebeck], 1960.) Contains essays published between 1950 and 1959.

───────────. *The Problem of Historicity in the Church and Its Proclamation*. Translated by Grover Foley. Philadelphia: Fortress, 1967. (Ger. Ed.: *Die Geschichtlichkeit der Kirche und ihrer Verküdigung als theologisches Problem*. Tübingen: J.C.B. Mohr [Paul Siebeck], 1954.)

───────────. *The Nature of Faith*. Translated by Ronald Gregor Smith. Philadelphia: Fortress Press, 1961. (Ger. ed.: *Das Wesen des christlichen Glaubens*. Tübingen: J.C.B. Mohr [Paul Siebeck], 1959.)

───────────. "Theology and the Evidentness of the Ethical." Translated by James W. Leitch. *Journal for Theology and the Church*, 2 (1960):96-129.

───────────. "Hermeneutik." *Die Religion in Geschichte und Gegenwart*. 6 Vols. 3rd ed. Tübingen: J.C.B. Mohr (Paul Siebeck), 1962. 3:242-262.

───────────. "Luther: Theologie." *Die Religion in Gerschichte und Gegenwart*. 6 vols. 3rd ed. Tübingen: J.C.B. Mohr (Paul Siebeck), 1962. 4:495-520.

───────────. "Verantworten des Glaubens in Begegnung mit dem Denken M. Heideggers: Thesen zum Verhältnis von Philosophie und Theologie," *Zeitschrift für Theologie und Kirche*, 58 (1961), Supplement 2:119-124.

───────────. "The Chief Problems of Protestant Theology in the Present." Translated by Alice P. Carse. *Journal for Theology and the Church*, 3 (1967):152-164.

───────────. "The Ground of Christian Theology: On Ernst Käsemann's Essay, 'The Beginnings of Christian Theology.'" Translated by James W. Leitch. *Journal for Theology and the Church*, 6 (1969):47-68.

───────────. "Theologies: Begriffsgeschichtlich." *Religion in Geschichte und Gegenwart*. 6 vols. 3rd ed. Tübingen: J.C.B. Mohr (Paul Siebeck), 1962. 6:764-769.

───────────. "Theologie und Philosophie: Problemstrukturen; Historisch; Dogmatisch." *Religion in Geschichte und Gegenwart*. 6 vols. 3rd ed. Tübingen: J.C.B. Mohr (Paul Siebeck), 1962. 6:782-830.

───────────. "Tradition VII: Dogmatisch." *Religion in Geschichte und Gegenwart*. 6 vols. 3rd ed. Tübingen: J.C.B. Mohr (Paul Siebeck), 1962. 6:976-984.

───────────. *Theology and Proclamation; Dialogue with Rudolf Bultmann*. Translated by John Riches. Philadelphia: Fortress Press, 1966.

(Ger. ed.: *Theologie und Verkündigung; ein Gespräch mit Rudolf Bultmann.* Tübingen: J.C.B. Mohr [Paul Seibeck], 1962.)

_____. "The Message of God to the Age of Atheism." *Oberlin College Graduate School of Theology Bulletin*, Oberlin College, Oberlin, Ohio U.S.A., 9 (1964):3-14.

_____. *On Prayer; Nine Sermons.* Translated by James W. Leitch. Philadelphia: Fortress Press, 1966. (Ger. ed.: *Vom Gebet: Predigten über das Unser-Vater.* Tübingen: J.C.B. Mohr [Paul Siebeck]. 1963.)

_____. *Luther; An Introduction to His Thought.* Trans. by R.A. Wilson. Philadelphia: Fortress Press, 1970. (Ger. ed.: *Luther; Einführung in sein Denken.* Tübingen: J.C.B. Mohr [Paul Siebeck], 1964.)

_____. "The New Hermeneutic and the Early Luther." *Theology Today*, 21 (1964):34-46.

_____. *The Word of God and Tradition; Historical Studies Interpreting the Division of Christianity.* Translated by S. H. Hooke. Philadelphia: Fortress Press, 1968. (Ger. Ed.: *Wort Gottes und Tradition; Studien zu einer Hermeneutik der Konfessioner.* Göttingen: Vandenhöck und Ruprecht, 1964.)

_____. "The Hermeneutical Locus of the Doctrine of God in Peter Lombard and Thomas Aquinas." Translated by David C. Steinmetz. *Journal for Theology and the Church*, (1967):70-111.

_____. "Time and Word." Translated by John Macquarrie. *The Future of Our Religious Past; Essays in Honor of Rudolf Bultmann.* Edited by James M. Robinson. New York: Harper and Row, 1971, pp. 247-266.

_____. "Existence between God and God: A Contribution to the Question of the Existence of God." Translated by James P. Carse. *Journal for Theology and the Church*, 5 (1968):128-154.

_____. *God and Word.* Philadelphia: Fortress Press, 1967.

_____. "Schleiermacher's Doctrine of the Divine Attributes." Translated by James W. Leitch. *Journal for Theology and the Church*, 7 (1970):125-162.

_____. *Wort und Glaube II; Beiträge zur Fundamentaltheologie und zur Lehre von Gott.* Tübingen: J.C.B. Mohr (Paul Siebeck), 1969. Contains essays published between 1960 and 1966.

_____. "Erwägungen zu einer evangelischen Fundamentaltheologie." *Zeitschrift für Theologie und Kirche*, 67 (1970):479-524.

_____. *Introduction to a Theological Theory of Language.* Translated by R. A. Wilson. Philadelphia: Fortress Press, 1973. (Ger ed.: *Einführung in theologische Sprachlehre.* Tübingen: J.C.B. Mohr [Paul Siebeck], 1971.)

_____. *The Study of Theology.* Translated by Duane A. Priebe. Philadelphia: Fortress Press, 1978. (Ger. ed.: *Studium der Theologie: Eine enzyklopädische Orientierung.* Tübingen: J.C.Mohr [Paul Siebeck], 1975.)

Heidegger, Martin. *Being and Time*. Translated by John Macquarrie and Edward Robinson. New York: Harper and Row, 1962. (Ger. ed.: *Sein und Zeit*. 7th ed. Tübingen: Neomarius, 1953.)

_____. *Kant and the Problem of Metaphysics*. Translated by James S. Churchill. Bloomington: Indiana University Press, 1962. (Ger. ed.: *Kant und das Problem der Metaphysik*. Bonn: Friedrich Cohen, 1929.)

_____. *The Essence of Reasons*. Translated by Terrence Malick. (A bilingual edition, incorporating the German text of *Vom Wesen des Grundes*.) Evanston: Northwestern University Press, 1969. (Ger. ed.: *Vom Wesen des Grundes*. Frankfurt am Main: Vittorio Klostermann, 1919.)

_____. "What is Metaphysics?" Translated by Werner Brock. *Existence and Being*. Edited by Werner Brock. Chicago: Henry Regnery Co., 1949, pp. 325-361. (Ger. ed.: *Was ist Metaphysik?* Bonn: Friedrich Cohen, 1929.)

_____. "The Age of the World View." Translated by Marjorie Grene. *Measure*, 2 (1951):269-284. (Ger. ed.: *Holzwege*. Frankfurt am Main: Vittorio Klostermann, 1950, pp. 69-104.)

_____. "Nietzsches Wort 'Gott ist tot.'" *Holzwege*. Frankfurt am Main: Vittorio Klostermann, 1950, pp. 193-247.

_____. *An Introduction to Metaphysics*. Translated by Ralph Mannheim. Garden City, N.Y.: Doubleday, 1961. (Ger. ed.: *Einführung in die Metaphysik*. Tübingen: Max Niemeyer, 1953.)

_____. *What is Called Thinking?* Translated by Fred D. Wieck and J. Glenn Gray. New York: Harper and Row, 1968. (Ger. ed.: *Was heisst Denken?* Tübingen: Max Niemeyer, 1954.)

_____. *Identity and Difference*. Translated by Joan Stambaugh. New York: Harper and Row, 1969. (Ger. ed.: *Identität und Differenz*. Pfullingen: Günther Neske, 1957.)

_____. *Nietzsche*. 2 Vols. Pfullingen: Günther Neske, 1961.

_____. *Phänomenologie und Theologie*. Frankfurt am Main: Vittorio Klostermann, 1970.

Works on Conscience

D'Arcy, Eric. *Conscience and Its Right to Freedom*. London: Sheed and Ward, 1961.

Bremi, Willy. *Was ist das Gewissen?; seine Beschreibung, seine metaphysische und religiose Deutung, seine Geschichte*. Zürich: Art Institute Orell Fussli, 1934.

Davies, W. D. "Conscience." *The Interpreters Dictionary of the Bible*. 4 Vols. New York: Abingdon Press, 1962. 1:671-676.

Jacob, Günther. *Der Gewissensbegriff in der Theologie Luthers*. Beiträge für historischen Theologie, No. 4. Tübingen: J.C.B. Mohr (Paul Seibeck), 1929.

Kähler, Martin. *Das Gewissen; die Entwickelung seiner Ramen und seines*

Begriffes, (Geschichtliche Untersuchung zur Lehre von der Begrundung der sittlichen Erkenntniss). Halle: Julius Frike, 1878.

Kierkegaard, Søren. *The Concept of Dread*. Translated by Walter Lowrie. Princeton: Princeton University Press, 1944.

Lehmann, Paul. *Ethics in a Christian Context*. New York: Harper and Row, 1963.

Maurer, Christian. "*sunoida*," "*suneidēsis*." *Theological Dictionary of the New Testament*. Edited by G. Kittel and B. Friedrich. Translated by G. W. Bromily. 9 vols. Grand Rapids: William B. Eerdmans, 1964-74. 7:898-919.

Engelberg, Edward. *The Unknown Distance; From Consciousness to Conscience, Goethe to Camus*. Cambridge, Mass.: Harvard University Press, 1972.

Scheler, Max. *Formalism in Ethics and Non-Formal Ethics of Values*. Translated by Manfred S. Frings and Roger L. Funk. Evanston: Northwestern University Press, 1973. (Ger. ed.: *Der Formalismus in der Ethik und die materiale Wertethik*. Jahrbuch für Philosophie und phänomenologische Forschung. Vol. 2. Edited by Edmund Husserl. Tübingen: Max Niemeyer, 1916.)

Stoker, H. G. *Das Gewissen; Erscheinungsformen und Theorien*. Schriften zur Philosophie und Soziologie. Vol. 2. Edited by Max Scheler. Bonn: Friedrich Cohen, 1925.

Wolf, E. "Gewissen." *Die Religion in Geschichte und Gegenwart*. 3rd ed. 6 vols. Tübingen: J.C.B. Mohr (Paul Siebeck), 1962. 3:1550-1557.

Other Works

Altizer, Thomas J. J. and Hamilton, William. *Radical Theology and the Death of God*. Indianapolis: The Bobbs- Merrill Co., 1966.

Baelz, Peter R. *Christian Theology and Metaphysics*. Philadelphia: Fortress Press, 1968.

Baillie, John. *Our Knowledge of God*. New York: Charles Scribner's Sons, 1939.

_____. *The Roots of Religion in the Human Soul*. London: Hodder and Stoughton, 1926.

_____. *The Sense of the Presence of God*. New York: Charles Scribner's Sons, 1962.

Ballard, Edward G. and Scott, Charles E., eds. *Martin Heidegger: In Europe and America*. The Hague: Martinus Nijhoff, 1973.

Barth, Karl and Brunner, Emil. *Natural Theology*. Comprising "Nature and Grace" by Emil Brunner, and "No!" by Karl Barth. Translated by John Baillie. London: Geoffrey Bles (The Centenary Press), 1946.

Baumer, Franklin L. *Religion and the Rise of Scepticism*. New York: Harcourt, Brace and Co., 1960.

Brown, James. *Subject and Object in Modern Theology*. New York: The Macmillan Co., 1955.

Brunner, Emil. *The Divine Imperative.* Translated by Olive Wyon. Philadelphia: The Westminster Press, 1947.

_____. *Man in Revolt; A Christian Anthropology.* Translated by Olive Wyon. New York: Charles Scribner's Sons, 1939.

Bultmann, Rudolf. *Faith and Understanding, I.* Translated by Louise Pettibone Smith. Edited by Robert W. Funk. New York: Harper and Row, 1969. (Ger. ed.: *Glauben und Verstehen, I*, 4th ed. Tübingen: J.C.B. Mohr [Paul Siebeck] 1964.)

_____. "The Idea of God and Modern Man." Translated by Robert W. Funk. *Journal for Theology and the Church*, 2 (1965):83-95.

_____. *Jesus Christ and Mythology.* New York: Charles Scribner's Sons, 1958.

_____. *Jesus and the Word.* Translated by Louise Pettibone Smith and E. H. Lantero. New York: Charles Scribner's Sons, 1958.

_____. "New Testament and Mythology." Translated by Reginald H. Fuller. *Kerygma and Myth, I.* Edited by Hans Werner Bartsch. London: S.P.C.K., 1965, pp. 1-44.

_____. "The Problem of Hermeneutics." Translated by James C. G. Greig. *Essays, Philosophical and Theological.* New York: The Macmillan Co., 1955, pp. 234-261.

_____. "On the Question of a Philosophical Theology." Translated by Orus C. Barker, Jr. *Union Seminary Quarterly Review*, 20 (1965):261-263.

_____. *Theology of the New Testament.* 2 Vols. Translated by Kendrick Grobel. New York: Charles Scribner's Sons, 1951.

Cavell, Stanley. *Must We Mean What We Say?* New York: Charles Scribner's Sons, 1969.

Christian, C. W. and Wittig, Glenn R., eds. *Radical Theology: Phase Two; Essays on the Current Debate.* Philadelphia: H. B. Lippincott Co. 1967.

Cox, Harvey. *Religion in the Secular City.* New York: Simon and Schuster, 1984.

Fackenheim, Emil L. *Metaphysics and Historicity.* Milwaukee: Marquette University Press, 1961.

Frank, Erich. *Philosophical Understanding and Religious Truth.* New York: Oxford University Press, 1966.

Feick, Hildegard. *Index zu Heideggers "Sein und Zeit".* Tübingen: Max Niemeyer, 1961.

Funk, Robert W. *Language, Hermeneutic and Word of God.* New York: Harper and Row, 1966.

Gadamer, Hans-Georg. *Philosophical Apprenticeships.* Translated by Robert R. Sullivan. Cambridge, Massachusetts: MIT Press, 1985.

_____. *Wahrheit und Methode.* 2nd. ed. Tübingen: J.C.B.

Mohr (Paul Siebeck), 1960.

Gelven, Michael. *A Commentary on Heidegger's "Being and Time"*. New York: Harper and Row, 1970.

Gendlin, Eugene. *Experiencing and the Creation of Meaning; A Philosophical and Psychological Approach to the Subjective*. New York: The Free Press of Glencoe, 1962.

Gilkey, Langdon. "Dissolution and Reconstruction in Theology." *The Christian Century*, 82 (1965):136-137.

_____. "The God is Dead Theology and the Possibility of God Language." Mimeographed. Chicago: The Divinity School of the University of Chicago, 1964.

_____. *Maker of Heaven and Earth; The Christian Doctrine of Creation in the Light of Modern Knowledge*. Garden City, N.Y.: Doubleday and Co., 1959.

_____. *Naming the Whirlwind: The Renewal of God-Language*. Indianapolis: Bobbs-Merrill, 1969.

Gogarten, Friedrich. *Verhängnis und Hoffnung der Neuzeit*. Stuttgart: Friedrich Vorwserk, 1953.

Harvey, Van A. *A Handbook of Theological Terms*. New York: The Macmillan Co., 1964.

Hefner, Philip. *Faith and the Vitalities of History*. New York: Harper and Row, 1966.

Herzog, Frederick. *Understanding God: The Key Issue in Present-Day Protestant Thought*. New York: Charles Scribner's Son, 1966.

Husserl, Edmund. *Cartesian Mediations*. Translated by Dorion Cairns. The Hague: Martinus Nijhoff, 1960.

Jonas, Hans. *The Phenomenon of Life; Toward a Philosophical Biology*. New York: Harper and Row, 1966.

Jüngel, Eberhard. *God as the Mystery of the World*. Translated by Darrell L. Guder. Grand Rapids, Michigan: William B. Eerdmans Publishing Company, 1983.

Kaufman, Gordon D. "The Meaning of 'God'; Transcendence Without Mythology." *New Theology No. 4*. Edited by Martin Marty and Dean G. Peerman. New York: The Macmillan Co., 1967, pp. 69-98.

_____. *God the Problem*. Cambridge, Mass.: Harvard University Press, 1972.

_____. *The Theological Imagination; Constructing the Concept of God*. Philadelphia: The Westminster Press, 1981.

Knauer, Peter. *Verantwortung des Glaubens (Ein Gesprach mit Gerhard Ebeling aus katholicher Sicht)*. Frankfurt am Main: Josef Knecht, 1969.

Kockelmans, Joseph J. *Edmund Husserl's Phenomenological Psychology, A Historical-Critical Study*. Translated by Bernd Jager. Pittsburgh: Duquesne University Press, 1967.

Küng, Hans. *Does God Exist?* Translated by Edward Quinn. New York: Random House (Vintage Books), 1981.
Løgstrup, Knud E. *The Ethical Demand.* Translated by Theodor I. Jensen. Philadelphia: Fortress Press, 1971.
Macquarrie, John. *An Existentialist Theology.* London: SCM Press, 1955.
_____. *God-Talk; An Examination of the Language and Logic of Theology.* New York: Harper and Row, 1967.
_____. *Studies in Christian Existentialism.* Philadelphia: The Westminster Press, 1965.
_____. *Three Issues in Ethics.* New York: Harper and Row, 1970.
Marcel, Gabriel. *The Philosophy of Existentialism.* Translated by Manya Harari. New York: The Citadel Press, 1968.
Marx, Werner. *Reason and World; Between Tradition and Another Beginning.* Translated by Thomas V. Yates and R. Geuss. The Hague: Martinus Nijhoff, 1971.
Mehta, J. L. *The Philosphy of Martin Heidegger.* Rev. ed. New York: Harper and Row, 1971.
Metz, Johannes B., ed. *Moral Evil Under Challenge.* New York: Herder and Herder, 1970.
Michalson, Carl. *The Rationality of Faith.* New York: Charles Scribner's Sons, 1963.
Moltmann, Jürgen. *Theology of Hope.* Translated by James W. Leitch. New York: Harper and How, 1967.
Mount, Eric, Jr. *Conscience and Responsibility.* Richmond, Virginia: John Knox Press, 1969.
Nabert, Jean. *Le Desir de Dieu.* Preface by Paul Ricoeur. Paris: Aubier-Montaigne, 1966.
_____. *Elements for an Ethic.* Translated by William J. Petrek. Evanston: Northwestern University Press, 1969.
Ogden, Schubert M. *Christ Without Myth.* New York: Harper and Row, 1961.
_____. "Introduction." *Existence and Faith: Shorter Writings of Rudolf Bultmann.* Edited and translated by Schubert M. Ogden. Cleveland: Meridian Books, 1963, pp. 7-21.
_____. "The Possibility and Task of Philosophical Theology." *Union Seminary Quarterly Review,* 20 (1965):271-279.
_____. *The Reality of God and Other Essays.* New York: Harper and Row, 1966.
_____. "The Significance of Rudolf Bultmann for Contemporary Theology," *The Theology of Rudolf Bultmann.* Edited by Charles W. Kegley. New York: Harper and Row, 1966, pp. 104-126.
Olafson, Frederick A. *Principles and Persons; An Ethical Interpretation of*

Existentialism. Baltimore: The John Hopkins Press, 1967.
Ott, Heinrich. *Denken und Sein; Der Weg Martin Heideggers und der Weg der Theologie*. Zollikon, Switzerland: Evangelischer Verlag, 1959.
_____. *Reality and Faith; The Theological Legacy of Dietrich Bonhoeffer*. Translated by Alex A. Morrison. Philadelphia: Fortress Press, 1972.
Palmer, Richard E. *Hermeneutics; Interpretation Theory in Schleiermacher, Dilthey, Heidegger, and Gadamer*. Evanston: Northwestern University Press, 1969.
Pöggeler, Otto. *Der Denkweg Martin Heideggers*. Pfüllingen: Gunther Neske, 1963.
Rahner, Karl. *The Church After the Council*. New York: Herder and Herder, 1966.
_____. "Theology and Anthropology." *The Word in History*. Edited by T. Patrick Burke. New York: Herder and Herder, 1966.
_____. *Hearers of the Word*. Translated by Michael Richards. Montreal: Palm Publishers, 1969. (Ger. ed.: *Hörer des Wortes*. Munich: Kösel-Verlag, 1963.)
_____. *Theological Investigations*, Volume XIII. Translated by David Bourke. New York: Crossroad, 1983.
Richardson, William J. *Heidegger; Through Phenomenology to Thought*. 2nd ed. The Hague: Martinus Nijhoff, 1967.
Ricoeur, Paul. *The Conflict of Interpretations; Essays in Hermeneutics*. Translated by Kathleen McLaughlin *et al*. Edited by Don Ihde. Evanston: Northwestern University Press, 1974. (Fr. ed.: *Le Conflit des Interpretations; Essais d'Hermeneutique*. Paris: Editions du Seuil, 1969.)
_____. *Essays on Biblical Interpretation*. Edited by Lewis S. Mudge. Philadelphia: Fortress Press, 1980.
_____. *Freud and Philosophy: An Essay on Interpretation*. Translated by Denis Savage. New Haven: Yale University Press, 1970. (Fr. ed.: *De L'Interpretation; Essai sur Freud*. Paris: Editions du Seuil, 1965.)
_____. "Religion, Atheism, and Faith." *The Religious Significance of Atheism*. New York: Columbia University Press, 1966, pp. 59-98.
_____. *The Symbolism of Evil*. Translated by Emerson Buchanan. New York: Harper and Row, 1967.
_____. "The Task of Hermeneutics." Translated by David Pellauer. *Philosophy Today*, 17 (1973):321-331.
Robinson, James M. and Cobb, John B. Jr., eds. *New Frontiers in Theology I: The Later Heidegger and Theology*. New York: Harper and Row, 1963.
_____. *New Frontiers in Theology II: The New Hermeneutic*. New York: Harper and Row, 1964.
Schmithals, Walter. *An Introduction to the Theology of Rudolf Bultmann*. Translated by John Bowden. Minneapolis: Augsburg Publishing House, 1967.
Schmitt, Richard. *Martin Heidegger on Being Human; An Introduction to*

"Sein und Zeit". New York: Random House, 1969.

―――――――――. "Two Senses of Knowing." *The Review of Metaphysics*, 18 (1965):657-677.

Shook, L. K., ed. *Renewal of Religious Thought*. Theology of Renewal Series, Vol. 1. Montreal: Palm Publishers, 1968.

Smith, Ronald Gregor. *The Doctrine of God*. Edited by K. Gregor Smith and A. D. Galloway. Philadelphia: The Westminster Press, 1970.

Spiegelberg, Herbert. *The Phenomenological Movement*. 2 Vols. 2nd. ed. The Hague: Martinus Nijhoff, 1965.

Thevenaz, Pierre. *What is Phenomenology? And Other Essays*. Edited and translated by James E. Edie, *et al*. Chicago: Quadrangle Books, 1962.

Toulmin, Stephen. *An Examination of the Place of Reason in Ethics*. Cambridge: Cambridge University Press, 1950.

Vahanian, Gabriel. *The Death of God; The Culture of Our Post-Christian Era*. New York: George Braziller, 1961.

West, Charles C., ed. *Consultation for University Teachers Report on "The Meaning of the Secular"*. Bossey: Ecumenical Institute, 1959.

Zaner, Richard M. *The Way of Phenomenology*. New York: Pegasus, 1970.

Index of Subjects

Alarm (*Erschrecken*) 66
Analogy, analogies 17, 20, 125, 140 n.93
Angst 66f.
  in Kierkegaard and Heidegger 78 n.10
Anthropology, anthropological ix, 1, 10, 16, 21, 24f., 40, 49, 56
  anthropological foundations 16
  anthropological hermeneutic 50
  anthropological ontology 21, 56
  Christian anthropology 14, 36 n.106
  philosophical anthropology ix, 2, 17, 21ff., 24, 49, 57 n.1, 108 n.101
  theological anthropology 1, 2, 11f., 15, 40, 49, 111
Anxiety (see *Angst*)
Assertion (*Aussage*) 89–91
Atheism 7ff., 9, 12, 14, 98, 113, 132 n.60, 133 n.61
Atheistic ethics 132 n.60
Aufklärung 27 n.11,
Authentic 6,
  authentic versus inauthentic existence 102 n.104
  authentic worldliness
Authority 130 n.16
Autonomy 4–6, 29 n.26, 30 n.28
Autonomous standpoint of reason 4, 5

Befindlichkeit (state-of-mind) 90, 91
Being
  Being-towards-death ix, 69f., 84f., 101–02 nn.43, and 46
  Being-guilty (*Schuldigsein*) 70ff., 84
  Being-a-basis 96f.
  Being-the-basis of a nullity 96
  Being the ground of Dasein's thrown possibilities 96f.
  Being in the world as a whole 120–122
  Care-Being 65ff.
  everyday being 10, 16, 67, 111, 121, 129
  potentiality-for-Being (*Seinkönnen*) 92, 96
"Before God" (see *Coram Deo*)
"Before himself" (see *Coram seipso*)
"Before the world" (see *Coram mundi*)
Bible 2, 8 n.11, 18, 29 n.18
Biblical faith 4, 8f.

Bultmann's influence on Heidegger's thought 52–53, 60 n.61, 62 n.63

Care (*Sorge*) 65, 84, 91, 131 n.39
Christian, Christianity 1, 4f., 16
  Christian faith 8, 13f., 97
  Christian talk about God 4, 113, 127ff.
  Christian theology 97f.
Christology, christological ix, xiii, 14, 15, 32 n. 71, 41
Church 1, 11–13, 15
Communication (*Mitteilung*) 88, 90–93
Community of faith xiii, 97
Concept 49, 60–61 n.55, 93f., 104–05 n.63, 111 (formation of concepts), 121
Conceptualization of God 16, 111ff., 125ff.
Conscience
  authentic "judgement" of conscience 73f.
  as an authoritative "court of justice" 82
  "bad" conscience (see "Good" and "bad" conscience)
  in Baillie's thought 37 n. 115
  in Barth's thought 37 n. 120
  in Bremi's thought 53
  brings man to "truth" 83f.
  brings into view the "wholeness" of man's Being-in-the-world 87–88
  in Brunner's thought 53–55,
  in Bultmann's thought 38 n.117, 50–51
  call of conscience 66–69, 78 nn.14, and 21, 88, 103 n.53
  call to "Dasein's original, ownmost potentiality-for-Being" 67ff., 78 n.21
  calling back by calling forth 86ff., 101 n.43
  as "a codex of general truths and commands" 45, 88
  as "the coming to expression of man himself" 45, 82
  the "condition" for understanding the meaning of the word "God" 46
  as "the connexion between man, the world and God" 81
  conscience (*Gewissen*) and certainty (*Gewissheit*) 83f.
  context of conscience 66ff., 69, 96f.

Conscience *(continued)*
  and death 41
  "decline" and "fall" of conscience 28, 36 n.109
  defines man/woman 81, 86f., 101 n.43
  as disclosure of non-mastery xi
  discourses in the mode of "keeping silent" 67, 78 n.14, 88, 94
  as "dissociation" in human nature itself 45
  in Ebeling's thought chapters II and IV, 48–50, 56f., 101–02 n.43
  as experience of identity and non-identity 83
  as an experiential locus for the understanding of "God" x, 23f., chapter V
  existential interpretation of conscience 55, chapters III and IV
  as a faculty or organ 45, 67
  and faith 40, 41
  and freedom 87
  in Freud's thought 37 n.111, 67
  as a general mode of self-disclosure 66
  in Gogarten's thought 38 n.118
  "good" and "bad" conscience 83ff., 101 n.28
  in Heidegger's thought 48–53, 83ff., 86–88, 101–102 n.43, chapter III
  in Heim's thought 38 n.115
  as "the hermeneutic principle" 43
  in Hirsch's thought 55
  historical demise of conscience 24
  history of the idea of conscience 36 n.108, 37 nn.108, and 109
  in Holl's interpretation of Luther 56
  "as the inmost being" 43
  in Jacob's thought 55f.
  as "joint-cognizance" xi, 52, 82
  in Kähler's thought 52f.
  in Kant's thought 37 n.109, 42, 82f.
  in Kierkegaard's thought 52
  as "the law written in the heart" 42, 88, 103 nn.53, and 54
  in Lehmann's thought 42 nn.107–09
  in Luther's thought 61 n.59, 103–04 n.54
  makes no speeches 88
  as "man himself in radical questionableness" 59 n.33
  " a mathematical point where everything meets" 41, 43
  as "a mathematical point between the *regnum Christi* and *regnum mundi*" 44
  misconceptions of conscience 45f., 67,
  as a moral law written in the heart 42f., 54, 88, 103 n.54
  as "the mystery of the world" 30 n.37
  as a primordial "*existentiale*" 66
  as a prismal plane in Ebeling's systematic thought 42, 81, chapter IV
  as a linguistic phenomenon 67ff.
  in Luther and Kierkegaard 52, 54–55
  Luther's view of conscience 46, 103 n.54
  as "that mathematical point where everything meets" 41, 43
  misconceptions of conscience 67f., 100, 111f.
  as a moral law written in the heart 42f., 54, 88, 103 n.54
  as the "mystery of the world" 30 n.37
  as not "an external authority over against man" 45, 82f.
  as not the voice of God 54, 67
  "this one point at which everything stands or falls together" 43
  ontological description of conscience 54, 57 n.1
  as ontological grounding for understanding "God" x, 23, 81f., 111f.
  Paul's view of conscience 42, 51, 103 n.54
  as the "place of man" 44
  as the place where it is decided what man truly is 44, 111
  as the place where God and the world meet 6, 43
  as the place where we experience what "God" means xvii, 43, 81, 111, 127ff.
  as "the plight of being in between" 41
  "the point at which everything stands or falls together" 43

in popular parlance 44
as "the question mark branded upon man: 'where art thou?'" 42, 88, 103–04 n.54
and "the radical questionableness of reality" 43, 85 (see Radical questionableness)
and reality 42f.(see Reality)
and the Reformers' doctrine of the law 42, 103 n.54
relating morality and faith 81
and responsibility 85, 87, 101 n.43
in Ricoeur's thought 106 n.86
in Scheler's thought 83, 100 n.21
as self-identity 85f.
in Söderblom's thought 37 n.112
as "the sphere of the world and of time" 40
in Stoker's thought 37 n.109, 53
as a summons 67f., 84.
as a "summons to Dasein's ownmost potentiality-for-Being-itself" 82–84
"summons to the interpretation of reality" 42
as a summons of guilt 70f., 85f.
as superego 67
as the supreme "*principium individuationis*" 87, 102 n.43
temporal aspect of conscience 41, 66f. 69, 84f., 104 n.58
in Thomas Aquinas' thought 37 n.109
in Tillich's thought 38 n.116
as the true hermeneutical situation of theology 41
as the truth of "who" and "where" man/woman is 42, 66f., 69, 84f., 104 n.43
and understanding reality as a whole 43
the "verbal placelessness of God" 30 n.37
voice of conscience (*Stimme des Gewissens*) 51, 66ff.
as the voice of God 37 n.110, 45
as "where it is decided what man truly is" 44, 81
as "where time is received as time" 40, 81
as "where the world is encountered as world" 40–41, 81, 111
as "where we experience what 'God' means" 42f., 81, 111
as word-event 87, 89
conscientia 45, 52, 62 n.72
in conscientia and *coram Deo* 124
Consciousness 9
Communication 14, 90–93
coram ("before")
  coram Deo ("before God") x–xi, 4, 6, 108 n.96, 124, 126–28, 138 n.81
  coram mundi ("before the world") 124, 127
  coram seipso ("before himself") x–xi, 124, 127f.
Cross of Christ 141 n.103
Culture, cultural 1, 112
  contemporary culture 1, 2, 113
  Western culture xiii, 106–07 n.91

Dasein (definition: 77 n.1)
  as always a possibility and never a mere object 67f.
  as Care-Being 65ff.
  Dasein's essential being as "possibility" 67
  as "fallen" 66
  as "potentiality-for-Being" 67
Death 13, 20, 69f., 101–02 n.43
De-divinization 4, 5
Debt, indebtedness 71ff.
Demythologizing 2, 19, 28 n.13
Deus absconditus ("absent God") 126
Dialectical balance 4
Dialogue 24
Di-polar theism 17
Discourse (also, see *Rede*) xiv, 92f.
Discursive principle of intelligibility 94f.
Distanz (Dissociation) 83, 123
Divine 1, 4, 14, 20, 27
Dread (*Grauen*) 66, 69f.

Ecclesiology xiii, 15
Enlightenment 4
Entwerfen (Projecting) 90f.
Eschatology, eschatological 9
Existence
  as fundamentally word-event 138

156 *Index*

Existence (*continued*)
  between "God" and "world" (see also *coram*) 123
Existentialist interpretation 49ff., 66ff., 103 n.54, 105 n.72
Existential rendering of theological concepts 49f., 105 n.72
Existential (or ontological) possibilities and *existentiell* (or ontic) possibilities 17, 27f., 33 n.75, 52, 66f.
Existential understanding 17, 22f., 33 n.75, 92
Existentiell understanding 17, 22f., 33 n.75, 71f., 73–75, 79 n.29, 92
Existenzialen (existentials or structures of being) 82, 90f.
Experience, experiential 9, 11–13, 16, 21, 23f., 25, 36 n.105, 93f., 120
  everyday experience 13f., 18, 24, 120f., 134 n.65, 123,
  experience given to man as conscience x, 23, 81f., 111f.
  experience what "God" means ixff., 123f.
  experiential locus ix, 124–29
  felt experience 93
  religious experience 17–20, 34 n.87
Explanation versus understanding 67

Facticity (*Faktizatät*) 71f., 91f.
Faith 1, 4, 16, 21, 29 n.18, 31 n.42, 36 n.106, 51, 97, 99, 109–10 n.108, 114, 118, 120, 125f., 129
  and unbelief 43, 109 n.108, 107 n.91
  and understanding 119
Fallenness 73–77
Fear (*Furcht*) 66
Feeling and meaning 93f.
Finitude 9, 20, 36 n.105
Fleeing 87f.
Forgiveness 51
Forms of life 93f.
Freedom 4, 6, 51f., 70, 87, 96, 133 n.61

German Idealism 24
Gewissen (Conscience) ixff, 62 n.72, 83, 101 n.22, 110 n.110
"*Gewissensreligion*" 56

God
  as absent reality (see *Deus absconditus*) 15, 126f.
  assertions about God 18
  being of God and being of man 140 n.102
  concepts of God 2, 17–25, 99, 108 n.101, 109 n.107
  as Creator xiv, 99, 128f.
  "death" of God 2–12, 29 n.25
  as *deus absconditus* 45, 126f.
  as direct object of thought 125
  as *ens perfectissimum* 120
  existence of God 22f.
  experience of God 2, 3–11, 13–17, 20, 32 n.53, 123–29
  experienced as a "question" 123
  God-language 125ff.
  "God" not a specifically "Christian" term xvii, 98, 112f., 129
  as ground of our personal being 23f., 127f.
  holy God 7
  idea of God 2, 16, 22f.
  image of God 2–12, 29 n.18, 36 n.105
  as "interjection" or a "'catcall' of existence" 41, 126
  idea of God in Heidegger's philosophy 99
  as Judge xiv, 127
  language about God 13, 15, 76, 123–29
  as limiting judge and savior 127f.
  as linguistic event 137 n.72
  meaning of "God" ix, xiii, 9, 13ff., 17–27, 31 n.42, 41, 122, 129
  meaning of "God" in Jesus' last outcry 41
  as object of philosophical analysis 17–25, 98f., 109 n.107, 125
  as personal creator and preserver 127–29, 141 n.105
  as "phenomenon" 46
  problem of God xiv, 1–12, 18–27, 35 n.104
  "proofs" for existence of God 133 n.60, 137 n.73
  question of God 7–12, 15, 22f., 27, 51

as a reality apprehended in its indirect presence 127f.
reality deemed "God" 10, 23f., 27, 111
reality experienced in conscience 128f., chapter V
reality of God 4, 16–25, 111, 122,
as savior 127f.
spoken to the conscience 124, 138–39 n.86
term (word) "God" xiii, xvii, 5, 12–15, 23ff., 124, 127f., 137 n.72
as Thou 52
transcendent God 6, 12, 14, 128
understanding of "God" 24, 41, 76, 86, 123, 129
'unsaid God' 12
voice of God 51
Word of God 129
God-language 19–27, 126ff.
the logic of God-language 23ff, 127ff.
the validity of God-language 127ff.
Godlessness 12, 31 n.42, 98, 130–31 n.25, 126, 140 n.101
Good (and evil) 51
Good conscience (see Conscience)
Gospel xi, 1, 18, 107 n.91, 133 n.61
Grace 12
Guilt, guilty 70–74, (see also Being-guilty)
ontological guilt 86
in relation to responsibility 70

Heart xi, 51, 88
Hearing (*Hören*) 75, 94f., 106 n.86
hearing as understanding 75
Hearkening (*Horchen*) 106 n.86
Heidegger
importance of the early Heidegger (*Being and Time*) 50ff., 57–58 n.1,
influence on Bremi's study 53
influence on Bultmann's thought 50–53, 61 n.61, 62 n.63
influence on Ebeling's thought 48–57, 64 n.101, 88, 106–07 n.91, 121f.
influence on Jacob's study 56, 64 n.101
interpretation of conscience chapter III, 83–86

Hermeneutic, hermeneutics, hermeneutical ixff., 2, 9, 13–16, 18, 39, 121, 129
biblical hermeneutics 2. 13. 15. 39
foundational theological hermeneutic 13f.
hermeneutic circle 90ff.
hermeneutical locus concerning "God" 13–15, 129
Historical reality 96f., 121, (see also Reality)
Historicality (*Geschichtlichkeit*) 97f.
History of language 96f.
Hören (hearing) 51, 90–93, 95, 106ff.

Ideology 6
Immanence x
Interpretation 13, 90, 93

Justification 4

Kerygma 9, 31 n.42, 51, 112, 125, 127
Kingdom of God, kingdom of Christ 44
Knowing by feeling 147f.
Knowledge (*Erkenntnis*) xiv, 90, 94f., 120
knowledge of God 22f., 26f., 36 n.106, 120–29
knowledge versus "understanding" and "action" 106 n.78, 116–18, 120–22
natural knowledge of God 138 n.81
objectifying knowledge 13
personal or existential knowledge (see Understanding)
as "theoretical reason" (*theoretische Vernunft*) 120

Language (*Sprache*) xiv, 90–93, 96, 105 n.71
about God 10, 13, 17–27, 35 n.104, 126–29
inclusive language 26 n.4
and history 96f.
language-games 93f.
"moral" language 19f.
religious language 19f. 33 n.87
representational language 126
"scientific" language 19f., 48f.
theological language 19f., 48ff.

Language (*continued*)
  and understanding 13, 91 (see also Understanding)
Law xi, 5, 51, 111
  law and gospel 50, 108 n.101, 139 n.86
  lex naturalis 51f., 103–04 n.54
  moral law 51f.
Limiting questions 20ff.
Linguistic, linguisticality (*Sprachlichkeit*) 49, 121, 123, 137 n.72
  linguistic paths 96–98, 106–07 n.91
  linguistic situation 50f., 112, 128
  linguistic tradition 49ff., 111f.
Logical positivism 12
Love 13

Man, man/woman, human nature 1, 30 n.1, 133 n.61
Meaning, meaningfulness 90, 93f.
Medieval scholastics 24
Metaphysics, metaphysical 11, 12, 16–18, 31 n.39, 33 n.79, 98, 109 n.102, 113, 117, 119, 132 n.60
  overcoming metaphysics 98ff.
Mood (see *Befindlichkeit*)
Moral, morality 5, 22f., 19, 132 n.60, 133 n.61
Mystery 141 n.104
Myth, mythology 2, 17

Nature and grace 12
Natural sciences 13, 111, 115, 119f.
Naturalism 12
Neo-orthodox, neo-orthodoxy 24f.
New quest of God 14, 16
New quest of the historical Jesus 13–15
New Testament 2, 50
Nihilism 1, 7ff., 30 n.34, 31 n.39, 120, 132 n.60
Nineteenth-century 2, 3, 16
Nothingness 68

Obedience 96
Objectivizing thought 13, 120ff.
Ontology, ontological 6, 9f., 135–36 n.69
Ontological-existential clarification of concepts chapter III, 137–38 n.78
Owing 73f., 85

Paradox 4
Passivity (*Passivität*) 123
Personal divine-human communication xv, 141 n.107
Phenomenology, phenomenological 18, 25, 52, 121f., 134 n.65, 140 n.102
Philosophical anthropology 49f.
Philosophical thinking and theological thinking 21ff., 25ff., 34 n.102, 48f., 60 nn. 46, 51
Philosophy
  Christian philosophy 110 n.108
  linguistic philosophy 93f.
  philosophy and theology xiiif., 17–25, 48f., 86f., 97f., 106 n.90, 106–07 n.91, 108, nn.100 and 101, 109–10 n.108, 110 n.110, 121f.
  process philosophy 17f.
Polytheism 113
Positivism 120
Prayer 141 n.107
Pre-understanding 11 (see Understanding)
Projection (*Entwurf*) 69, 78 n.27, 92f.
Prolegomenon, prolegomena ix, 10, 23f, 124, 141 n.109
  prolegomenous "anthropology" 11f.
  prolegomenous theological anthropology 10, 12f., 23ff., 127
Protestant, protestantism xiiif., 16, 29 n.18

Questionableness 51
  radical questionableness (*radikaler Fraglichkeit*) 68, 77, 123, 137 n.72, (see also *Distanz*, (dissociation)

Reality (*Wirklichkeit*) xv, 21, 25, 49, 76, 89, 114, 121
  deemed "God" xvii
  of God 11f., 17–27, 44f. 111
  historic reality 96
  natural science's concept of reality 122
  physical concept of reality 115
  reality as a whole 24, 88f., 111, 113f., 115ff., 119, 122f.
  transcendent reality 126
  as two spheres 114f.
  wordliness (*Worthaftigkeit*) of reality

137 n.72
Reason 30 n.28
  objectifying reason 122
Rede (discourse or talk) 90f., 94, 105 nn.72, and 73
Reformation 3, 113
Reformed heritage xv, 108 n.101, 112
Religion. religious 5, 20, 29 n.27, 31 n.45, 35 n.103, 87
Religiosity 6, 9
Renaissance xiii, 3, 5
Responsibility 85f., 96, 127, 130 n.16, 132 n.60
Reticence (*Verschwiegenheit*) 88, 92, 94, 96
  as an authentic mode of disclosure 95
Revelation 10, 125, 129
Righteousness 51
Ritschlian school 24
Ruf (call) 90ff.

Salvation xi, 50, 114, 127
Saying (*sagen*) 90, 105 n.71
Schweigen (keeping silent) 142ff., 148ff.
Science, scientific 19f., 119
Scripture, scriptural xiii, 15, 17f., 39
Second Vatican Council 12–14
Secular, secularistic 1–4, 9, 29 n.18, 31 n.45, 35 n.104
  "secularistic godlessness" 5, 113f.
Secularism xiii, 3–5, 25 n.1, 27 n.8
Secularization 3–6, 25 n.1, 29 n.18, 130–31 n.25
Selfhood 82f., 86
Self-understanding 12, 82, 120
Sensus divinitatis xiv
Silence (*Schweigen*) 88, 94ff.
Sin 51
State-of-mind (*Befindlichkeit*) 90ff.
Subject
  Cartesian model of the subject 91
  Kantian "theoretical subject" 91
  Subject in Heidegger's *Being and Time* 92ff.
Subjectity (*Subjectität*) 4f., 8, 29 n.25, 30 n.37, 120
Subjective 30 n.37
Summons (*Aufruf*) 51, 67, 78 n.21, 83f.
synderesis 24, 28

syneidēsis 45. 52. 62 n. 72, 82

Temptation 102 n.44
Terror (*Entsetzen*) 66
Testimony (*Temoignage*) 100 n.15
Theology
  biblical theology 49,. 112
  Christian theology 129
  Ebeling's view of theology and philosophy 41, 48f., 97–99, 106–07 nn.91, 92, 93, 108–09 nn.100, and 101, 110 n.110
  fundamental theology (*Fundamentaltheologie*) 121, 134 n.66, 136–37 n.70
  Heidegger's view of theology 109–10 nn.107, and 108
  Luther's view of "*theologice*" 47
  methodological starting point 2, 6, 8, chapter I, 49f., 122
  modern theology 131 n.51
  natural theology xi, 9f., 11f., 15, 49, 51
  neo-orthodox theology xiii, 1, 24f.
  nineteenth century theology 1, 19, 132 n.60
  philosophical theology 19, 21f., 34 n.101
  protestant theology 1, 19ff., 111f.
  Rahner's view of theology's starting point 11f.
  revealed theology xi, 10
  revelational theology 9–12, 41, 113
  systematic theology 12f., 118, 129
  theology as hermeneutic 15ff., 49
Theological method 2, 10, 13, 15f.
Theological prolegomenon 15
Theological situation (present) 1–12
Thinking 97
  as "non-objectifying" 13
Thrownness 68, 85
Transcendent x. 1. 6. 12f. 15, 68
Truth xiv, 13, 84, 87, 120
  truth and reality 84, 116f., 119

Uncanniness (*Unheimlichkeit*) 68, 78 n.13, 85
Uncanny anxiety (*unheimliche Angst*) 66–68

Understanding (*Verstehen*) 13, 15–18, 92f., 104 n.62
  existential understanding 92
  existentiell and existential understanding 17, 22f.
  in Heidegger and Ricoeur 104 n.62
  prereflective understanding 2, 20, 35 n.102, 92f.
  prior understanding 126
  "reality as a whole" and understanding 115–17
  understanding oneself as a whole 126
  "understanding" versus "knowledge" (or perception") 94f., 116f.
  understanding and faith 115

Value 5, 31 n.39, 132 n.60
Verschweigenheit (reticence) 88, 92
Verständnis (understanding) 90–94
Voice of conscience (*Stimme des Gewissens*) 66

Word (*Wort*) 10, 89
Word-event (*Wort-geschehen*) xiv, 39, 87, 89, 92f., 125
  word-event of conscience versus word-event of kerygma 125
World 5–8, 115f.
  Cartesian world of *res extensae* 120
  world as a whole 120

Index of Names

Adam xiv, 128
Altizer, Thomas J. J. 25 n.1, 26 n.2
d'Arcy, Eric 37 n.109
Augustine, St. xi, xiv, 15, 18, 28 n.13, 34 n.94, 37 n.114

Baillie, John 20, 24, 34 n.94, 37f. n.114
Barr, James xv
Barth, Karl 9, 24, 27 n.9, 28 n.13, 38 n.119
Baumer, Franklin L. 26 n.1, 28f. n.18
Beach, Waldo 57 n.1
Blamey, Kathleen xv
Blanke, Fritz 53
Bonhoffer, Dietrich 27 n.10, 31 n.42, 98, 109 n.105
Braun, Herbert 28 n.16
Bremi, Willy 53, 55
Brunner, Emil 53–55, 63 nn.85–92
Buytendijk, F. J. J. 134 n.66
Bultmann, Rudolf xiiif., 1–12, 14, 16, 19ff., 22, 24, 26, 27 nn.9 and 11, 28 nn.12 and13, 28 n.17; 29 nn.19–28; 30 nn.35 and 36; 31 nn.38 and 40–43, 32 nn.69, 71,. 75; 34 nn.101–103; 35 n.105, 51, 52, 62 n.63, 63 n.78, 75, 79 n.47, 99, 108 n.101, 135 n.67, 140 n.93
van Buren, Paul 1ff., 27 n.9
Butler, Joseph xv

Calvin, Jean xiv–xvi
Camus, Albert 7, 9f., 134 n.66
Cavell, Stanley 93, 105 n.77
Cobb, John 47
Cox, Harvey 27 n.8

Dilthey, Wilhelm 15, 18, 104 n.62
Dostoevsky, Feodor 20
Dowey, Edward Jr. xv, xvi n.1
Duke University 57 n.1

Ebeling, Gerhard ix–xi, xivf., xvii 24f., 29 n.28, 32 n.58, 36 n. 108, 42 n.107, 49ff., 58 n.1, 64 n.94, chapters II, IV, and V, and *passim*
Engelberg, Edward 37 n.109

Flew, Antony 21
Fuchs, Ernst 14, 16, 40, 47f., 56, 99
Funk, Robert 39, 58 n.7, 62 n.63
Franz, Helmut 99
Freud, Sigmund xv, 24, 28, 37 n.111, 48, 82

Gadamer, H. G. 9f., 62 n.63, 134 n.63
Gendlin, Eugene 93, 105 nn.74–76
Gilkey, Langdon xv, 14, 16f., 26–27 nn.1, 7, 8, 32 n.66, 105 n.74
Gogarten, Frederick 3, 10, 24, 27 n.10, 28 n.18, 43 n.116, 44 n.117, 55, 56
Gustafson, James 57 n.1

Index

Hamilton, William 25 n.1, 26 n.2
Harnack, Theodosius 56
Haroutunian, Joseph xv
Hartshorne, Charles 17, 20ff., 34 n.102
Harvey, Van 31 n.47, 38 n.75, 108n.95
Hefner, Philip 39, 47, 49, 58 n.5, 60 n.45,
Hegel, F. W. H. 52, 63 n.75
Heidegger, Martin ix–xi, xiv, 4, 7, 17, 19f., 24, 27, 30 n.34, 31 n.39, 32 n.75, 34 n.96, 36 n.108, 37 n.108, 47ff., 96ff., 109 n.107, 120, 140 n.93, chapter III, and *passim*
Heim, Karl 24, 43 n.114
Herzog, Frederick 13–16, 32 nn.59–67
Holl, Karl 55f.
Hölderlin 107 n.91
Husserl, Edmund 122, 134 n.65
Huxley, Julian 7, 9f.

Jacob, Gunther 55f., 64 n.101, 103 n.54
James, William 20
Jaspers, Karl 75
Jesus Christ 9, 97, 107 n.91, 112, 126f., 139 n.86
Jüngel, Eberhard 26 n.1, 35 n.37, 36 n.42

Kähler, Martin 52, 100 n.13
Kant, Immanuel xv, 29 n.27, 37 n.109, 63 n.75, 82, 132 n.60, 133 n.60, 134 n.62, 137 n.73
Kaufman, Gordon 26 n.1, 31 n.25, 35 nn.104, and 105
Kierkegaard, Søren 52, 54f.
Knauer, Peter 139 n.86
Küng, Hans 26 n.86

La Place, Pierre 4
Lehmann, Paul 24, 28, 36 n.108, 37 nn.111, and 112
Lombard, Peter 86, 139 n.86
Luther, Martin x, 4, 47f., 50, 55f., 60 n.45, 64 nn.101, and 104, 107 n.91, 108 nn.101,113, 124, and 125, 133 n.61, 134 n.66, 139 n.86

MacIntyre, Alasdair 131 n.31
Macquarrie, John 74, 76, 77 n.1, 79 nn.45, and 48
Marcel, Gabriel 29 n.26, 141 n.104
Melanchthon 107 n91, 134 n.66, 136 n.69
Michalson, Carl 101–02 n.43, 135 n.69
Moltmann, Jurgen 137 n.73
Mount, Eric, Jr. 57 n.1
Müller, Hans 56

Nabert, Jean 100 n.15
Niebuhr, H. Richard 57 n.1
Nietzsche, Friedrich xv, 7f., 24, 29 n.25, 30 nn.34, and 37, 37 n.111, 63 n.75, 98, 104 n.62, 120, 132 n.60, 133 n.61, 134 n.62,
Novak, Michael 27 n.8

Ockham 134 n.62
Ogden, Schubert 16–25, 26 n.7, 27 n.9, 28 n.12, 32–33 nn.68–79, 34 nn. 87, 95–97, 101, 103 n.54, 108 n.95
Olafson, Frederick 133 n.62
Oxford University xv

Palmer, Richard 134 n.63
Pascal, Blaise 20
Paul, The Apostle xiv, 4, 23, 36 n.106, 42, 51, 103 n.54
Paul, Jean 6
Plato 31 n.39
Princeton Theological Seminary xv

Rahner, Karl 11–14, 31 nn.47, and 48, 32 nn.49, 50, 52–55, 69, 100 n.15,
Regis College, Toronto 64 n.94
Richardson, William J. 58 n.1
Ricoeur, Paul xvi, xi, 96, 100 n.14, 104 n.64, 106 n.86
Rilke, R. M. ix
Ritschl, Albrecht xv, 28, 132 n.60
Robinson, John A. T. 2, 32 n.69, 62 n.63

Sartre, Jean Paul 133 n.61, 134 nn. 62, and 66
Scheler, Max 83, 100 n.21
Schleiermacher, Friedrich 15, 18, 35 n.104, 108 n.95, 129, 139 n.86
Schmithals, Walter 61 n.60
Schopenhauer, Arthur 63 n.75

Seeburg, Erich 56
Smith, Ronald Gregor 26 n.1, 29 n.18, 136 n.69
Söderblom, Nathan 24, 37 n.112
Staten, John ix–xi, xvi
Stoker, H. G. 37 nn.108–111, 53, 63 n.76, 100 n.13

Tillich, Paul 24, 28, 35 n.104, 38 n.116
Tolstoy, Leo 20
Toulmin, Stephen 18, 20–24, 36 n.105
The University of Chicago xv

The University of Marburg 50ff., 62 n.63
The University of Zürich 53ff., 136 n.70

Vahanian, Gabriel 26 n.1, 28 n.18, 31 n.40

West, Charles 33 n.18
Wilder, Amos 40, 58 n.4
Winter, Gibson xvi

Yahwist, The xiv

Index of Biblical References

Genesis
2-3   128, 141 n.106
Matthew
3:7   60 n.45
John   15
Ephesians
2:12   130 n.22

Galatians
5:1   47
5-6   60 n.45
Romans
1:18f.   23, 51
1:32   51
2:14ff.   42, 51

JAN 3 1 1990

JAN 0 3 1989